A FAMOUS AUTHORITY ON ENTERTAINING . . .

reveals her secrets for successful parties. With this book, a hostess or host has everything necessary to make entertaining gracious, imaginative—and easy!

Worried about whom to ask?
What to serve and how much?
Will the party swing?
How to serve—and clean up?
Using the same old menus, invitations, decorations and gimmicks?

Here are answers to every possible party problem, whether you are managing on a tight budget or have all the money in the world.

And the entire Part Two of this fabulous book is devoted to the author's own tried and tested recipes for appetizers, dips and dunks, fancy sandwiches, soups, main dishes, vegetables, salads and sauces, all kinds of desserts—with a special chapter devoted to mixing drinks.

Make all your parties memorable, mishap-free—and fun!—with this wonderful entertaining-and-cooking guide.

"If you are looking for a book on how to enjoy your own party, and how to give parties that your friends enjoy as well as your family, get 'The Complete Book of Entertaining.' "
—*Dallas News*

"This book is just what its name says it is; it offers a guide for every hostess with plans, charts and etiquette tips for parties from two to 200."
—*Hackensack Record Call*

"I enjoyed every single page of this book. It is full of tips and hints on what successful hosts and hostesses have found to be workable under a variety of circumstances, and is stuffed with menus and recipes that make you want to run right down to your corner grocery and stock up."
—*Chattanooga Times*

"Has the latest ideas for hostesses; for the woman who entertains often—or even fairly frequently—this is a most worthwhile acquisition."
— *San Rafael Independent Journal*

"Drawing on nearly 40 years of entertaining, the author tells how to make a success of any occasion, from a clambake to a coming-out party."
—*New Orleans States Item*

"This book should provide all the help necessary in making plans for (any party). The author, in a down-to-earth manner, makes the whole thing simple."
—*Sacramento Bee*

"There are ideas galore here. If you want to make your next party a real production, you need this book."
—*Colorado Ad Exchange*

ABOUT THE AUTHOR:

Nata Lee is one of America's most famous party-givers. She planned—and baked the three-ton birthday cake served at—the late Mike Todd's Madison Square Garden party; she has organized receptions for the Duke and Duchess of Windsor. She has been giving parties—and helping other people give theirs —for the past 35 years.

THE
COMPLETE
BOOK OF
ENTERTAINING

Nata Lee

AWARD BOOKS
NEW YORK

TANDEM BOOKS
LONDON

FIRST AWARD PRINTING 1969

FOR Marc, Debbie, David,
Bobbie, Danny, Amy,
plus the grand six

Library of Congress Catalog Card Number: 67-24662

AWARD BOOKS are published by
Universal Publishing and Distributing Corporation
235 East Forty-fifth Street, New York, N. Y. 10017

TANDEM BOOKS are published by
Universal-Tandem Publishing Company Limited
14 Gloucester Road, London SW7, England

Manufactured in the United States of America

Contents

Part One

HOW TO GIVE A PARTY

Preface to the Revised Edition

From the moment the first copy of the first edition of this book came off the presses in 1961, subconsciously I have been cutting, rearranging, and adding to it, in order to keep pace with the rapid changes of the nineteen-sixties.

In a recent Department of Agriculture bulletin, I was astonished to read that ninety per cent of the products on the shelves in the markets today were not there ten years ago. This statement underlines the fact that our food habits have changed—and how quickly! For example, we now eat less sugar and less fat; we eat smaller portions; we use more convenience foods.

To be of continuing value, therefore, a book on entertaining, which naturally encompasses the art of cooking, must take note of these changes. Many people—the woman in the supermarket who told me about a new (to me) bologna fantasy (p. 202); the customer who gave me the stuffing recipe I named for her, "L.L." (p. 240); and many of my friends who bring me details of the fabulous parties they attend—all of these and many others have helped me with this book.

In the first edition I wrote:

It is not possible to mention by name, and to thank personally, all those many people who helped me to acquire that party know-how that has gone into this book.

I cannot, however, pass by the old friends from the shore, who started my penchant for parties, and those good friends in Westchester who nurtured my food knowledge by letting me practice on them. Or the many of my customers who constantly inspired me to new ideas. And particularly my staff, who by their loyalty and efficiency helped me on my way.

Now I must give a special "thank you" also to my friend Irma Hyams for her help in revising. How grateful I am for her editorial skill, her eagle eye, and her logical mind!

N.L.

1. Your Party—A Successful Production

All hosts and hostesses want to win applause for their parties.

The only way to get a rave review for a party—just as for a hit theater production—is to plan every detail before opening night. A smoothly run performance (on- or off-stage) comes only after many rehearsals. Whether it's tea for two or an extravaganza for two hundred, the host and hostess should be where the guests are—not behind the scenes. When you see a relaxed hostess enjoying her own party, you can be sure that she has done plenty of advance planning and preparing.

Make a Guest Chart

Here is an easy way to organize your party planning, and it works as well for the inveterate as for the occasional party giver. Buy either a loose-leaf notebook or a card index. This will be a kind of party diary—a permanent record of all the parties you give, the dates, and the people you invite. You can make it as detailed as you wish. The more parties you give, the more notes you'll have for future references. (See sample charts on pp. 291-303.)

Start your party diary by listing alphabetically all the people you want to entertain in the next few months. Break the list down into couples, single women, and single men. You'll be using this as a master guest chart—as the basis for lists for specific parties—so be sure to keep it intact. As you invite people, simply fill in the dates on which you've entertained them. Leave plenty of space between the names so that you can insert others and still keep them arranged alphabetically. Also, leave space to jot down comments about each person—special diets, food preferences, who likes or doesn't like whom. You may want to make notes like "Don't have fresh flowers, they make him sneeze." Then too, there is nothing so flattering as to have a hostess remember such preferences as "He loves strawberry shortcake," or allergies like "Capers make her ill."

Now that your party diary and your master guest list are set up, you are ready to start planning parties.

Start with a Plot

Frequently, the first thing people ask me about a party is what the menu should be. They are often amazed when I say the food is almost the last consideration. The exception is when the party is built around the food, for example, when a hunter has bagged some wild ducks or a fisherman has made a big catch. Usually the menu hinges on the answers to who and how many people will be asked? What is the occasion? What type of party is it to be? Where and when and how is it to be given? Once these questions are settled, you will easily decide what to serve.

If you were a movie or TV producer, the first thing you would do is block out every bit of action and business. So pretend your party is a play. Sit down at your desk and outline every phase of the party. Make notes of every detail that might cause last-minute jitters.

Your guests can make or break a party, so study your master guest list and map out the best possible cast for your production.

Who

Some hostesses feel that if their party is centered around someone in a particular field—a novelist, let's say— they should round up all the other writers they know. To me, this is a fallacy. The honored author, more likely than not, would prefer entering into discussions with a doctor, lawyer, or Indian chief than going into theories of the written word with another author. For no matter how congenial a group may be, if they are all of one profession the result is apt to be a dull shop-talking party. Such gatherings should be saved for annual professional conventions.

If the party is in honor of any type of celebrity, it's always a good rule to ask impressionable people rather than those who have a penchant for impressing. Another hint about guest selecting: If you have a compulsive talker or an exhibitionist on your list, balance the party with a few good listeners or people who make a good audience.

If it's a duty party, you have a built-in cast—people you have to pay back. Some hostesses do this at one fell swoop —to have it over and done with. It's cheaper, too. But the result is usually dull, because the guests are not hand-picked. It is always well to intersperse the have-to list with a few gay, owe-nothing-to characters. Unless you have a ready-made list for such a must party or for a special occasion—wedding reception or shower, birthday, anniversary party, etc.—you can start from scratch and have fun predicting who will go best with whom.

If the purpose of the party is match-making, you'll be a wise cupid if you ask a few dullards who will make your targets sparkle. Otherwise, your arrows may go askew.

An even number of males and females is the aim of most hostesses. Although this is important to girls in their teens and early twenties, it becomes progressively less important as the years go by, especially for large, not seated parties. Some hostesses even waive this biological balance for dinners. The main concern of any party is that *the people enjoy themselves*. And this is up to you, first, in selecting good go-togethers, and second, in seeing that they mingle effectively. This doesn't mean breaking up an earnest conversation to introduce a new subject or person. But it does mean watching guests with an eagle eye, and rescuing someone who needs you.

How Many Guests?

The number of people you invite depends on the size of your home and your budget. But it also depends on what you wish to accomplish. If it's to be an intellectual, talky evening, the guests should be selected with particular thought and care. And they should not outnumber the seating capacity of your furniture conversation groupings. But if you are planning a medium-sized cocktail party which you want to be especially gay, be sure to have half again as many people as you have seating space. If the chairs and sofas are too comfortable and too many, it takes a very clever hostess to get the guests to circulate. If the party is a large reception or cocktail party, don't be afraid of asking too many guests, for when people speak of a party as a "crush," they usually are saying it in a complimentary way.

The "Whys" for Giving a Party

Parties can be as impromptu as calling in the neighbors to share the large pot of soup you have just cooked or the first successful bread you've ever baked; or they can be as prearranged as a debutante ball, with the date set and the country club engaged a year in advance. They can be as informal as a last-minute get-together to celebrate your husband's new raise or a spontaneous "Come home for potluck" after a football game or horse show. They might be as elaborate as a costume extravaganza with a Hawaiian motif.

Many people feel that a party is more successful if it has a gimmick. If there is no particular reason—like the time of the year (Halloween, Valentine's Day, Easter), or occasion (wedding, graduation), or the arrival of visiting firemen— they will invent one. The reasons for a party, whether planned or impromptu, are as varied as your whims. Later in the book you will find descriptions of parties for every known occasion as well as for some of the "fantasies" I have invented which may spur your imagination.

What Type of Party? Where?

After you have decided the reason for giving a party and whom and how many you'll ask, it will be easy to decide on the type. Of course, your natural resources—your budget and the size of your home—are important factors. If you have decided to ask a large group of women and your apartment is small, a luncheon is not to be considered. But you can give a coffee in the morning, or a tea in the afternoon. If you are having a mixed group, settle for a reception or a cocktail party.

If your home is large but your dining room cannot seat all your guests, you can rent small folding tables and chairs and place them all over. Even though your own home is the ideal place for a party, if the guest list runs out of bounds there is always your favorite club. But there is also the risk of anonymity when a party is given in a public place. In a Midwestern city, it became the custom for each debutante to have her coming-out party at a certain country club. At the end of the season it was difficult to remember who gave what party when. So, unless an enormous party is essential, it is more gracious to give a series of smaller parties of the size you can accommodate right at home.

Another way to handle a large group in a relatively small space is to give a continuous party. For instance, you could be "At Home" on New Year's Day from two to six. Divide your guest list in half and send invitations to each group for different hours—two to four, and four to six.

One determined hostess who would not compromise on the size of her list and was adamant about having everyone at one time in her city apartment went so far as to hire a van to move most of her furniture away for the day. This may seem extreme to some people. However, she found the cost was less than the rental of a hotel party room. There are simpler and less expensive space savers, however. Sofas and chairs can be pushed back against the wall, and bulky pieces from the living room moved into a bedroom.

If you are planning an outdoor barbecue or a garden party, you must always consider the vagaries of the weather. If your house is large enough to handle the guests, make an alternate indoor party plan. Of course, the foolproof (though more expensive) way to plan an outdoor party is to rent a waterproof tent or marquee.

When?

The time of day or night at which you give your party helps determine the kind. And where you give it depends on the availability of the people you want to ask and the place you happen to be when you get that party-giving urge. It can be a farewell party on an ocean liner. It can be a gathering of new acquaintances in your temporary home at a resort hotel. It can be a roundup of delayed passengers at an airport. Or it can be at your office, your kitchen, your studio. Wherever there's space for a group of people to gather, that's the place for a party. And, no matter how small and informal, it's a party when friends get together, break bread, and have fun.

What to Serve?

Before you decide on the menu, examine your guest list. If it's a hen party, figure out whether the girls would appreciate low-calorie food rather than a whipped-cream binge. If it's a tea and men are coming, have on hand a supply of stronger refreshments. If it's a meal for men and women (luncheon, supper, dinner), stick to sturdy food—and plenty of it. If it's a cocktail party on a weekday in the city, serve substantial snacks so theater-goers won't need to stop elsewhere for supper.

Now look at the individuals on your list. Do any of them have food allergies or particular preferences? Are any of them on diets? Just in case someone has an allergy to fish or shellfish, better keep some chops or cold chicken in reserve. Are any of the guests on the wagon or teetotalers? Be sure to have a supply of tomato juice and soft drinks on hand and some good strong coffee. And in reverse, if *you* are a teetotaler, don't expect your guests to be.

You may get your inspiration for the main course of the menu by glancing through your guest list. If one of your friends has just written a book, you might fashion the hors d'oeuvre in the shape of a book made of bread and appetizer foods with the title squiggled on in cream cheese (see p. 209, "Book Hors d'Oeuvre"). Or you may want to flatter a particular guest by serving Lobster Newburg in the copper chafing dish he gave you for Christmas.

Serving what comes naturally is a good rule to follow for any party. And trying to outguess what your guests will like is a foolish practice. The wife of an Italian diplomat at the United Nations once entertained a group of American friends. She served the most American dinner she could think of—turkey with cranberry sauce and all the fixings. All the guests were tremendously disappointed that she had not dished up one of her mouth-watering Italian specialties —spaghetti, lasagna, or her marvelous ravioli.

The *specialité de la maison* is always the best best when ordering in a strange restaurant. And so your specialty, no matter how simple, will be more enjoyable to the guest than an untried concoction. A familiar dish is easier to prepare and makes for an unharried and happier hostess.

Don't run the risk of trying out a new recipe on guests. Of course, you can add zip to your old standby by making variations on a familiar theme. For example, if meat loaf is your specialty, try baking it in a ring mold instead of an oblong pan. It will not only have a new look, but can be further enchanced by filling the center with vegetables. And why must pie always be round? Try baking it in a square or oblong pan. Such variety is the spice of cooking.

Different shapes are extremely versatile. Through the years, I have devised a group of recipes I call "Basic Helpers" (see pp. 179-185). They are my party wardrobe—much like a basic outfit you can dress up or down—and they are one answer to a large repertoire for parties. One of them, cheese dough, has only three basic ingredients, but with an added this or that its usefulness has been expanded to many separate recipes (salt appetizers and sweets, plus as many pies as you can dream up). If you cultivate a few dependable basics, you will use them so often that making them will be almost automatic and you can use your imaginative talents to devise exciting variations.

Serving a familiar and unostentatious meal is usually the best formula if the guests happen to be the boss and his wife. If you go over your head (and budget) and attempt to serve the fare you think *they* are used to (but *you* are not), they are apt to sense a false note. And the boss might look askance on the imported caviar you can't afford on the salary he pays.

Of course, if the party is planned for your husband's good customer, it is quite understandable to put on the dog. But don't go so far overboard that the effort will show. And be sure to acquaint your husband with the menu so he won't spoil the impression you're trying to make by mumbling, "These are good, what are they? . . . Escargots? . . . Look like snails to me."

If the party is a large seated one—a luncheon, supper, or dinner—it is always wise to serve food that the majority of people like. Save your imagination for smaller parties. When there is only one main course and there are a hundred guests, resist your impulse to serve a delectable curry. Chicken—creamed, broiled, or in salad—may seem dull to you. But it's a safe choice—few people really dislike chicken— and if it is prepared in an interesting way, it can appeal to the most finicky gourmet.

It may be wise for you to consider what other hostesses in your group have served recently. And avoid duplicating their menus. People who go to many parties sometimes wince at the thought of *another* pseudo-*boeuf bourgignon*.

The same rules apply for dinner at home for a foursome or banquet for forty. Pick the main dish first. Then surround it with accessories that will set it off. In any party I plan, I try to create drama in the menu with an exciting contrast of color, texture, taste, and form. For instance, if the main dish is bland in color, contrast it with the green of string beans and the red of tomatoes. If the texture is creamy, supplement it with the crispness and crunchiness of a mixed green salad, and be sure that the dessert is not gooey or creamy. If the meat is salty or fatty, include something sweet and something sour on the menu. If the main dish has shape or form, like a turkey or a crown roast of lamb, let the dessert be a bowl of pudding.

How Much to Serve

The amount of food you have at your party is a personal matter. Some people provide bountifully and some are skimpy. I have worked out charts (pp. 298-301) which suggest a happy medium. But the best bet for any hostess is to keep a full record of every party she gives and use these as her guides for future parties.

Two charts (pp. 295, 303) have proved particularly help- ful in party planning. They will not only simplify your organization and remind you to make notes of every detail, but will also be useful for future parties *and* the income tax authorities.

One is a pre-party work chart. The other is a recapitula- tion and permanent record of your expenses. After the party, fill in all details, clip the two lists together, and file them away in your party diary.

The pre-party chart includes not only the type of party, the date, the people, the invitations, and the menu, but even has a space to make a note of what you wore. This is

not as frivolous as it may sound. For what hostess can remember exactly what she wore to a party given weeks
before? And what woman lacks the vanity of wanting to
wear something different when she entertains even a few
of the same people again?

The post-party chart is a permanent record of how many
people came and how much they ate and drank. This chart
is an excellent way to keep an account of all expenses, and,
if business is involved, it will be essential for income tax
purposes. Make a note of all business people and the names.
Also attach all sales slips and bills that have to do with
the party.

Be sure to fill in all of the blanks on each chart, and do
it the day after the party, when everything is fresh in your
mind. Check off the people who didn't show, and enume-
rate any extras. The percentage of refusals will be a good
gauge as to how many you can safely ask when you want
to end up with a certain number of guests. The amount of
food and beverages consumed by a given number of people
will also be invaluable in future planning. However, never
judge by the party where everything was consumed. Chances
are, some went hungry. It's always best to have extra quantities on hand, especially if the party is on a Sunday or if
the source of supply is not conveniently around the corner.
There is no greater embarrassment for a hostess than for
something to give out and she has to whisper "F. H. B.,"
which translated means "family hold back." Far better to
have left-over-food, which can always be camouflaged for
the family later, and too many bottles, which can be returned
to the store.

Consumption of food and beverages at a party is as
variable as the people who attend. For example, if you plan
a cocktail buffet along the lines of an extremely successful
one you gave a few months before, you may run into trouble
if you use the previous party as an *exact* guide. Even if you
ask practically the same group of people, it might turn out
that the turkey should have been larger and the ham smaller
or vice versa. Or you may wonder why the black olives
disappeared so quickly and the celery not at all. It might
also seem surprising that martinis were the pets this time,
when scotch starred before. And why was it that you had

to phone the delicatessen to rush over soft drinks and beer when not a single soul asked for them last time?

No hostess can foresee these seeming whims. Perhaps the largest eaters at the party recently had their fill of ham at home. The turkey may have looked and tasted more delectable this time. And wasn't that a new and perhaps better brand of olives? Maybe some of the scotch-loving guests had been to a party where they didn't like the brand of scotch and so switched to martinis. And guests hardly ever notify the hostess in advance that they have suddenly gone on the wagon or that they have developed an ulcer. In comparing charts of past cocktail parties you may find that there is an inconsistency in the eating and drinking ratio. If people ate more and drank less at a certain party, a little detective work might reveal that a number of the guests were going to the theater. The reverse may be true if many of them were headed for a dinner party.

A hostess who says, "I figured the quantities exactly right —there wasn't a scrap left on the buffet table," should examine her concepts. If there was nothing left, how in the world could she be sure that more food would not have been welcome, or that some guests may not have left with un-satisfied appetites?

Round Up the Players

The cast is picked, the theme is planned, the scene is set, so you are ready to start putting the show on the road. But before going into production, the actors must be invited.

Whether you send engraved invitations or use the tele-phone, be explicit. Give the time, the place, the kind of party, and whether it's formal or informal—your guests will want to know how to dress. Don't keep them in the dark about the Saturday night dance at the country club. If it's going to be a countrified, rugged weekend, tell them, so that they won't have to walk your mountain roads in spike heels.

Don't keep it a secret if you are having a substantial buffet at your cocktail party. But if abundant food is not involved, and you don't want your guests to be misled, it is perfectly correct to say, "Cocktails—from 5 to 7." Al-though some hosts and hostesses actually close the bar at the hour they have stated, it is generally used to indicate "no supper."

If the party is given for a particular reason or person, tell the guests about it. It will put them in the mood of the party in advance. If it's a birthday party but you don't want to seem greedy for gifts, just tell them *not* to bring presents, or to bring the silly dime-store kind. If you're asking friends you met on your vacation, they'd like to know ahead that you are showing the movies of them you took in Bermuda.

Invitations by Telephone

Although it is time-consuming, the telephone gets faster results about who is or is not coming than invitations by mail. And it is essential if the party is less than two weeks away. Also, the enthusiasm in your voice can get the party off to a good start. You can chat about who else is coming and what the party is about. If there is a guest of honor, you can tell interesting things about him or her. (Before the party begins, be sure to give the guest of honor a list and a thumbnail sketch of each of the guests.) The pitfalls of a telephoned invitation are that the prospective guests may feel trapped. Always give them an out by telling them what type and when the party is *before* you ask if they can come. Of course, if you're just asking a couple for dinner and you can't stand the embarrassment of an immediate refusal, give alternate dates. This will give "Mrs." a chance to check with "Mr." and either accept one of the dates or dream up an excuse. Unless your list is long and the time short, it is always best to talk directly to the person involved and not leave a message about the party with a servant or a child— unless you are sure of their dependability. Better to find out when the person will return and call back or leave your name and phone number and say you want to talk to him about a party you are giving.

Invitations by Telegram

This is the lazy way, because all you have to do is supply a list and one message to the telegraph company. Even though telegram invitations are generally accepted for business functions, they seem a cold way to ask someone to a private party. Naturally there are exceptions. A bachelor who is not quite up to the niceties of life can be forgiven, especially if the invitation is worded wittily. And there are last-minute occasions—the surprise arrival of a guest, the sudden departure of friends, an unannounced marriage— when time is of the essence and a telegraphed invitation is the answer.

Invitations by Mail

Whether they are engraved (see pp. 100-104 for wedding invitations), partly engraved with the guest's name and date filled in, or handwritten, invitations by mail should be sent at least two weeks before the party. Less than that doesn't allow enough leeway for receiving responses, and an R.S.V.P. or "Kindly Reply" is a must for a meticulous hostess.

Informal Invitations

The greeting-card people have done an excellent job of designing invitations for all types of parties. And the ever popular informals have taken on a new party look. Whether printed or engraved, they can be ordered in gay color combinations complete with name, address, and telephone number. If there is an artist in your family, he can design invitations using sketches of your country home or maps showing how to get there. (Miniature stationery has many other uses—short thank-you notes, acceptances, as well as invitations.) One of the virtues of the fold-over informal is that the actual invitation can be written on the outside and a little note can be written inside the fold. Like this:

Outside:

To meet
*Mr. and Mrs. Robert Black**

MR. & MRS. PERCIVAL J. JOHNSON
Monday, October 3
Tea 4-7   *21 East 67th Street*

* (Italics means filled-in handwriting.)

Inside:

> *The Blakes are the ones I told*
> *you about—met them in Nassau*
> *last winter. Hope you can come.*

This informal was engraved with only the name of the wife. Double informals can have both Mr. and Mrs. However, the former has more uses, and it is perfectly correct to fill in the "Mr." in ink when the party is given by both. Or if the party is very informal, a line can be drawn through the entire engraved name and then signed informally:

> *Surprise birthday party for Jo*
> *Dinner at 7:30, May the ninth*
> *Hope you can come—but don't*
> *bring presents!*
> *Love, Mary*
> *21 West 54th Street*

Invitations by Gag, Gimmick, or Theme

Fun parties are even funnier if the invitation can be related to a theme. One birthday party was to be a surprise for Ann. Since only close friends were to be asked, her husband, Tony, sent invitations written in black crayon on brown paper grocery bags: "Come to a party for my old bag"—with responses directed to his office. Decorated paper bags blown up and attached to plants and crazy, impudent, or risqué signs all around made a hilarious evening.

One enthusiast invited friends for an Origami evening with invitations written on a folded flying bird. An invitation for a musical evening was handwritten on music paper, the letters being notes. A barn dance invitation had a swatch of blue denim and a few stalks of hay stapled to a plain card with time and place written in orange ink. Playing cards (the miniature ones are novel) pasted to heavy paper enhanced an invitation to a card party.

You can always be on the lookout for props. For example, last December I saw tiny Santa Clauses on skis and was able to find a skiing enthusiast to use them on invitations for a ski party.

Invitations to Formal Functions

Most people today prefer informality, except for wedding invitations and announcements, which are discussed on pp. 100-104. A few general rules will suffice here.

Invitations to a formal function may be handwritten or engraved, and they are always worded in the third person with all names written out. In the days of Mrs. Astor's "400," people who entertained frequently kept on hand engraved invitations with spaces to be filled in:

> Mr. and Mrs. T. Carter Jones
> request the pleasure of
> . . . . 's
> company at . . . .
> on . . . .
> at . . . .
> 979 Fifth Avenue
> R.S.V.P.

Of course, there may be some very special occasions, like a debutante ball or an embassy reception for a visiting dignitary, which will require formal engraved invitations:

> Dr. and Mrs. Charles Cuttle
> request the pleasure of your company
> at a reception in honor of
> Dr. Amos Hayes Watson
> Friday, the first of March
> at five o'clock
> Englewood Hospital

R.S.V.P.
325 South High Street

The How of Producing

Your party is now beyond the planning stage. Opening night has been announced, and the show must go on. A complete outline has been plotted, and now is the time to fill in all the details. Consider every phase of the party to avoid stage fright at curtain time. Start by measuring the talents you have at hand against the size and type of party. Is it small and informal enough for you to handle it unaided? Will you need one or more helpers? Or is it so large and unwieldy that you'll want to call in a professional party producer?

If you can afford to hire outside help, nothing will give you greater dollar value. For instance, if it is a cocktail party for thirty, you *can* answer the door, empty the ash trays, and pass the hors d'oeuvre. And your husband *can* be bartender. But at the end of the party you are both likely to be exhausted and will discover that neither of you had a chance to talk to so-and-so. So if your budget can take it and you can find capable people, do bring them in.

Frequently, however, eager friends can be enlisted. And they love it. It makes them a real part of the party, and if they are gregarious, it gives them a means to meet all of the guests. A designing, single female can look over the men while she's passing cheese and crackers; a cagey bachelor can start or stop a conversation at will with, "May I fix you a drink?"

But no matter how much service she has for a party— unpaid guests or paid help—the hostess is responsible for coordinating all the details. Unless, of course, she has a professional party producer who brings a staff and takes over completely.

The number of helpers needed for any party is another extremely variable factor. It depends on the size and the layout of the home, the type of party, and how elaborate or informal it is, but mostly it depends on what the hostess wants to achieve. Here is an example of two parties I catered for one hundred guests. At party A, I furnished four helpers. One was at the bar, another was in charge of the food, the third opened the door and directed people where to leave their coats (later she helped out wherever needed), and the fourth was clean-up man—policing ash trays and abandoned glasses. Party B was given by a famous milliner. There were the same number of guests, but this hostess wanted service with a capital S. Instead of four, I used ten helpers. Two were assigned just to her. One man's sole function was to keep an eagle eye on her and to understand what she meant when she lifted her eyebrow in a given way. His assistant was then instructed to run and fetch whatever was the need of the moment.

It's sometimes discouraging when people engage me because of my experience and are then adamant about not taking my advice. In some cases I am strong-minded, but in this particular one I was not. It was a tea for three hundred and fifty guests. The people giving it agreed to every detail about the food and the serving of it. However, they were absolutely firm that they wanted only six coat racks and two hat-check girls. I strongly advised more, but they held firm. The result was a shambles. Everyone came at once. Not only did I have to pitch in to allay the emergency, I was forced to steal help from the food and serving units.

Beg, Borrow, or Rent

Now you must count your guests, study your menu, and list what tableware and serving equipment will be needed. Then check what is needed against what you have on hand —and always allow a few extras in case of breakage. If it is not convenient to borrow the extras you need, catering firms that supply coat racks, chairs, etc., also rent table accessories.

No matter how careful a checklist is kept, almost everyone is likely to forget something, sometime. I found this out to my horror early in my catering career. I was doing a press luncheon in a cosmetic manufacturer's showroom. As there was no real kitchen on the premises, the chicken salad and so forth was prepared in advance and delivered complete with serving appointments. Or, I *thought* complete—until someone asked for salt. The bottom of the box of salted nuts yielded enough for this emergency, but to ensure "never again" I developed a master inventory list. I check it personally for every party I cater. It's been a great boon to me in both my business and my home.

The inventory is nothing more than an organized list of everything that may be needed for any party, at any time. I drew it up by checking back over the equipment lists for parties over a period of years and writing down each item I had ever used. After categorizing them, I double-checked my memory and filled in any omissions.

This list is included in the book even though it is perhaps too detailed for the average home party giver (see p. 296). It can be useful as a guide in drawing up such a list to fit your personal needs.

When you make a complete inventory of all the equipment you own, you may find it better to catalog your possessions in a different way. For instance, if you have colored table linens, you might list each color separately along with the china, glassware, vases, etc., that go well with each.

I have also devised a simplified planning chart that should be a helpful guide against omitting any important detail (see p. 295). It has space to fill in the ingredients for each dish on the menu; a shopping list for the ingredients you don't have on your supply shelves; the equipment needed to serve; and a space to jot down what you have in your personal inventory and what will have to be borrowed or rented. It also has space to remind you of decorations—flowers, party favors, and so on.

Dress Rehearsal

Once you have made all your lists and know what you need to supplement your own tableware and equipment, you can heave a sigh and relax. But not for long. You can *buy* most of your needs the day before or the day of the party (depending on perishability). But it's wise to *order* several days ahead. If you have your heart set on a very special kind or color of flowers, tell your florist about it way ahead. And if you plan to serve squab or Cornish hen, your poultry man would like advance notice. This is true of any food specialty—strawberries or asparagus out of season, and even alligator pears, if you want them to be the perfection of ripeness.

Do-aheads

It is also well to order in advance any equipment you may want to rent. The supply people don't usually run out of coat racks, hangers, folding chairs, and cocktail glasses. But if you are entertaining at the height of party-giving time—Christmas and New Year's, particularly—they just might. If you are borrowing glasses or silver from a friend, it's

well to pick them up before the day of the party, for washing and polishing.

To lessen the chance of mix-ups, make a list of all borrowed items. But don't, for goodness' sake, do what a well-
intentioned friend did to me: On returning flat silver, he
kept the knives, forks, and spoons separated by rubber bands.
It took a year of hard rubbing to remove the discoloration!

And in your own home, that pretty pink linen tablecloth
may not have a crease because you have rolled it on a tube.
But you'd better examine it—there's just a chance it might
need a washing or even a dye bath. If you take a look, those
crystal goblets you save for company could do with a deter-
gent bath to give them the sparkle they deserve. And what
about all the silver you have decided to use? And the copper
chafing dish? Even if you're not going to have a fire in your
fireplace, the brass andirons will give a glow to the hearth
if they are polished. Better round up all your ash trays, too.
Are there enough for every nook and cranny?

If you can come up with an inspiration for a menu no one
else has had, so much the better. Be sure, though, to try it
out on the family first. It also helps to have a dress rehearsal,
so you can make a time chart for "opening night." Don't
lay too much stress on housecleaning before the party. See
that everything is in reasonable order, but save thorough
cleaning for the day after.

Another little chore for the day before is to write down
specific instructions for each of the servants you have engaged. And have you thought about their uniforms? Does
Mary have a simple black or gray dress, and do you have
a crisp white apron for her to wear? And does Tom have a
butler's jacket and Joe a bar coat? Or must you order these?
And if it's a dinner party, the seating chart must be made
and the place cards written.

The Day of the Party

Try to leave the day of the party for lady-like chores.
(This is the ideal which few hostesses accomplish.) If the
party has been carefully planned, the hostess should be able
to pinpoint her attention to simple, nonharassing, last-minute
details. She should be able to spend as much time as she

wants in arranging the flowers. Then there is the inspection tour to see that no dust has dimmed the luster of the mahogany overnight or the ash trays cluttered, that the powder room is still spick and span, and that there are adequate guest towels in evidence. Now, after these charming tasks, she will have time to rest with moistened pads over her eyes. Then to relax in a tepid, scented tub, put on her make-up in an unhurried way, and dress—with plenty of time left over to make a thoughtful decision about which jewelry looks best.

This sounds ideal, and it could be true. However, no matter how well the plans are laid, there always seems to be something that goes awry. The maid is taken with a virus at the last minute, and the hostess has to track down some-one else. She may not have a uniform, so there is that to find. The ice does not arrive on schedule, and the ice dealer's phone does not answer. Only nine squabs arrive for a dinner for ten. The hothouse strawberries are lovely on top but moldy at the bottom of the basket. And the laundry forgets to deliver your husband's dress shirt.

So even though you have used all of the planning suggestions in this book, you have to be ready to cope with any emergency. For no matter how upsetting the day's happenings have been, the show must go on.

Keep Calm

Even when I have been in complete charge of a party —with all of the burdens on *my* shoulders—I have seen a host and hostess have opening-night jitters. They had no worries about the production, every single detail was my problem, and yet they were worried sick about whether the party would be a success. We had planned the menu together. Everything was just what they wanted. They had a squabble over nothing just before the guests arrived. With all my experience, I was truly worried about the outcome. However, with the first ring of the doorbell, the distraught hostess who was quivering with nerves and still putting on an earring rushed ahead of the butler to greet the guests. Like magic she had changed into a relaxed and gracious human being with true warmth.

Curtain Time

The producer is waiting and wondering. Will the show be a hit? If it's a cocktail party or tea—will too many come, or too few? Will they all come in a crush, making introductions difficult? Or will they straggle in? If it's a dinner, will they arrive so that there is time for cocktails and the food won't be overcooked? These are the worries of the producer—you, the host or hostess.

But even though the guests are your best actors, how can you depend on their performance? John, who is usually the life of the party, may get stoned and become a bore. Food is the way to a man's heart, they say. But even the most divine food cannot pull a faltering party together. Nor can drinks.

What makes a successful party are the intangibles. And believe me, they amount to about ninety per cent—leaving only ten per cent for the tangibles (the food, the drinks, the decor). The tangibles you can study in a book (this one, please!) and learn to master them, as you would any technique, by practice. But the intangibles have to come naturally.

What makes a party click can easily be narrowed down to something as elusive as good will. Actually, it's the hostess' innate talent, first to select a combination of people with potential rapport, and then to see that they meld well.

It starts with a warm greeting when guests arrive—making them feel welcome and wanted and a little special. And then it's the complimentary and very personal touch in introducing—to get the conversation ball started and to keep it rolling.

Introductions

Even the most poised individual is apt to feel self-conscious when entering a room full of people. And a mass introduction not only adds to the newcomer's embarrassment but causes an awkward pause in the general conversation. So when there are more than six or seven present, it's better to introduce the new guest to a small group or a single person. Further introductions can come later, after you've seen to the newcomer's refreshments. If it's a large party and several people arrive at once, introduce them before they enter the room so they'll have their own little group until you have time to bring others to meet them. If you have just greeted a single man or a couple who are old friends and the doorbell rings again, it's perfectly all right to ask them to get a drink at the bar, tea at the tea table, or go talk to so-and-so until you get back.

A man is always introduced *to* a woman, and youth *to* age. The woman's or older person's name is always said first. "Miss Brown, this is Mr. Black." Or "Mrs. White, do you know Nancy Green?" Also, ". . . I'd like you to meet . . ." or ". . . may I introduce . . .?" Although first-name introductions used to be frowned upon, this informality has become correct by usage—"Mary Brown, I'd like you to meet George Black." Or just "Jean Lowell, do meet Barbara Black. You're both such opera buffs that I've meant for some time to bring you together."

In large cities, especially New York, it has become commonplace for the hostess to tack on an identification tag to her introductions. "She's promotion manager at Saks Fifth Avenue." Or "He's on Wall Street—with Something, Something, Something, and Someone." This direct method is sometimes embarrassing to the individuals and slows up rather than starts conversation. Better to divulge these vital statistics ahead of time or whisper them before the introduction. This is particularly true if a person is famous—or thinks he is.

However, a more subtle opening wedge is good for conversation making. "Mary, this is George Black. George, Mary Brown is almost as dedicated to the theater as you are. I'll bet you know lots of the same people." Or "Mrs. White, may I present Mr. Green? I believe you are both from New England, aren't you?" Or "Mrs. Span, this is my husband, John Jones. He's a great admirer of your volunteer work for ANS." If there is no mutual interest to bring up, the hostess can throw in a talk-starter like, "Mr. Jones has just moved to our city—you came from Chicago, didn't you?" or "How tan you are, Mary, did you just get back from vacation? Where did you go? . . . John, are you going to hire a boat again?"

As previously mentioned, a hostess must keep an eagle

eye on the various groupings, and particularly on twosomes. She must be able to sense if a man is boring a girl to tears or a woman is talking a man's ear off. In the first case, take an attractive male to meet the girl and ask the talkative fellow to help you in some small way. In the second, excuse yourself to the man and say that you must steal Mrs. So-and-So away as the group over there is just dying to hear about her trip to Egypt. As it is difficult to transport a small group from one part of the room to the other, it is perfectly all right to take a woman to them. However, it is obviously not correct to usher a lone woman to a single man—unless, of course, she is a new arrival, or the man is elderly or eminent, or the guest of honor.

Complimenting a guest is fine. But it must be done so that it does not smack of flattery and spoil sincere good will. So don't say that a particular group wants to hear the effusive Mrs. So-and-So tell about Egypt unless it's true. Think of another excuse to get her away from the young man.

When to Leave Your Guests Alone

Just as it is important to separate people who are boring each other, a hostess must be wary of breaking up a couple who are deep in an interesting conversation. Keeping a party circulating can go out of bounds when an avid hostess disturbs a romance in the bud.

The clever hostess knows that she has to keep a delicate balance between solicitude and indifference. Indifference seems like an odd term to be applied to a hostess. However, it couldn't be more important. Guests should be looked after and babied up to a point. Then, when they are doing fine alone, they should be left strictly to their own devices.

Leaving guests alone is particularly important on weekend parties, and that will be taken up later. But "leaving alone" has another aspect, which really means letting well enough alone.

A Case Against Regimentation

No matter how thoroughly every detail of a party has been organized, a hostess must recognize that there may *have* to be changes. She must keep a certain flexibility in her plans and in her thinking. For example, if the party is in full swing, but the prearranged hour to serve the buffet supper has arrived, what should the hostess do? Should she stick to her schedule, disturb the gaiety, and herd everyone into the dining room? Or should she adjust to the circumstance and either postpone the supper announcement or tell people individually that the buffet table is ready and they can eat when they choose? Certainly a foresighted hostess would leave out of her menu any dish that could not keep —either cold on ice or hot on an electric warming tray.

A young hostess once saw that the living room was becoming jammed at the height of her cocktail party. She thought of breaking up the crowd by placing an attractive array of hors d'oeuvre on the desk in the study. It was her notion that this would lure many of the guests into the other room. If she had been firm about regimenting the people, she probably would have succeeded in breaking up not only the crowd but the party as well. Instead, she decided to relax and enjoy the living-room crush (everyone else was) and to pass the hors d'oeuvre with the help of a few friends.

Remember, the party's the thing. The guests, not the hostess, are the ones to be pleased. If you regiment them, you're likely to spoil their fun. And if the guests are having fun, that's the party where you'll find a happy hostess.

Hospitality, according to the dictionary, is the friendly and generous entertainment of friends. But all good things can be overdone. And forcing your generosity upon your guests can be worse than not giving enough.

The distaste most people have at being urged to eat probably started in childhood. Grandma's coaxing—"Eat the carrots so they'll make your hair curly!"—left its mark. And the insistence of a host or hostess can become very annoying indeed. "Just one more drink . . . not even a little one? . . . Come on—one for the road." "Try this hors d'oeuvre, I made it myself . . . well, try this . . . try that." "Do have some more chicken . . . more potatoes? . . . more asparagus? No? My dear, you eat like a bird!" And "my dear" wishes she were a bird and could fly away.

The gracious hostess limits her urging to the immediate

family, and allows her adult friends to make up their minds about what and how much they want to eat and drink.

Urging can take another form, too. It's fine to compliment a guest about his talents, to rave about his piano playing, his adeptness at photography, his clever way with tricks of magic. And it's usually all right to suggest mildly, "John, how about playing that new tune for us?" (Or take a picture, or do a trick.) That is all that's needed for an exhibitionist. But the shy person who would rather sink through the floor than show off resents being urged. If he is a professional he is apt to feel, and rightly so, that he is being exploited; just as a lawyer guest might react to being asked a legal question or a doctor a medical one.

Coping with the Unexpected

No matter how well a party has been planned or how smoothly it seems to be going, there is always the possibility of a minor calamity. A good hostess needs to be ready with tact and resourcefulness to cope with the unexpected. Humor, too, is a good thing to have on tap for parties as well as for daily living. One working hostess came home at the last minute from her office. When she found that there would be thirteen at table instead of the eleven she had carelessly counted, the two extra places were quickly laid. To her guests, the hostess said: "It's good, isn't it, that thirteen is my lucky number! Now, you will have a great story on me." Even professionals make mistakes, for I must confess that I was that hostess.

Some small tragedies can be forestalled with a little advance thinking. If it's a large party and space is limited, have small flowers. Or at least see that huge gladioli don't brush your guests' noses. If children will be present, put your prized bric-a-brac away or place them on high shelves. Even if *you* are not a smoker, put ashtrays every place that guests will be. And even if you don't approve of smoking at the dinner table, give your guests a break and put a cigarette tray at each place or between every two guests.

But even with forethought, something may break or burn or spill, and it's up to the hostess to hide her distress and alleviate the embarrassment of the guest. I'll never forget the graciousness of Fay Bainter when my small boy tipped over the Cape Cod Lighter at her fireplace. She looked at the horrified child and said soothingly, "Oh! That kerosene is good for the floor. I have it oiled every week. Now you've saved me the trouble!" Not only the child but we parents were made comfortable and set at ease in the midst of disaster.

A hostess who can manage to be gracious when her prize extra man arrives with an uninvited girl deserves a Hostess Oscar. Of course, this young man makes a dreadful blunder. He *must* ask the hostess if he may bring someone along; thereafter it is up to her. If she doesn't want an extra girl, she must be firm and say "no" with whatever reason she has: "We are very crowded," or "It is a seated dinner."

Resourcefulness is a much needed asset when, let's say, the very special fresh jumbo asparagus burns. The stores are closed and the frozen vegetables in the freezer and cans on the shelf seem so dull. It is amazing, though, what a crisis and a little ingenuity can do. Many exciting recipes have been born this way. Here are a few examples:

Gertie had a moment of panic when her husband called that he would be home in half an hour—with three guests for dinner. The pot roast would stretch, for luckily she had planned to use it for two meals. But vegetables? In the freezer she found extra string beans, a package of French fried onions; on the shelf was a can of cream of mushroom soup. She calmly put them all together, creating Gertie's Green Dish (see p. 241).

Once, when the asparagus really did burn and had to be discarded, I found that I had a large bunch of carrots. It was an emergency, so I saved time and shaved the carrots into long thin strands with a vegetable scraper. They took no time at all to cook. They were the hit of the dinner and no one knew they were a substitute. "Carrot Noodles" (see p. 242) are now in my recipe repertoire.

Another time, a child "Calamity Jane" sat right smack on the pie that was to be served for dinner. My friend Ruth did not seem dismayed. She put canned peaches into a greased oven dish and then put slices of the dough (which was fortunately left over) over the top. She had no time to roll it out. At the end of dinner we had a lovely peach cobbler.

The kind of resourcefulness I suggest is enhanced by a good emergency shelf and an inner calm.

Be a Hostess to the End

The party is almost over, there are a few stragglers left. They may be good friends with whom you can let down your hair, kick off your shoes, and re-hash who said what to whom. Or they may be near strangers whom you wish would GO. However, you are *still* the hostess, and you can't do anything that would spoil the wonderful illusion of graciousness you've built.

So try to be relaxed and not worry about the dishwashing. And even though you are tired, get the most out of your party until the very last minute.

Obviously, if it's a supper or dinner party, you have removed the soiled dishes and scraped and stacked them. But you did all this in such a deft way that you were never behind scenes for long. Because, as any good hostess knows, her place is with her guests—not elbow-deep in a dishpan.

Even toward the end of the party, the living room looks fairly neat, considering you weren't a Mrs. Fussbudget. Do you remember that old classic, *Craig's Wife,* a play which dwelt on a housewife with a compulsion for order and cleanliness? Neatness became such an obsession that she nagged her husband right out of her life. This case against obsessive neatness points out the necessity of not making your smoking guests uncomfortable by trailing them with a silent butler. Nor should you forever plump up cushions or wipe up glass rings from the coffee table. Instead, you should be so unobtrusive about removing empty glasses and disposing of ashtray debris that no one realizes that you are cleaning up. These are accomplishments hostesses should learn. There is nothing more disconcerting to guests than for the hostess to make an obvious display of neatening up the mess they have been responsible for. Guests like to be comfortable and relaxed—not kept so tidy that they feel they're in a straitjacket.

After the Party is Over

The last guest has left. They all gave rave reviews. So you can heave a happy sigh knowing your show was a smash hit and you a successful producer. Now it's understandable for you to crow over your prowess.

You plotted the details like a stage director. You planned the food with the know-how of a chef. You invited and combined the guests with the grace of a social director. You mustered up the tact of a diplomat and the resourcefulness of a magician to cope with the unexpected. And throughout you glowed with the graciousness and warmth of an angel.

So go to sleep feeling the contentment of success, without a worry in your head—except for tomorrow's cleanup.

And, oh! yes—that formal dinner party you're giving two weeks from Friday.

2. Parties Around the Clock

Any time is a good time for a party. And the time of day or night determines the type of party and the kind of food and drink to be served.

More or less, that is. A "coffee" can be in the morning or afternoon, and a child's cambric tea party can be any time at all. A breakfast can be given from dawn to noon. And a cocktail buffet can be a luncheon, supper, or late snack. So here are parties around the clock.

Breakfast—Parties and Otherwise

People are more set in their ways about what they eat for breakfast than for any other meal. Breakfast idiosyncrasies are varied. They can be as simple as one man demanding coffee the minute he wakes up or another demanding tea. To some people fresh orange juice is a must; others must have piping hot cereal. While pie may seem normal breakfast fare to some people, it might seem unusual to the Philadelphian who insists on scrapple.

Some people "can't eat a thing in the morning," while others claim "breakfast is my best meal." Breakfast can mean prune juice, two three-minute eggs, toast, and coffee to a business man; oatmeal and milk to a school child; Danish pastry and hot chocolate to a teenager; or merely grapefruit, Ry-Krisp, and tea to a calorie-conscious housewife. Yet, almost all these stubborn individuals who are unswervingly persnickety about what they eat and the time they eat it—Monday through Friday—turn traitor to their pet meal when the weekend comes around.

On Saturdays, Sundays, holidays, and at vacation time, breakfast becomes an entirely different kettle of victuals. It takes on an informal party-like air when time is no object.

It becomes leisurely instead of rushed, talky instead of quiet, bountiful instead of skimpy. And there is no thought of calories when the table is laden with berries and thick cream; sausages, creamed beef, or chicken; waffles, griddle cakes, French toast, muffins, or popovers. Breakfast now has the bountiful atmosphere of a party—even if there are no guests.

When breakfast is really a party, it becomes even more varied. It can be served from early morning to afternoon, and *what* is served can resemble any other meal of the day or night. A wedding breakfast is like an elaborate luncheon. A hunt breakfast, complete with champagne, could double for an after-theater supper. And there are breakfasts that seem to be lunches; people sometimes refer to this meal as brunch.

Petit Dejeuner

In France, breakfast usually consists of *café au lait* with a *croissant* or *brioche* and is sometimes called *café complet*. It is similar to the continental breakfast some hotels leave outside your door. This European invention is particularly useful when you have houseguests. Coffee, fruit juice, and perhaps a sweet roll is an easy way to stay them until you serve a hearty breakfast at noon. In this way you skip lunch entirely, which not only simplifies meal planning but minimizes cooking and dishwashing.

All-American Company Breakfast

However, there are times when an early breakfast is indicated. Perhaps you have overnight guests who hope to get an early start the next morning. Or you have asked everyone to your house for breakfast before a hunting or fishing trip. Perhaps a friend who has weekend guests is having an elaborate party on Saturday night, and you have decided to help her out by asking her guests for breakfast so she can prepare for her party without guests under foot.

In any of these cases you will want to serve a substantial meal. It is a good plan to set the table the night before—complete with electric percolator and toaster, a chafing dish ready to be lighted, and an electric hot tray. You can even measure the coffee into the pot beforehand. Make the coffee

before the guests are scheduled to arrive, then you can
greet them with a steaming cupful. And be sure to have a
big pitcher of fruit juice and serve it in generous glasses.
While they are drinking this, the bacon strips can be kept
crisp on the hot tray and the scrambled eggs can be made
in the chafing dish. Here is the menu—as American and as
easy as pie. Look in the recipes, p. 225 for my scrambled
eggs recipe.

ALL-AMERICAN COMPANY BREAKFAST
Coffee
Orange Juice
Scrambled Eggs* and Crisp Bacon
Wild Mountain Blackberry Jelly
Toast
Coffee   Coffee   Coffee

The "Coffee" and the Kaffee-Klatsch

When someone is sending invitations for a tea it is
almost superfluous to add that it will be held in the afternoon. However, the hour for a coffee or a kaffee-klatsch
may differ considerably according to where you live. And
either of these two functions has a close relation to the
coffee break so dear to the white-collar set.

The idea for a coffee originated in the Deep South, where
entertaining the ladies was pleasanter in the cool of the
morning than in the heat at afternoon tea-time. Although
the usual hour for such get-togethers in the South is elevenish,
the food served with coffee is almost exactly the same as
that for an afternoon tea. The manner of serving is also
similar—the silver tea or coffee service, the honored guests
who pours, the table laden with platters of dainty little sandwiches and trays of delectable cakes.

One hostess who had a long list of duty pay-backs had a
double-duty coffee. Fifty women were asked from eleven
to twelve, and another large group from twelve to one. You
can gather that it's convenient and relatively inexpensive to
entertain this way—without liquor, and with simple "tea"
foods. A mob of guests can be served in two fell swoops.

* Asterisks refer to recipes in Part II of this book.

But the so-called coffee has moved from the South. In the North it is sometimes used to express a before-bridge-lunch-without-cocktails. Also, people have been known to serve coffee instead of tea in the afternoon (very good, too—especially if it is iced in the summer).

In Europe, where it obviously started, the kaffee-klatsch (literally "coffee-gossip") has always been an elaborate afternoon gathering. But American women have relegated it to the morning. Usually it's given after the children have been sent off to school, the dishes done, the small household chores accomplished. Then Mrs. Doe, Mrs. Jones, and Mrs. Smith can gather at the home of one of them at approximately ten o'clock and dunk doughnuts in coffee while they gossip about how amazingly rotund Mrs. So-and-So has become. The "klatsch" usually winds up with more cups of coffee and another round of doughnuts or Danishes ("O, my, I shouldn't!") and a discussion of the most recent and popular diets.

Brunch

Brunch covers a multitude of menus that are strictly neither breakfast nor lunch, but have some of the good qualities of each. But instead of holding to Webster's stolid "a combined breakfast and lunch" description, let's consider it in an entirely different way.

I like to think of brunch as a direct descendant of the old German *Gabel Frühstück*, literally "fork early piece" or, freely, fork breakfast. It was the German custom to have a hot beverage before going to chores on the farm or to the office. And then, at about eleven o'clock, the family gathered for the *Gabel Frühstück*.

This is a charming concept. But when you invite people to a brunch, don't assume that they have had a hot beverage. Be ready with a steaming pot of coffee. From then on, the menu is up to the hostess, who can be as daring or conventional as she pleases. For the usual breakfast orange juice, substitute broth of the sea. Instead of sunny-sides-up with bacon, there could be a variety of main dishes as wide as anyone's imagination. Here are a few that have proved most successful. The first one is a good choice for a holiday.

HOLIDAY BRUNCH
Coffee
Juice of the Sea*
Curried Shrimp Pancakes*
Marble Coffee Cake*
More Coffee

SATURDAY BRUNCH
Coffee   Coffee   Coffee
Fresh Dill Tomato Juice*
Sweet and Pungent Tongue (Orange Almond Sauce)*
Flaky Crescents
Munster Cheese Apples*
Coffee

SUNDAY BRUNCH
Coffee   Coffee   Coffee
Minted Pineapple Juice
Sautéed Chicken Livers   Mushrooms and Onions
Rye Toast
Wild Strawberry Preserves
Walnut Coffee Cake*
Coffee

Party Luncheon

Whether elaborate or simple, luncheon parties fall into two distinct categories—with or without men—and the menus for each can be chosen accordingly. When men are included, the food must be substantial rather than dainty. And the menu must be planned so that an extra round of cocktails for the boys won't spoil the pudding.

But lunch for the ladies can be prettified and frivolous and can include creamy dishes for the non-calorie-counting guests. A ladies' luncheon usually calls for more imagination than any other party meal. Small clubs and committees abound everywhere, and when the members take turns at entertaining, the female competitive urge reaches the boiling point. But there is no ill will in this type of competition among friends. Even though jealousy may try to raise its ugly green head, most guests are sincere in their compliments to a hostess who has provided a delicious lunch in an original style. They may, however, be double-thinking all the while about how they can top it when their turn comes around.

Lunch for the Ladies

A luncheon does not have to be large or elaborate to be considered a party. Even if the hostess has asked only three guests, with or without bridge afterward, it's more fun for everybody if she thinks of it as a party. The menu may be perhaps a bowl of soup and a sandwich. But a party mood can be set with the accoutrements—a special flower arrangement, pretty linens, china, glass, and silver.

In the following menus, the hostess with little or no help was kept in mind. The changing of first-course dishes has been eliminated. However, any one of them can be preceded by hot or iced bouillon and/or hors d'oeuvre. Not included here are the several-course country club or hotel luncheons which are too elaborate for home. Later in the book, luncheons for such special occasions as holidays, business, weekends, and wedding showers will be covered.

Serving and clearing up are the bugaboos of a maidless hostess. And there are several ways to cope with both. If there is a dining area in your home, the fuss and bother of clearing can be minimized by serving the main course there and then moving into the living room for dessert and coffee. If there is no dining room, the smart hostess can have a serve-yourself buffet luncheon which the guests can eat standing or seated—with the aid of the ubiquitous stack table. Or she can serve on trays set with a plate of food, beverage, cutlery, and linen.

But for true unconcern at party time, that popular all-American word "prepackaging" crops up. A box lunch is a simplified and gay way to serve an informal gathering, and there is no reason for a hostess to be boxed in with the concept of a cardboard carton. As you will find later in the book, the containers for such a luncheon can be anything from a shoe box, a basket, or a bandanna knapsack to a see-through plastic handbag. More about these later.

Here are several menus for ladies' luncheons.

TWO SEATED LUNCHEONS
IN THE DINING ROOM
LUNCHEON #1

Cheese Soufflé*   Bacon Strips
Asparagus Salad
French Bread
Schnecken*   Coffee
(Dessert served in living room so dining table
can be left uncleared)

LUNCHEON #2

Cream of Mushroom Soup
Toast Fingers
Avocado, Grapefruit, Watercress Salad
Apricot Linzer Squares*
Coffee

TWO BUFFET LUNCHEONS FOR THE LADIES
LUNCHEON #1 (HOT)

Curry of Chicken
Rice
Chopped Peanuts   Grated Coconut   Chutney
Mixed Green Salad
Lime Pie
Coffee

LUNCHEON #2 (COLD)

Crab Meat Salad garnished with Pink Shrimp
Tomato Aspic   Bedeviled Eggs*
Alaskan Dressing*
Sliced Fresh Pineapple
Orange Pecan Cookies*
Coffee

TWO LUNCHEONS FOR THE LADIES
LUNCHEON #1 (HOT)

Individual Sizzling Plates
Broiled Double Lamb Chops
Chicken Livers   Crisp Bacon
Broiled Tomato Halves   Savory French String Beans
Lemon Pie   Parachute Cookies*
Coffee

LUNCHEON #2 (COLD)
Individual Chilled Multi-salad Plate
Tuna Salad   Egg Salad with Chives
Cottage Cheese with Watercress
Cherry Tomatoes in Endive Boats
Ry-Krisp   Sesame Crackers
Orange Walnut Torte*
Coffee

Lunch on a Tray

Trays are an ideal way to serve few or many. Perhaps only four friends are going to a matinee. Everything can be put right onto four trays. And a thoughtful hostess can include a cup of hot bouillon, just in case there is no time for coffee before curtain time.

When many are involved and there are more chairs than tables, trays again save the day. A young hostess used them to save *her* day when she was entertaining twenty members of the Women's Symphony Committee. Her living room could seat that many persons but there weren't enough tables to go around. Black lacquer trays set the theme for her luncheon. To create the mood, she greeted the guests with tiny cups of sake and her record player spun continuous Oriental rhythm. The trays were set with lacquered bowls of Eastern-type food and chopsticks.

ORIENTAL TRAY
Fried Shrimp*   Apricot Sauce*   Snow Peas
Hot Mustard   Soy Sauce
Jasmine Tea
Fortune Cookies

BEFORE-THE-MATINEE TRAY
Hot Tomato and Beef Bouillon
Baby Chicken Legs*   Avocado and Watercress Salad
Buttered Roll
Thin Mints

Box Lunches

These are as old as Sunday School picnics and go back
to the days of the original square dances, when young
swains bid on the prettiness of the girl rather than the
quality of food contained in her box. Nowadays, the prettiness is in the box and there is no bidding, as all of the food
within is good. Sometimes the box lunch reverts to its original
idea—a picnic meal. But frequently it is elaborate both in con-
tent and appearance. I have been asked many times to
dream up box lunches for lavish entertaining in elegant
homes as well as in showrooms of big companies. I have
used boxes, baskets, and all types of containers—including
beautiful lacquered bowls from the Orient, hollowed-out
styrofoam snowballs, and even gold-sprayed workmen's pails.
One of the easiest to produce and most effective was a
simple shoe box with flat green leaves stapled over its
entire surface. It brought an aura of picnic-in-the-woods
into a New York City apartment.

But, even though the container may be pretty enough to
take home as a souvenir, it is only as successful as the food
it contains. It can be fun to eat picnic-style in the living
room—but not unless it can be accomplished daintily. Sandwiches are but one easy way. They should be fairly small and
must be wrapped in wax paper and then foil so they will
remain fresh. Anything drippy like cole slaw or relish should
be deleted from the menu. There should be disposable plastic
eating implements, plenty of paper napkins, and individual
containers of salt, pepper, and mustard.

Unless the box lunch happens to be served in a school
or a workman's tin box (complete with thermos) is used,
the serving of after-lunch coffee must be reckoned with. The
two simplest ways to handle this are to pass mugs of coffee
or to include a cup in the box and then make the rounds
with a steaming pitcher and the sugar and cream.

Once I did a box lunch with a see-through plastic handbag as the container. The hostess had just returned from
California and mentioned rather casually that she had
brought back some unusual plastic bags to give each of the
guests. She thought I was daft when I suggested using them

as containers for the lunch. She finally went along with the idea, which turned out to be a great success. The foil-wrapped food looked pretty gleaming through the plastic. For an amusing finale, the change purse was filled with chocolate "money" wrapped in gold foil.

LUNCH IN THE BAG
Slim Turkey Sandwiches   Half-moon Tongue on Rye
Whole Bedeviled Egg
Celery Hearts   Carrot Slivers
Stuffed Olives   Sweet Pickles
Salt   Pepper   Mustard
Tangerine
Spanish Cake*
Chocolate Pennies
Coffee in Mugs

One of the most successful box-lunch parties ever was for a famous display designer. We call it "Turkey in the Straw." This is the party where we used gilded lunch pails as containers. We covered the bottom of the pail with a bed of gold cellophane "straw" on which the food was arranged. In the top of the box (which usually holds a small thermos) we put a split of champagne. Every bit of food that went into the lunch pail was wrapped in cellophane or foil.

TURKEY-IN-THE-STRAW BOX LUNCH
Champagne
Roast Turkey Leg
Crab Flake Salad in Cream Puff Shells*
Watercress Sandwich   Tomato and Egg Sandwich
Tiny Rich Cake Squares

Another successful box lunch was held at Easter. The box in this case was sizable (7" by 8" by 6") and was covered with chintz in a spring-flower pattern. The gimmick of this box was that, on opening the box, the luncher first saw a cellophane-covered paper plate which contained the main part of the meal. When he lifted this out, he saw the extras and eating implements beneath. This is what the box contained (incidentally, the boxes were so pretty that most guests took them home):

EASTER BOX LUNCH
On Cellophane-wrapped Plate
Half Broiler cut into Bite-sized Pieces
Parsley Sprigs   Plum Tomato
Underneath on Green Cellophane "Grass"
Two Paper Napkins   Plastic Fork and Spoon
Paper Cup with Handle
Cellophane Bags with
Stuffed Olives   Celery Hearts   Carrot Sticks
Salted Nuts
Cookies   Candy
Foil-wrapped Cake Squares

Basket Buffet

Another way to use baskets for lunch is to substitute them for platters or trays. They should have flat bottoms, and handles large enough for guests to swing them on their arms while selecting from the buffet. They should be lined with aluminum foil. If the baskets are wide enough and flat enough, they can be used as trays and can accommodate coffee mugs. Although cutlery could be provided, it's more fun to plan the menu so that the food is pick-uppable and non-drippy. And, of course, have lots and lots of large paper napkins.

PICK-UP BASKET LUNCH
Fried Chicken Pieces
Small Ears Corn on Cob   Cherry Tomatoes
Kebabs of Spiced Cantaloupe, Raw Pea Pods, Stuffed Olives
Small Buttered Rolls
Danish Pastry Midgets
Coffee

Dessert Luncheons

Sometimes, at the women's auxiliary of a large organization, the members arrive bringing their own sandwiches for a meeting at eleven A.M. At about 12:30, they sit in foursomes at card tables that have been set with a paper doily, plate, and napkin, and eat their own lunches while they discuss what went on at the meeting. Then they are served a dessert of cake or cookies and coffee or tea, for which each contributes twenty-five cents. This is a very efficient and simplified pay-as-you-go method. It's easy on the budget, and its informality is quite enjoyable.

Another kind of dessert lunch came into being when so many acceptances to an organization luncheon were received that it became cumbersome to serve a complete meal. The menu was quickly changed to coffee and cake. The one P.M. time was kept when it was pointed out that many women with pressures of dinner to prepare and school children to greet found it better than tea time to be away from home. So the dessert luncheon idea was born and, as with most good ideas, it prospered.

It is wise to provide two types of dessert in order to please both nondieters and the calorie-conscious. An interesting fruit platter—so pretty with contrasting colors, form, and texture—will leave even the dieters satisfied. One suggestion is my Basket Arrangement.

DESSERT LUNCH FOR DIETERS
Fruit Platter   Basket Arrangement*
Ry-Krisp
Coffee
Tea

DESSERT LUNCH FOR NONDIETERS
Fresh Coconut Layer Cake*   Dutch Apple Cake*
Jam Tarts*   Chocolate Nut Torte Squares*
Coffee
Tea

Luncheon with Men

When men are included at a luncheon party, it is usually on weekends, holidays, or special occasions like weddings, or anniversaries. And if the male is asked on an ordinary weekday the reason is usually business. All of these luncheon categories will be covered in later chapters. The chief thing to remember when men and food are involved is heartiness and simplicity. Avoid frou-frou in the main course. But remember that many men have a sweet tooth.

Here are two menus that men seem to enjoy. The first one has many courses and might seem rather hearty for the ladies. The second one makes up in quantity for far less variety.

SIT-DOWN LUNCH WITH MEN
Sectioned Grapefruit
Filets of Prime Rib Roast
Curried Corn Pudding
Fresh Asparagus   Lemon Butter
French Rolls
Brandied Apple Raisin Pie
Coffee

LUNCHEON BUFFET WITH MEN
Bouillabaise*
(plenty of it)
Hot Garlic Bread
Cheese Torte
Coffee

Tea and Empathy

There is something particularly festive about an afternoon tea. Whether it's an intimate gathering or a large reception, a tea somehow combines sophistication with Old World charm. Even in the small living room of a modest city apartment, a tea manages to seem elegant. The tea leaves stir up the illusion of a fanciful drawing room draped in mauve brocade. The hostess is *really* wearing a wispy tea gown, firelight flickers on the antique Sheffield tea service as she pours, the guests are trading witticisms over the tinkle of the bone-china teacups ...

A tea party is forthright and correct. Everybody knows just what to expect when they arrive—friendliness, charm, talk, a bit of food, a spot of tea, and much empathy. The invitation announces that the beverages will be nonalcoholic. So that settles the serving problems—unless dear Uncle Joe whispers demandingly, "Just a smidgin of rum in my cup, my dear."

Ladies of all ages seem to love tea parties for many reasons. They intrigue seven-year-old Wendy because they make her feel grown up—even though it's merely cambric tea (hot water, milk, slight tea flavoring). Her grandmother likes them because they're a good way to get together with old friends. Wendy's mother likes them because they are a simple way to entertain her garden club. And a debutante would far rather settle for a tea than for any other function a teetotaler relative might want to give ("Oh, Grandmother, what will everybody say when there's not even *wine* at my coming-out reception?").

Teas are an easy and inexpensive way to entertain either few or many people. Like cocktail parties, they can be termed "receptions" and a large group of people can be entertained in limited space and time. But teas have two advantages over the cocktail gathering—they are more economical and they are timesavers. The four-to-six or five-to-seven time schedule is taken much more seriously. Who ever heard of a tea-goer expecting dainty sandwiches and delicate cakes to substitute for her evening meal? She knows when she's had her cup of tea. And when she's tea-ed to the gills and has gathered all the gossip, she's away and gone before the hostess could possibly think of suggesting, "Do have just one more cup for the road."

The Large Tea or Reception

Before the guests arrive, the hostess must allow plenty of time not only to prepare the food but to arrange the dining-room table in a grand manner. It may be well to extend the table with extra leaves—much better to have the table too big than too small to avoid a clutter when the guests are serving themselves. The table is covered with a linen or lace tablecloth—the finest. In the center is a lovely flower arrangement and silver candlesticks. At one end is a tea service on a tray with a bowl of sugar lumps and tongs, cream pitcher, a plate of paper-thin lemon slices (some of them pierced with cloves), and a small fork. To one side are cups, saucers, and silver spoons. At the other end of the table is a tray with coffee urn, sugar lumps, cream, cups, saucers, and spoons.

On each side of the table are platters of dainty sandwiches, small cakes or tiny pastries, salted nuts, and mints. There are also linen tea napkins. Some hostesses find it convenient to provide salad plates for their hungrier guests.

At each end of the table there should be a comfortable chair for the two friends you have honored by asking them to pour. An old-time custom is to place an extra chair near each end of the table so that someone can sit and chat with the pourer. And be sure to relieve your "honored guest" from her "duty" after the first hour.

Aside from the volunteer help, there should be kitchen help at a large tea. The food platters must be replenished so that the table maintains a fresh, attractive look for new-comers. And used cups and saucers must be removed and washed.

A tea menu can be varied, but it almost always stays within the limits of dainty, pick-uppable foods. Some hostesses cannot resist showing off their baking skill by serving a large cake. In this case, cake plates and forks are a must.

The Tuesday Tea or "At Home"

There is a revival of old-time customs going on in our modern, sophisticated civilization. The "At Home" was charming and rewarding way-back and is gradually becoming a modern innovation. An At Home is not to be confused with the "open house" prevalent in many sections of the country on New Year's Day. It means that a hostess picks an afternoon—let's say Tuesday—when she will serve tea to any friends who drop in.

At the beginning of the season, she gives a blanket invitation, "Come by for tea any Tuesday at about four." Of course, until word gets around about weekly events, she may just sit and wait, and drink a lone cup. But once they catch on there is the mystery. Who will come? How many? And how will an unplanned party group mix? More often than not the party that's not planned ends up in a pleasant, informal get-together.

Because the number of guests is unpredictable, it is impractical for the hostess to make a quantity of sandwiches in advance. Her best bet is to have plenty of nonperishable cookies on hand and the wherewithal for the guests to make their own cinnamon toast or simple sandwiches. Of course, if she has a maid, these can be prepared as the guests arrive.

A do-it-yourself buffet makes for congeniality, and this

should be uncomplicated for everybody concerned. At one end of the buffet have all the setups for tea making, including a container of water simmering over a flame. At the other end have an electric toaster, bread, butter, cinnamon sugar, knives, and plates. Or, a loaf of datenut bread and a plate of cream cheese. The rest of the buffet table should consist of nonperishables—nuts, mints, cookies, wafers, and cheese sticks.

The Small Intimate Tea

The intimacy of a tea party depends on the seating arrangement in the living room. Because, to be truly intimate, there must be only one conversation group, with the hostess more or less in the center. So count the chairs before inviting the guests.

A tea is the kind of party a girl gives to whisper the news of her engagement or a suburban wife to launch a new neighbor or introduce a very special houseguest.

The hostess always pours with the completely equipped tea tray placed on a table in front of her. If the table is large enough, plates of food also can be placed on the table. A maid is certainly necessary when hot food is involved, because it's awkward for the hostess to be dashing in and out of the kitchen. For cold sandwiches and small cakes, the modern version of the rolling tea table is the perfect answer for small parties.

The Tea Dance

A dance in the afternoon was particularly popular with young people in the twenties, when it was dubbed *thé dansante*. The Plaza Hotel did a whopping afternoon business back in those days when Scott and Zelda Fitzgerald were among the habitués. Since that time, the popularity of the tea dance has been down and up. And now its name has more to do with the time of day than with the amount of tea imbibed, even though the currently favorite beverage, punch, may have tea as a basic ingredient.

Few homes nowadays are large enough to accommodate an impressive tea dance. And even though young people may have a Saturday afternoon party at home to the tune of rock and roll, they'd probably rather call it a coke dance. The greatest advocates of tea dances at the present time are doting uncles, who, remembering the twenties, give them at clubs for their debutante nieces.

Menus for Tea

THE LARGE TEA #1
Sandwich Assortment
Watercress Rolls*   Date-nut Checkerboards*
Paté Pinwheels*
Cheese and Olive Squares   Chopped Chicken Triangles
Chocolate Nut Torte Squares*
Tea Buttons*
Mints   Salted Nuts
Tea   Coffee

THE LARGE TEA #2
Sandwich Assortment
Minced Chicken Envelopes*   Paté Cornucopias*
Asparagus Rolls
Chopped Egg Triangles
Jam Tarts*   Old Dutch Cookies*
Chocolate Mints
Tea   Coffee

THE SMALL TEA (WITH MAID)
Narrow Strips of Hot Cinnamon Toast
Hot Biscuits with Wild Strawberry Jam
Tea

THE SMALL TEA (WITHOUT MAID)
(This is an easy one—the sandwiches are semisweet so that no cakes or cookies need be included in the menu.)
Sandwiches
Cream Cheese on Date-nut Bread
and/or
Cream Cheese and Jelly on Whole Wheat Bread
Tea

THE SUMMER TEA
Sandwiches
Thin Cucumber Slices with Dill on White Bread
Tomato Rounds with Tarragon on Whole Wheat Bread
Watercress Rolls
Iced Tea with Fresh Mint
Cookies (crisped in the oven)
and
More Iced Tea

Cocktail Parties—from Noon to Midnight

The extreme flexibility of a cocktail party has made it the most popular form of entertaining. It's a drink in one hand and a snack in the other. It may be for three thousand people or for three. There is no worry about seating arrangements because people mingle better when they are standing. And more people can be accommodated in less space than at any other type of party. "The more the merrier" is an applicable truism. The cocktail party can be formal or casual, elaborate or simple; and it can be given for business or pleasure. Its many advantages have released it from the tight confines of late-afternoon entertaining. Now cocktail parties go around the clock, and cocktail party foods are used for informal lunches and even for afternoon entertaining.

In planning a cocktail party of any appreciable size, a bar is a must—whether improvised or real. And if the party room is very large, it is well to have a bar at each end, which, of course, necessitates bartenders. If the group is small, the host can fix the drinks in the kitchen or the hostess can ask one of the guests to act as bartender—just as she would ask a friend to pour tea.

Before considering the edibles, the guest list should be studied to determine the quantities and types of beverages that are needed. Although your dearest friend may simply adore a frozen daiquiri when she goes to a restaurant, she most certainly will not ask for one at a party in your home. Even when there is a bartender, serving fancy concoctions has become passé. Unless you have very finicky guests, the three-way rule should be adequate—scotch; gin or vodka;

and bourbon, rye, or a blend. There should also be a supply of soft drinks and mixes—cola, ginger ale, club soda and, in summer, tonic. Don't forget a good supply of ice, plenty of glasses, and last but not least, dry vermouth for martinis.

If you've asked people from five to seven, don't make the mistake of whispering to a few special friends, "Stay for supper when the rest leave." Either plan a forthright cocktail party with snacks or make it a cocktail buffet—for everybody. Which brings us to the subject of cocktail foods.

Webster's New World Dictionary says that a canapé is a "toasted slice of bread or cracker spread with spiced meat, sardines, cheese, etc., served as an appetizer, often with drinks." The dictionary people obviously never attended a party where little, open-faced, fancifully cut, and bejewled bits (called canapés) were served.

For years I went along with the fad and spent hours upon hours concocting them, and privately thought of them as tortured tidbits—a lot of everything but not much of anything. It was by chance that I finally bucked the trend. It was a Saturday morning in the mid-40's. My staff was particularly harried. We had orders for hundreds and hundreds of canapés—and for two parties. Then the phone rang. It was Grover Whalen's office and one of his many secretaries confessed that someone had goofed. They needed a cocktail party that very afternoon for sixty guests in honor of the Duke and Duchess of Windsor. The guests had accepted, but ordering the party had been forgotten. I had arranged many parties for Mr. Whalen, and it was unthinkable that I should say "no" in such an emergency.

It was a tension-filled experience. I had to produce a party in not much more time than we usually had for packing the food and equipment and trucking it to the party scene. That's when I really decided that canapés were out.

We had only roast turkey and baked ham in our commissary, so they had to do for this party. Since time and hands were so short, I went along to help my staff. My butler was just about to carve the ham into wafer-thin slices when I had an inspiration that has served me well for many impressive parties since. I cut a huge slab from the bottom of the ham, almost half of it, right up to the bone. Then I cut this bottom piece into cubes, stuck them onto the top side with toothpicks, and placed the "ham pincushion" on a large silver tray.

Next, I had the breast from the turkey cut into "sticks." Each turkey piece was toothpicked, dipped into Russian dressing, and then into sliced toasted almonds. We placed the turkey sticks close together in neat rows around the ham and I immediately dubbed it "Ham Porcupine with Breast of Turkey Fingers."

This was the beginning of a new trend for me in my party business. Gone forever were the canapés I secretly despised. By luck, I had stumbled on a way of presenting pick-up foods in a dramatic fashion. And I was thrilled with the possibilities of devising new and different hors d'oeuvre in this way.

Later we devised other porcupine platters with different meats and cheese. We made ice-bowl gardens, which started out as a method of keeping shrimp cold during a party. In lieu of dreary old canapés, we used smoked salmon and sturgeon in platter arrangements as a smart presentation of foods that are pick-uppable.

Hot Hors d'Oeuvre

As our repertoire of hot appetizers also began to expand, we were constantly creating new ideas. Inspiration seemed to come with need. For example, a hostess in the fashion world almost always invited the same group to her parties and asked me to give them something novel. Walking home from the interview with her, I passed a poultry store and was inspired to use tiny chicken legs.

Appetizers served piping hot from the oven are always compliment-getters. But many hostesses shy away from them, feeling they require too much time in the kitchen during the party. Actually many hot hors d'oeuvre can be prepared in advance and popped in the oven for a quick heat-through. Some can be prepared days or weeks ahead and then frozen. Others can be made the morning of the party—partially baked or not cooked at all and kept in the refrigerator. It's much more impressive to produce hot tidbits than crackers and the cheese that happens to be left over in the refrigerator.

In preparing for any party, make extras. These can be held back for an emergency in case the guests are hungrier than expected. And, if not eaten, they can be filed in the freezer for future use. Asparagus Cheese Rolls* are excellent for this purpose. Any left over from the original party can be frozen and served toasted later. Mini-Pizzas* are another example—they can be frozen at any stage after the dough has been rolled and cut. Other suggestions are given in Part Two.

Do-it-yourself Appetizers

Dips are much like punches—they are made "to taste." Choosing ingredients for such cocktail fare is a challenge to the venturesome hostess. It seems to me that those two little words, "to taste," are the most adult and the most demanding in the whole lexicon of food literature. Should a recipe include them, it does not mean that the author is being negligent about giving information. She *is* saying, "Go ahead and make this your own very personal dish. Have courage. Add this or that. By using ingenuity you will make this your own personal recipe." This is what it means to be a creative cook, and it is this variation that makes food exploration so fascinating.

Dips and Spreads

The consistency makes the difference between a dip and a spread. Dips are usually light and fluffy—like whipped cream or mayonnaise—and can easily be scooped up with even a fragile potato chip. Spreads are slightly more solid, e.g., cream cheese or *foie gras*. Little butter knives or spreaders are a must for them.

Mediterranean Caviar* should be an honored member in anyone's guess-what-it-is taste club. Its origin is the Near East, where eggplant is a favorite vegetable. When it is cooked, combined with other ingredients, and chilled, it is apt to defy detection. Especially when it contains the surprise element of freshly chopped dill.

It's not only fun to include surprise ingredients in dips; when well chosen, they can add that something-special flavor that makes guests exclaim, "Oh, I know it's basically clams —what else?" This has happened with Clam Dip Bari when dry vermouth is the added extra, or with Crab Dip Bombay with grated coconut. And hardly anyone has guessed that chopped red apple is what gives Eggs Lido that crunchiness.

Tartar steak is easy to make—no cooking. Chopped liver is an old cocktail party stand-by that can be served in numerous ways. (See recipe section.)

Dunkers

The foods to dunk into dips or to be spread with them are legion, and many ideas are given in the appetizers section of Part Two. Also in Part Two are some novelties for cocktail parties—a collection I call fantasies. Along with them are ideas for emergencies.

Cocktail-party Fork Foods

Presentation is a tremendously important factor in the serving of food. And variety in serving is surpassed only by variety in seasoning. Finger foods, dips, and spreads are the rule at most cocktail parties. But no rule prevents the use of a fork and small plate at a drinking party. Of course, fork foods are more manageable when the party is small because there's always the problem of *that* glass, and perhaps *that* cigarette. But if the food is good enough and the guest hungry enough, he will not mind the handling problem.

Cocktail-party fork foods are first cousins to dishes served at a buffet supper. And, just as a little breakfast is called *petit déjeuner,* so could cocktail food that's eaten with a fork be called *petit souper* or *petit buffet.*

Two hot dishes that always make a hit at a cocktail party are Oysters Casino and Cheese Soufflés. The oysters are baked and served on a bed of rock salt. Plates and oyster forks (and perhaps some asbestos mitts) are needed. The soufflés are baked in individual soufflé dishes or ramekins. When they are puffy and golden, they are whisked from the oven, placed on a plate, and served piping hot.

A cold dish popular with men is Ham and Potato Salad Torte. It's just what the name says, a "cake" of salad.

Hors d'Oeuvre Cakes are fun to make for special occasions. And when you let your imagination run riot, the guests "oh" and "ah" and hesitate to cut into them. The basis for these cakes (sometimes called sandwich loaves) is layers of bread with appetizer fillings spread thickly between them. The outside of the cake is covered with softened cream cheese and decorated to suit the occasion with strips of green pepper and pimento and radish slices.

Hors d'Oeuvre Cakes can be made in any shape that suits your fancy. I've made them round, square, oval, triangular, even in the form of a three-tiered wedding cake. For an author's birthday party, I made a cake that turned out to be a dramatic success, with a literary flavor—an open book.

For the Big Crush—Sandwiches

Since the Earl of Sandwich gave his name to this whole family of pickup foods, the variety of fillings is limitless. Inventiveness is the fun of cooking and there is no end to the combinations of ingredients a sandwich chef can dream up or to the unusual shapes that can be devised.

The size of cocktail sandwiches may vary with the type of party. If it is an all-male function, they are apt to be quite large, probably with the crust left on. If it is an impromptu office celebration, they may be served just as the delicatessen sends them or hero sandiches cut in hunks. Usually, however, cocktail sandwiches are fairly small and are made of thinly sliced bread.

A simple sandwich made with the standard square sandwich loaf can be given an air of novelty just by the way it is cut. After the crusts are removed, it can be sliced into triangles, oblongs, tiny squares, thin strips, diagonal strips, etc.

Loaf sandwiches are extremely practical as they can be made three days ahead of the party. They will be fresh as long as they are kept in damp towels in the refrigerator. And there is little last-minute work—just cutting and trimming.

There will be more specifics about these in the recipe section of the book. Other novelty sandwiches which will be described in detail are pinwheels, checkerboards, cornucopias, envelopes, and tiny roll-ups.

Dinner Parties—Formal and Otherwise

Dinner has always been the principal meal of the day. Noon used to be the time for a hearty meal—when the man of the house would come in from the fields or home from his business. This was particularly true in the summer. The major cooking could be done in the cool of the morning. In the sizzling afternoons, the housewife could relax on a shaded veranda or behind drawn curtains in the cool sitting room. The evening meal at six would be cold left-overs from dinner and glasses of iced tea.

Midday dinner still prevails in some areas on Sundays. It is almost a necessity for farm hands who have had breakfast at dawn and need hearty sustenance at noon to replenish their physical energies. But in urban and suburban areas, dinner has been relegated to late in the day. With the modern tensions and strains of business, it's the only time that the worker can relax, put his feet up, and enjoy a home reunion. Since evening dinner can be eaten leisurely, it's a good time to have company.

Spontaneous little dinner parties are fun because there is no pretext of grandeur. They are potluck—and that is it. The casual "Stay for dinner, won't you?" is a heritage from our grandmothers' generous, open-door hospitality. It represents the kind of impromptu entertaining that requires merely an extra plate or two. Some meals lend themselves readily to an extra guest—lamb casserole or a curry, for instance, can be divided or expanded. More bouillon can be added to make them juicier, and more rice can be cooked for a solid base.

Four lamb chops, however, would require higher mathematics and ingenuity to make them stretch to feed five guests. They can be cut off their bones, cubed, marinated, and become shish kebabs—on a skewer with the addition of whatever vegetables are on hand. And, again, that old stand-by, rice, could act as an additional filler-upper. Or, the entire menu could be changed—that's when an emergency grocery shelf or freezer comes in handy.

"Come on over for dinner!" is another type of last-minute invitation. It usually doesn't have the emergency element—because there is time to scrounge around for needed ingredients. The reasons for this type of little party are many. The husband of a friend has left on an unexpected business trip. A relative arrives in town out of the blue. That attractive couple who were so nice to you in Haiti are stranded between planes at the airport.

To my way of thinking, whenever you ask a guest it's a party. Aside from the spontaneous dinner parties just mentioned, a dinner should be carefully planned. Small or large, formal or informal, elaborate or simple, whether for a visiting dignitary or for simple homebodies, there are three important elements (besides the food) which are of prime importance. There should be invitations in advance, a seat for each guest, and adequate service. Invitations need not be engraved— they can be handwritten, telephoned, or wired. A seat for each guest does not mean matched, upholstered dining chairs. The seat might be a sofa or a step on the stairs, it might be a folding chair or a picnic bench in the yard. The serving might be done by liveried butlers or French maids, or it might be accomplished by your anxious, slightly awkward, but very willing teen-age progeny.

Here are the ways, means, and menus for various kinds of dinner parties—from the really informal to the very, very formal.

The One-platter Dinner

One hostess I know had a very tiny dining space—so small in fact that necessity gave her the idea for one-platter dinners. When I say the whole meal was dished up on one platter, I do not mean a stew or a casserole. Here is a typical example of one of her pretty-to-look-at-and-good-to-eat meals. Down the center of an oval platter were overlapping slices of rosy roast beef. On one side of the meat, browned potatoes staidly stood guard, with slivered green beans on the other side. A big bunch of watercress was tucked into the meat at one end—a colorful accent for the picture.

Another favorite was served by the same hostess on a large round chop plate. In the center was a mound of feathery rice. The asparagus was arranged, tips pointing up, around the rice. Portions of roast chicken bordered the platter. What an easy way to serve! And, there was only one serving platter and one set of serving tools to wash.

Seated Buffet Dinner Party—No Maid

Jean gives some of the nicest informal dinner parties I know of, usually with six or eight guests. At cocktail time she wheels in a cart on which are several kinds of dips and crackers. Her living room is so arranged that the guests can cluster around the cart with their drinks.

When Jean calls you to dinner, the first course is already on the table. It may be a soup or a fruit. While you are finishing this, Jean will quietly disappear and before you know it the sideboard is covered with the complete main course.

You are asked to help yourself from the sideboard buffet. You do—then sit down again to eat in comfort at the table. If you want a second helping, it's no great effort to help yourself again, because there is everything sitting pretty and warm on the hot trays.

She has a simple way of clearing the table, too. Each guest passes his plate to Jean, who stacks them onto the service cart and wheels it into the kitchen. In short order, she reappears with the cart, bearing coffee and dessert. The entire party seems effortless, informal, and relaxed. Here are two of her menus:

INFORMAL BUFFET DINNER (NO MAID) #1
Honeydew Melon
Roast Prime Ribs of Beef
Mashed Potatoes   Oriental Eggplant*
Buttered Rolls   Torino Olives
Green Salad
Natsapple Cake*
Coffee

INFORMAL BUFFET DINNER (NO MAID) #2
Clam-Tomato Broth
Crackers
Stuffed Baked Whitefish*
Baked Potatoes with Sour Cream and Chives
Broccoli with Lemon Butter

Rolls
Sliced Cucumbers with Dill
Chocolate Cake
Coffee

Dinner Party for Eight—One Maid

An informal dinner can have a dramatic and formal air, even with limited help. It all depends on the hostess. The excellence of the menu, of course, is even more so. One smart hostess, Lil, starts planning two weeks in advance. That's when she phones her invitations. She usually asks eight people—the number her dining table will comfortably seat. She takes great pains in setting the table and always works out a color theme to combine the linens she has on hand with the flowers or fruits that are available.

She has an excellent maid, who has been trained to serve a dinner for eight smoothly. After cocktails, when the guests go to the table, the soup is on. So are the bowls of salad, rolls, and relish. When the soup course is finished and the plates removed, the maid places a stack of warmed dinner plates to the left of the hostess. Then the meat platter and vegetables are set in front of her. Lil carves and dishes the food onto the plates. As each plate is filled, the maid serves it—honor guest first, then clockwise around the table. When the main course is finished, she removes the dishes, tidies the table, and serves the dessert in the same way.

Here is an example of one of her dramatic menus:

DINNER PARTY FOR 8 (ONE MAID)
Gazpacho*
Scallions   Radish Roses   Gherkins
Crown Roast of Lamb Rousseau*
Whole Baby Carrots   Fresh Green Peas
Rolls   Butter Curls
Imperial Salad*
Cup-up Fruits   Sauce of the Angels*
Thin Cookies
Coffee

Patio Dinner Party, California Style— Teen-Age Help

Outdoor eating is no novelty to Southern Californians. It has long been a way of life for much of the year. A patio dinner is planned and served in much the same way as an indoor meal. A typical example was a charming party given for me by Betty and Bill. The glass-topped patio table was candle-lit and was set for twelve people. At each end there was a huge bowl of salad. Salad is customarily eaten as a first course in California, and so, as soon as the guests were seated, they started.

Meanwhile the host was busily occupied at the barbecue grill. Carving steaks into individual portions before cooking is another practical California custom. The host becomes a short-order cook so that each guest can have his steak done to the exact degree desired.

Bill kept the stack of dinner plates warm at the side of the grill. As each steak was cooked to a turn, he placed it on a hot plate, then a teen-aged son or daughter hustled it over to Betty's end of the table. The young waiter or waitress stood at attention until Betty had filled it with its supplement of vegetables, then served it pronto to the guest it was intended for. It is standard operating procedure for the children of the household to get up immediately after a course and clear the table. I like the idea—and their California menu:

PATIO DINNER PARTY FOR 12 (TEEN-AGE HELP)

Valley Salad*   Hazel's Roquefort Dressing*
Buttered French Bread
Barbecued Marinated Steaks*
Grill-roasted Potatoes   Tomato Mystery Pudding*
California Flaming Oranges*
Coffee

Formal Dinner Parties at Home—for Twelve or More

Invitations for a formal dinner party are much the same now as they were in Victorian days. They must be written or engraved, and they must be sent by mail or messenger two weeks before the party. Aside from diplomatic or government functions, the average standard of formality takes only what is practical from the Victorian customs. For example, the traditional books of etiquette rule that *only men* should serve at a formal dinner and there should be *one footman for each two guests*. This style would be out of place (and above the budget) in most American households. In fact, should an average citizen follow the book to the letter, he would be considered a show-off or a *nouveau riche*.

Obviously, if the invitations are formal and "Black Tie" is designated, the dinner must be elegant—with the finest silver, crystal, china, and linen the hostess can furnish. It must be a seated party and expertly served. It is possible to accomplish this with three rather than the prescribed six people in service for a dinner party of twelve. Mrs. X has worked this out successfully for the formal parties she gives. She has two people, male or female, in the dining-room and one in the kitchen. The dining-room help are always spotlessly and smartly uniformed.

She is a marvelous executive hostess. She hires bright, competent help to whom she can delegate food and service responsibility. When the party starts she seems not to have a care. But even when she is in fascinating conversation with the guest of honor, she has an eye on everything. With a wave of her hand or a nod of her head she can indicate that someone needs wine, water, or whatever.

Although it has become customary to serve the guest of honor first, there are two schools of thought on the matter. Mrs. X prefers the older one—having the hostess served first. This dates back, no doubt, to the Middle Ages, when the king had a taster to assure him that his wine and food were not poisoned. She, then, plays the king's taster. Either method is correct.

At formal dinners, no food is carved or served at the table. The platters of meat, vegetables, and salad are served individually to the left of each guest. A silver serving fork and spoon are placed on each platter in a position that makes it convenient for the guest to serve himself.

The maid or butler stands at the left of each guest. She or he holds the platter on top of the left palm with a folded napkin between hand and bottom of dish. The person serving goes first to the woman at the right of the host with the meat or fish platter, then clockwise around the table. The second serving person follows with the vegetables. The platters may be passed again for second helpings. When the main course is finished, the dinner plate is removed with the right hand and the salad plate is set with the left hand.

It is perfectly correct for the table to be cleared just before dessert is served by removing two plates at one time—one in each hand. A clean, folded napkin is used to brush crumbs onto a small tray or plate. The only exception to the left-handed serving rule is for pouring coffee, water, or wine. This is always done from the right.

Before dessert is served, a dessert plate with doily, finger bowl, fork, and spoon is set in front of each guest. The *guest* picks up the finger bowl, with doily, and places it in front of the dessert plate. The fork is put to the left and the spoon to the right of the plate. The dessert is now served to each guest. Wine may be served with it as well as with the meat course. Demitasse—from a gleaming silver service—is served in the living room with liqueurs. This is the type of formal dinners Mrs. X would serve:

FORMAL DINNER PARTY FOR 12 #1 (BUTLER, MAID, COOK)

Clear Consommé   Sesame Crackers
Hearts of Celery   Colossal Stuffed Olives
Beach Plum Jelly
Breast of Guinea Hen   Black Cherries
Small Browned Potatoes
Fresh Green Asparagus   Lemon Butter
Small Rolls   Butter Balls
Green Salad   French Dressing
Raspberry Ice   Chocolate Wafers*
Demitasse

FORMAL DINNER PARTY FOR 12 #2 (BUTLER, MAID, COOK)

Lump Crabmeat Cocktail
Black Olives   Celery Curls
Filet of Beef
Small Browned Potatoes

Whole Artichokes   Hollandaise Sauce
Small Finger Rolls
Chocolate Roll*
Demitasse

Suppertime

Supper is the last meal of the day, eaten in the evening. Actually suppertime depends on the occasion, and on
the hunger or age of the guests. Midnight suppers are for
people who prefer to eat after rather than before the theater
or concert. Earlier suppers are for bridge or poker players
who have to get to work the next morning. A seaside cot-
tager I know frequently serves supper to her weekend guests
in midafternoon so they can drive back to the city at a
decent hour. Actually, it's a combination of lunch and
supper—and she has dubbed it "lupper" (with apologies to
Noah Webster).

The old-fashioned supper was always about six o'clock.
Adults from various sections of the country can dig into
their memories of childhood to recall, and mentally savor,
the dishes that were supper specialties in their particular
regions. Saturday-night supper in New England was oven-
baked beans and brown bread, or clam chowder made with
cream. In Maryland, it was likely to be freshly baked rolls,
straight from the oven (Saturday was baking day) with a
bowl of thick vegetable soup.

In some regions, corn pone or Sally Lunn is the favorite
Sunday-night supper dish with thin slices of ham. A winter
Sunday supper treat in Virginia is baked oysters. They don't
have to be shucked—just put them on a pan and leave them
in a hot oven until they pop open. The addition of butter,
lemon, or Worcestershire sauce is entirely up to the guests.

Maryland crabs are wonderful supper fare. Deviled crabs
mean more work for the hostess, but steamed hardshell
crabs are practically no trouble. She steams the crabs in a
minimum of water, flavored with vinegar and black pepper.
Then she dumps them onto a newspaper-covered table—
and the guests are on their own. How they love it!

Both in the southern and midwestern states (and perhaps elsewhere) the covered-dish supper has been popular
in many church groups as a way to raise money. The ladies

are asked to bring their particular cooking specialty—a casserole, roast, potato salad, etc. The emphasis is on sturdy food instead of the sweets they would contribute to a bazaar or food fair.

The church-supper idea spurred a young Westport, Connecticut, housewife into giving a private party, which turned out to be a great success. The birthdays of three husbands in her group fell within a certain week. The wives decided to give one large party (they invited thirty people) to cover the three celebrations. Instead of each person bringing presents for the three birthday boys, it was decided that each wife would bring her particular food specialty. No one was given a hint about what anyone else would bring. Each wife was merely asked to bring enough for four servings. Amazingly, there were no duplications. The supper buffet was spread on a long table covered with red checked tablecloths. There was so much more food than needed that there was a return buffet party on the following night.

Invitations, both formal and informal, are covered in another section of this book. But off-beat ones will have to be described in conjunction with imaginative parties. For example, the invitation for the "covered supper" was written on a small paper plate encased in a square of red checked gingham. The four corners were tied like a knapsack, and the whole thing was mailed in a manila envelope.

Suppers can be simple, like those mentioned, but they also can be highly elaborate. Many times I have been asked to produce a cocktail-buffet party, which is virtually two parties in one. The first part features solid hors d'oeuvre which are extremely sustaining. The supper buffet menu is also ample—but everyone seems to be happy.

COCKTAIL PARTY AND BUFFET SUPPER
Hors d'Oeuvre
Deviled Nuts
Grilled Steak Kebabs
Hot Asparagus Cheese Rolls*
Ham Porcupine with Breast of Turkey Fingers*

BUFFET SUPPER
Veal Fiesole*   Green Noodles
Tossed Green Salad with Chinese Water Chestnuts

Small Buttered Rolls   Spiced Cantaloupe
Tri-Fruit Bowl*
Walnut Divine Squares*
Coffee

For people who have simple eating habits, here are a few supper buffet menus that will satisfy the starving guests. Obviously, the hostess will serve small snacks with the drinks before supper. And she will have generous amounts of the few dishes she serves. For instance, if it is a dish that deserves rice, she will be sure that the entrée has enough juice to saturate the rice. Although some people love rice for its own sake, most prefer it as a sop for succulent accompaniments.

Here are five tasty and easy menus for supper buffets which could be served any time from six to midnight.

BUFFET SUPPER FOR THE CROWD #1
Hors d'Oeuvre
Drinks
Beef Maria*   Potato Dumplings
String Beans, cooked with ground Savory
Small Buttered Rolls
Spiced Peaches
Walnut Roll*   Coffee

EASY BUFFET CASSEROLE FOR THE CROWD #2
Snacks and Drinks
Creamed Chicken Mr. A.*   Rice
Green Salad
Toasted Rolls   Sweet Butter
Blueberry Pie
Coffee

EASY BUFFET FOR ANY NUMBER #3
Finger Food and Drinks
Chicken Anita*
Gingered Rice with Almonds
Frenched String Beans
Melba Toast   Chive Butter
Pistachio Ice Cream
Parachute Cookies*
Coffee

CASSEROLE SUPPER BUFFET #4
Oysters Casino*
Drinks
Shrimp Creole
Rice   French Peas
Crisp French Bread   Sweet Butter
Cheese Torte*
Coffee

SUMMER SUPPER BUFFET #5
Crisp Vegetable Appetizers
Long Cool Drinks
Chicken Salad Henshaw*
Cucumber Sandwiches
Lime Ice
Iced Tea   Iced Coffee

Theater Suppers—Before the Show

A *petit souper* before curtain time is an excellent way to entertain theater-goers who are also commuters. As it is on a strict time schedule, it is far from a leisurely party and the hostess must plan with clocklike precision so that each guest will be fed without fluster or confusion. There should be enough time left before the departure deadline to allow for primping, coating, and hatting. A nice touch, if the budget can bear it, is to have transportation ready to whisk all of the guests to the theater door—a limousine or two for a small group, a bus for a crowd.

The food for this kind of party should be fairly substantial. It should also be easy to eat and easy to serve. A buffet table spread with finger foods or foods that require a minimum of eating implements is the best bet for the hostess who has no servants to clean up after the party. When this is no problem, fork foods can be served—but tables can be eliminated and no knives need be used.

SMALL BUFFET SUPPER (FINGER FOODS)
Cocktails
Shrimp Garden Platter*   Zippy Cocktail Sauce*
Tiny Drumsticks*   Stuffed Mushrooms*

Assorted Small Cakes
Demitasse

LARGE BUFFET SUPPER (FORK FOODS)
Cocktails
Bouchées* of Marine Mix*
Cherry Tomatoes   Black Olives
Celery Heart Curls
Nova Scotia Salmon Platter*
Ham and Potato Salad Torte*
Assorted Fruit Tarts
Demitasse

Theater Suppers—After the Show

Many people in the performing arts and those who
live on off-beat schedules eat their main meals late at night.
That's when they can relax and enjoy themselves, because
their mornings are for sleeping. A midnight supper party is
practically the only way to entertain such people.

How a midnight supper is served depends on space and
the number of guests. It can be seated with full service, or
it can be a buffet with or without small tables. The menu
can be elaborate or simple; there can be light, delicate viands
and rich concoctions. But the term "midnight supper" con-
notes elegance—the ladies in silks and satins, the gentlemen
in glistening white shirtfronts and tails, the buffet table with
silver candelabra and chafing dish.

Here is the way three different types of people entertain
at midnight:

Mr. A. has one of the few large mansions left in New
York City. It has become traditional for him to give a large
supper after the opening night of the opera. His invitations
are as prized as a bid to a cotillion. His buffet table is
bountiful, and small round tables with gilded chairs are
distributed throughout the parlor floor.

AFTER THE OPERA
GALA MIDNIGHT SUPPER FOR 200
Champagne
Hearts of Celery   Colossal Stuffed Olives

Carrot Sticks   Watermelon Rind   Radish Roses
Blinis—Fresh Beluga Malossal Caviar   Sour Cream
Pastry Crescents   Small Buttered Rolls   Tissue Rye
Lobster Thermidor
Creamed Chicken Mr. A.*
Vegetable Mélange
Tossed Green Salad
Bel Paese   French Brie
Ice Cream Balls   Marrons
Rich Little Cakes
Demitasse

Mrs. B. is chairman of the woman's committee of her local symphony. She likes to entertain the visiting conductor or soloist after an important concert. Her buffet menu might read:

AFTER THE SYMPHONY
MIDNIGHT SUPPER FOR 50
Chilled Rhine Wine
Fresh Lobster Chunks in Lobster Bisque   Cheese Puffs*
Large Open Sandwiches cut in Halves
Beef Tongue   Turkey   Swiss Cheese
Molded Fruit Salad
Jam Tarts*   Tiny Danish Pastries
Coffee

Mrs. C. is an inveterate first nighter, and she loves to throw a midnight supper afterward. She asks a nucleus of friends in advance, and has enough food prepared. But if the show is a hit, her enthusiasm runs away with her and she's likely to ask as many of her friends in the audience and cast as she can corral. She has an ace in the hole to meet such a circumstance. She makes a quantity of thermidor sauce and tucks it away in the refrigerator. As the guests gather, all she has to do is to warm the sauce in a double boiler and drop a hard-cooked egg cut in half for each new arrival.

Here is her impromptu supper menu:

AFTER THEATER
IMPROMPTU MIDNIGHT SUPPER
FOR 20 OR MORE
Ale
Glazed Canadian Bacon
Baked Beans
Hard-cooked Eggs   Thermidor Sauce*
Hot Buttered Biscuits   Celery Hearts
Fruits Tri-color*
Sponge Cake*
Coffee

Actually, this supper menu (minus the sweets) could become a wee-hour breakfast after a debutante ball or New Year's Eve party. It would be an interesting switch from the usual scrambled-eggs-bacon-or-sausage fare. The beans could be kept warm indefinitely in a very low oven. The Eggs Thermidor could be handled at the last minute—just as Mrs. C. did.

3. Parties Around the Calendar

A sudden whim is all that's needed to put some people in a party-giving frame of mind. But almost everybody finds that the incentive of a national, religious, or traditional holiday gives impetus to the party spirit. If it's an official holiday, when all businesses are closed, both the guests and the hosts have time on their hands and are more relaxed and gay. Even if it's a holiday which may fall on a work day (St. Valentine's or St. Patrick's), the decor and the menu have a built-in theme.

So here is a fiesta calendar with food and decorating suggestions intended to spur a hostess into giving a year of successful parties.

A Yearful of Parties

Let's get a date book for the coming year and flip the pages from month to month. And, before checking off the obvious occasions, jot down the little personal holidays that are dear to you and your friends. Make a note of all the birthdays and anniversaries of people you know. Though a party may not necessarily be indicated, these jottings will be wonderful reminders to send cards.

Now let's turn back the pages to the beginning of the date book and start plotting parties by the calendar.

January—the Beginning of a Party Year

A hostess who has been up late on New Year's Eve can be "At Home" on New Year's Day with little work. New Year's eggnog parties originated with the Dutch Nieuw

Amsterdam burghers, and the tradition, which survived in the New York area, has been carried far and wide.

The fruitcake, made weeks ago, has been aging nicely in its airtight tin, with occasional cups of brandy added to keep it moist, and is now waiting to be sliced. A sprig or two of holly salutes the season. The eggnog base, made several days ahead to meld the flavors, is ready to be poured into the punch bowl. Then the stiffly beaten egg whites are folded in, and nutmeg lightly sprinkled on top. The food and drink await the guests. So simple and so festive!

January One is not the only New Year celebration in this country. The Chinese New Year is a spectacular event in large cities with a sizable Chinese population. The date is variable, but is usually in January. There is a street festival that is brilliant with lanterns, firecrackers, and huge fish kites. Foodstands abound with delectable morsels for sale.

The Jewish New Year comes much later—September or October. And the tradition is to dip bread in honey to sweeten the year ahead.

Whatever the New Year, it is a time to rejoice together with relatives and friends, to eat, drink, and be merry—and hope for a good year ahead.

February Was Made for Parties

If it weren't that February is our shortest month, or that George Washington was born within its limits, or that St. Valentine blessed it—most people would gladly chuck it right out of the calendar. Especially in the northern United States, February is a cold and blustery and sometimes slushy time of year. It is a month that extends winter twenty-nine days too far—without a hope that spring is on its way.

Therefore, February is an excellent time to perk up everyone's spirits with colorful parties. This is an obvious way to keep young fry happy and out of mischief. But it also can be amusing and fun for adults. The most sophisticated people are often delighted with a bit of "corn." Even though they may explain away their enthusiasm with, "It reminds me of my childhood days!" they are really relaxing and having fun.

February 14 is the day to entertain a pair of new romancers with hearts and flowers and sentimental gadgetry for invitations and decorations. A pretty centerpiece for such a party—luncheon, supper or dinner—would be a mass of flowers in two shades of pink interspersed with a few pink heart doilies wired to florists' sticks. A variation could be a tight mass of pink carnations with garnet roses in the center or in reverse, deep red carnations with sweetheart roses. A pretty addition would be an edging of pink paper doilies to make an old-fashioned nosegay.

VALENTINE LUNCHEON OR SUPPER
Tomato Juice   Heart-shaped Garlic Toast
Celery Hearts   Stuffed Olives
Salmon Mousse*
Pickled Beets   Sweet Onion Slices
Tiny Rolls
Butter Cake with Pale Pink Icing
(Decorated with Red Heart Candies)
Coffee

VALENTINE DINNER
Cold Borscht on the Rocks
Radish Roses   Pimento Olives
Boiled Beef Tongue
New Potatoes with Paprika
Creamed Spinach
Buttered Rolls   Red Shell Pistachios
Open Cherry Pie*
(Decorated with Lacy Whipped Cream)
Coffee

VALENTINE COCKTAIL PARTY
Valentine Cocktails
Vodka and Cranberry Juice
Hearty Sandwiches
Open Turkey with tiny Hearts cut out of Pimento
Closed Heart-shaped Salmon Sandwiches with a
Heart "Window" cut out of top piece of Bread
Garden Platter
Fresh Shrimp in Red Cabbage Cups   Cocktail Sauce I*
Celery Hearts   Pickled Onions
Unhulled Strawberries
Pimento Stuffed Olives
Salted Nuts
Coffee

YOUNG GIRL'S VALENTINE PARTY
Box Supper
Tongue and Mayonnaise Sandwiches on White Bread
Pickled Red Eggs
Pink and White Candy Hearts
Easel Cake*
Cola   Hot Chocolate

The easel cake made a great hit at one February party. A high round cake, iced white and decorated in red, made the bottom. The top was a low heart-shaped cake backed by firm cardboard and slanted against a small easel, as would a painting. The heart, also white and red, told the story "Be My Valentine." Details for making easel cakes are on page 256.

February 22 is another wonderful time to give a party. It is not only a national holiday, but provides ready-made ideas for both food and decorations. Red again is the key-note color, but now it can be combined with blue and white. Stationery and variety stores always have a supply of novelties for the occasion—favors, decorations, place cards, invitations. Cherries are the obvious answer for the dessert course. And Cherry Upside Down (see p. 272) is not only delicious, but can have an added George Washington theme by drawing the outline of a hatchet on top with whipped cream and a pastry bag.

WASHINGTON'S BIRTHDAY
LUNCHEON OR SUPPER
Cups of Cream of Tomato Soup
Radish Roses   Celery   Pimento Olives
Tongue Salad
(Mixed Greens, French Dressing, tossed with
Cubes of Boiled Beef Tongue)
Hot Garlic French Bread
Cherry Upside-down Pie*

March—the Wearing of the Green More Than the Growing

A woman of eighty-five once said, "I have always felt that March meant spring was here. But aside from a few crocuses, I have been disappointed every year. You'd think I'd have learned better by now."

Nobody seems to know better—there's always the hope that spring is around that gusty corner. The gayest event in March is St. Patrick's Day, and it is a day for a party. In New York City, the Irish have a grand parade down the green stripe on Fifth Avenue, rain or shine, and there is much festivity afterward. But Irish, Catholic, or not, March 17 is a gay and great time. Though it's not a national holiday in the United States, all nationalities seem to take on a bit of the Irish and wear a sprig of green.

Celebrations go on at restaurants all over town, or at homes where hostesses who've never seen the Emerald Isle use green as the gay theme of the evening.

Each dish in this St. Patrick's Day menu has an in-the-mood name, but don't let this make you feel that the food will be "corny."

ST. PATRICK'S DAY DINNER
Erin Pipe Dreams* (Anchovy in Cucumber)
Wheels of Chance* (Spinach Ring* Fried Oysters)
Fruited Cobblestones*
(Fruits—round side up, tinted green)
Emerald High Hat*
Coffee

Here is an idea for place card props for this dinner: Cut scraped carrots into squat one-inch pieces and stand them up. Scoop out the tops. Then fill with a bit of cream cheese and stick in four-leaf clovers (if unavailable, use parsley sprigs). They make darling little flowerpots and are edible, too. Paste them onto cards with cream cheese.

April—Easter's Here and So Are Parties

The sight of little girls in straw sailors and navy blue coats pinned with a bunch of violets means spring is truly here. With older girls it may be flowered hats, navy blue suits, and a spray of orchids.

But whatever the finery, spring is in the air. It's a time for rejoicing after the austerity of winter. It's a colorful time with chocolate chicks and bunnies, baskets with green grass, and hard-cooked eggs dressed up in all the rainbow's colors.

April sometimes seems to be the most perfect month in the year. It's a time of new thought and new life, a time people of many faiths revere. It is a family time—and anyone asked to an Easter party knows that he is considered a close friend.

In every culture there is a spring festival to celebrate the reawakening of life. The Last Supper was a Seder, which Jews celebrate in memory of their march of freedom from slavery in Egypt and their rebirth as a nation in the Promised Land. Seders are traditionally held on the eve of the first day of Passover.

Eggs—the symbol of new life—are the focal point in many Easter parties. An egg-rolling party on the lawn has long been a White House custom, enjoyed by both children and the adults who watch the colorful spectacle. Egg hunts are always a treat for the very young, who are usually told that a rabbit has hidden them. This stems from a European tradition that bunnies bring good things to children.

Eggs also feature in pre-Easter do-it-yourself parties for children—egg coloring, candy making. Both are held in the kitchen with an adult or two to supervise. Spread plenty of newspapers on the kitchen table and floor, because vegetable dyes, although pure and harmless, can stain, and young artists are not noted for their neatness. Old clothes or plastic aprons are also recommended.

Fondant is a happy choice for an Easter candy-making party, as it is so easy to make and can be molded into shapes to suit the occasion. Chocolate eggs are easy, too. Use any dipping chocolate you like. First make a hole in each end of an egg shell, then blow the egg out. Now seal one hole with Scotch tape and pour the chocolate into the other. Set aside in egg boxes to harden, peel off the shell, and you have a perfectly shaped chocolate egg which looks fine as is, but can be made even prettier with squiggles of white cake icing made with a pastry tube. These make attractive "place cards" for a children's (or even adults') Easter party—with the first names or initials of each guest in icing on top.

Here are three Easter menus—a luncheon, a dinner which features the traditional Easter baked ham, and a Seder dinner:

EASTER LUNCHEON PARTY
Half Avocado
with Half Hard-cooked Egg, Fresh Caviar
Stuffed Cornish Game Hen
Wild Rice
Fresh Asparagus   Lemon Butter
Tiny Rolls   Currant Jelly
Lemon Ice Box Cake*
Coffee

EASTER DINNER MENU
Salted Almonds
Grapefruit Segments
Small Rolls   Raspberry Apple Sauce
Baked Ham
Tiny New Potatoes
Broccoli
Vanilla Ice Cream with Sliced Strawberries
Coffee

PASSOVER SEDER DINNER
Ceremonial Platter
Charoseth*   Roasted Hard-cooked Egg
Horseradish Root   Watercress   Roasted Lamb Bone
Matzos
Hard-cooked Egg   Salt Water
Gefüllte Fish Balls*   Matzo Balls*
Chicken Soup*   Matzo Balls*
Roast Spring Chicken
Tiny New Potatoes   Fresh Asparagus
Fresh Strawberries   Matzomeal Sponge Cake
Coffee
Salted Nuts   Raisins

May—Flower-time, Party-time

The first day of this cheerful month and the next to last day are both party-giving occasions. And in between there's Mother's Day for good measure. May is the month when the profusion of flowers prove right the jingle about April showers. It's a month that opens with a party for the children, that honors the mother and grandmother midway, that offers a holiday celebration for the whole family at the end.

Probably as far back as pagan days, small boys left little baskets of flowers on the doorsteps of their favorite little girls' homes on Mayday morning. It has always been a sweet and sentimental idea. But young Lotharios dislike admitting they have a sentimental streak.

A Mayday party has a built-in decor, either for children or adults. The tall maypole with colorful ribbons which the children dance around is also charming in miniature as a centerpiece for a First of May dinner table or buffet for adults.

Here is a springlike dinner party idea for the May 1 party that plays up the season both in decorations and in food. Ideally, the dinner table should be round. In the center is a twelve- or eighteen-inch dowel thrust into a circle of styrofoam. Both dowel and base are covered with flowers. As many varicolored ribbons as there are guests are stapled to the top of the dowel. A small bouquet of flowers is then tied to the top. The ribbon streamers are looped down to each place setting. On the end of each is tied a flower and a place card.

The color scheme for this party should be like a nosegay —varicolored flowers with ribbons to contrast. The food should include all of the delights of spring.

MAYDAY DINNER
Fresh Artichokes Vinaigrette
Rare Roast Leg of Baby Spring Lamb with Marjoram
New (unpeeled) Potatoes—Parsley Butter
Fresh Asparagus   Lemon Butter
Rolls   Mint Jelly
Mixed Green Salad   French Dressing
Linzer Diamonds   Pineapple Water Ice   Salted Nuts
Coffee

Mother's Day offers a special way to entertain. If mother has teen-age children, it gives them a chance to do something special in the way of repaying her for all her efforts. One way they can do this is to say, "Mother, you are not to do a lick of work on the day that has been designated as yours."

They could then plan all the meals for the Sunday on which Mother's Day falls.

Start with a fine breakfast before church, then a luncheon or midday dinner for just the family or for relatives and friends too. This midday feast should be planned so that there are enough left-overs for supper—Mother should not have to do a thing on *her* day.

Here is a full, three-way menu—breakfast, luncheon-dinner, supper—for teen-agers who want to help their mothers.

MOTHER'S DAY BREAKFAST
Orange Segments
Grilled Canadian Bacon—Fried Egg on each Slice
Popovers (made from mix)
Strawberry Jam
Coffee

MOTHER'S DAY DINNER
Tiny Artichokes on Lettuce Leaf
Black Olives   Celery
Roast Leg of Veal
Baked Potatoes with Sour Cream
Frozen String Beans
Small Rolls
Frozen Raspberries on Sponge Layers   Whipped Cream
Hot Tea with Lemon

MOTHER'S DAY SUPPER
Sliced Cold Veal   Anchovies
Sliced Tomatoes
Rye Bread
Brownie Squares (made from mix)
Root Beer

Memorial Day, or Decoration Day, marks the beginning of Summer fun for the family. It sets the mood for vacationing, and often it falls conveniently at the end or beginning of the week so that it becomes a long weekend. Frequently the weather turns warm enough to allow the year's first outdoor eating—picnics and barbecues.

Whichever way the weather turns, you will be fortified with these menus:

MEMORIAL DAY PICNIC FOR WARM WEATHER (OUTDOORS)
Apricot Nectar with Lemon Juice
Grilled Chicken Parts   Frozen Corn Rounds, Grilled
Garlic Bread
Pick-ups
Celery   Carrots   Raw Peas   Lettuce Wedges
Apple Cake*   Coffee

MEMORIAL DAY PICNIC FOR COOL WEATHER (INDOORS)
Hot Beef Bouillon
Celery   Dill Pickles
Macedonian Mélange
(short ribs of beef, rice, eggplant, tomatoes,
oregano, pine nuts)
Sesame Rolls
Tossed Green Salad
Fruit Gelatin Dessert   Walnut Divine Squares*
Coffee

June's Parties

There are graduations for all ages in June and this means that father is on the giving end of presents and entertaining rather than on the receiving of such—even though *his* day falls in the middle of the month.

Although graduations are celebrated from grade school to college, the best time for a party is after a high school commencement, before the big senior dance. This is a most memorable time—when teen-agers are approaching adulthood.

BUFFET PARTY BEFORE THE SENIOR DANCE
Cranberry Orange Punch
Olives   Gherkins   Celery
Ham Polynesian
(Cubed ham, pineapple chunks on bamboo skewers)
Buttered Rye Rolls
Lettuce and Tomato Salad
Blueberry Tarts   Coffee

Even though Flag Day, June 14, is not a national holiday, it affords food and decorating ideas for a party. Here is a buffet supper which I arranged for a large group. Flags are the easiest props to come by, and in the center of the buffet table there was a large bouquet of them in varying sizes. Because of the type of menu, it was a seated party, and each little table for four had a small bouquet of flags.

FLAG DAY SUPPER BUFFET
Cold Boiled Lobster Halves   Mayonnaise
Cold Roast Prime Ribs of Beef   Baked Ham*
Sweet Potato Soufflé*
Tossed Green Salad   French Dressing
Flag of Fresh Fruits
Parachute Cookies*   Coffee

The Flag of Fresh Fruits was arranged on a large oblong pan placed in front of the flag bouquet (slightly tilted) and was not only the centerpiece but the high spot of the meal. Chopped ice was placed in the large drip pan, then the flag was made with:

Red stripes   —strawberries
White stripes   —fresh pineapple
Blue background   —blueberries
Stars   —honeydew melon balls

Summer Is for Casual Parties

Although Memorial Day is the prelude to summer entertaining, real summer parties start with July Fourth and continue through Labor Day in September. July, August, and September are carefree vacation times when everyone has a relaxed point of view. Except for parties at some tennis, golf, or country clubs, and private parties in such places as Southampton, Long Island, the mood and the dress are informal.

Outdoor cocktail parties on the terrace or lawn and outdoor eating by the barbecue pit, on the beach, in a shaded glade, on a sailboat or yacht are the backgrounds for summer entertaining. Last-minute invitations to any summer gathering are expected and accepted with pleasure.

Since summer entertaining is in the great outdoors, refer to that chapter for specifics on clam baking, barbecuing, and picnics. The section on weekend planning might also be useful to summer cottagers. Here is a festive Fourth of July supper in two versions—#1 for indoors, #2 for the terrace. The decor can be the same for both. Red blotting paper makes handsome firecrackers. Roll a sheet of it into tubes, fasten with Scotch tape, stuff with raw cotton, and use a white pipe cleaner as a wick. They can be made in many sizes and heights—but don't allow anyone to light them.

In each menu I have featured salmon, which has become a traditional Fourth of July dish. The story goes that George Washington was especially fond of salmon because with his troublesome dentures it was easy to chew. Since Martha Washington is supposed to have invented strawberry ice cream, I have included it. (It seems that she put a dish of crushed strawberries and cream in her ice box, which was so cold that the mixture froze.)

FOURTH OF JULY SUPPER—INDOORS
Chilled Cream of Tomato Soup
Sesame Crackers
Fresh Poached Salmon   Lemon Sauce
Mashed Potatoes
Fresh Peas
Strawberry Ice Cream   Old Dutch Cookies*
Coffee

FOURTH OF JULY SUPPER—OUTDOORS
Tomato and Clam Juice
Cold Boiled Salmon   Hollandaise Sauce
Cold Baby Potatoes Marinated in French Dressing
on Bibb Lettuce
Strawberries and Whipped Cream
(chilled until almost frozen)
Coffee

October Is Full of Surprises

Fall may seem to be in the air in October, but Indian summer may arrive and give it an aspect of summer—warm enough to dunk in the ocean and acquire an off-season tan. Columbus Day comes on the twelfth. It's a day when

Italians parade and stores have special sales of fall and winter coats. It's in no way a national holiday. But it is a good day to give a party—Italian or not. Here's an appropriate buffet supper menu:

COLUMBUS DAY BUFFET SUPPER
Appetizers
Broiled Mushrooms   Stuffed Olives in Garlic Sauce
Thin Italian Salami   Boston Lettuce Leaves
(Guests make sandwiches of leaves and salami)
Columbus Day Covered Casserole*
Green Salad   Italian Dressing*
Penelope's Pears in Wine*
Imported Bel Paese
Espresso

Now we come to Halloween, which is a holiday for both children and adults. Even if there is no children's party planned, mothers enjoy making costumes for their youngsters' "trick or treat."

Actually, a Halloween party for small fry is simple to plan, as the decorations and the games are traditional. Apple-bobbing may be messy, but is nondestructive when done in the cellar. In fact, a cellar is an excellent place to hold all the games for such a party. It can be made dim and mysterious with the lighting produced by candles in hollowed-out pumpkins carved into smiling or grotesque faces. Corn stalks can be heaped in corners and ghost stories can be told. Then, upstairs for the food—Jack o' Lantern sandwiches and soft drinks. The sandwiches are cheese on whole wheat bread—the top layer of bread has goblin face cutouts. The dessert can be chocolate ice cream served in orange shells. And if there is a fireplace, marshmallows can be roasted.

Adults too can decorate with candlelit pumpkin faces. Their lanterns, however, might be made from large rounds of Edam cheese by cutting off the top, scooping out the cheese, cutting out the face, and putting a candle in the cavity. The scooped-out cheese can be grated and seasoned to use for cheeseburgers.

One way to keep in the spirit of the occasion is to use a hollowed-out pumpkin as a bowl for a dip. Or a mound of paté can be formed into the shape of a pumpkin, the surface covered with grated carrots and knife marks to indicate the face.

A wonderful way to entertain in late October—for both adults and teen-agers who live near the wide open spaces—is a Harvest Festival. The ideal place to hold this is a barn decorated with fall vegetables and corn stalks. The guests wear clothes appropriate for square dancing—blue jeans, plaids, and bandanna neckerchiefs for the men; bright colored full skirts and peasant blouses for the girls. It can take the form of an old-fashioned box supper, with the men bidding for their dinner partner and her box of goodies. Rustic games like cornhusking contests fit in well.

November—the Winter Social Whirl Begins

There's excitement in the air—the entertainment season is on. In large cities there are new shows to see, the opera and symphony open, there are charity balls. Everyone is dressier and more formal. There are formal dinners before the ball, buffet suppers before and after the show. For the younger crowd, there are gay college weekends and gala dances after the football game.

All of this leads up to the first big winter holiday—Thanksgiving. No matter how this day is spent—a sentimental twosome in front of an open fire or a jolly crowd at the Army and Navy game—it should be festive. The meal of the day may be Thanksgiving dinner at a large country home, or it may be a simple buffet in a small city apartment for away-from-home acquaintances. But simple or bountiful, it's a time to share—and to be thankful that you can.

TRADITIONAL THANKSGIVING DINNER
Salted Almonds   Hearts of Celery
Oysters on Half Shell
Lemon   Crackers   Horseradish
Roast Turkey*   Chestnut Dressing   Giblet Gravy
Cranberry Orange Relish*
Candied Sweet Potatoes
Creamed White Onions   Frenched String Beans
Brandied Mince Pie
Coffee

THANKSGIVING BUFFET DINNER

Celery Hearts   Black Olives
Roast Turkey Legs
Shaved Carrots*   Fresh Broccoli
Spiced Peaches
Rolls
Pumpkin Ice Cream   Chocolate Sauce
Orange Mints   Raisin Clusters
Coffee

December—Get Set for the Biggest Parties of the Year

The first of December is not too early to start readying the house and the larder for end-of-month festivities. Fruit-cakes and puddings will keep perfectly when stored in tins. Cookies, too, will last for weeks in closed containers. And while you are on this pre-holiday baking spree, stock the freezer with an assortment of pies—mince, pumpkin, apple raisin—and don't forget Christmas candies.

"Do your Christmas gift shopping early" is an old saw, but it's a good one. With presents wrapped and safely stored by midmonth, the week before Christmas can be devoted to decorating the house and to last-minute party preparations.

Try trimming the tree in the old-fashioned way. Let the children get in the act. They can string cranberries and pop-corn into long ropes to loop like garlands among the branches. These can be interspersed with molasses popcorn balls wrapped in bright colored cellophane.

A tree-trimming party is fun for young and old. And it can be followed by carol singing. The refreshments can be as simple as cider and cookies—but not too many because there's a big day of eating ahead.

As with Thanksgiving, Christmas is a time for large family get-togethers. And it's also a wonderful time to round up all the people who for one reason or another might be lonely. It's not a day for anyone to be alone, and there is great satisfaction in sharing good will and good food. A grab bag is an icebreaker at this kind of singles party. Ask each guest to bring two wrapped presents, one for a man and one for a woman. Be sure to limit the cost to a trifle. Have ready two foil-covered cartons marked "His" and "Hers" in which arriving guests may deposit their gifts. When all are present and have sipped some Christmas cheer, they take turns choosing two packages each. You'll be amazed at the humor and good cheer created by the nonsense. When all the gifts have been opened, it is time to bring on the buffet.

CHRISTMAS BUFFET
Celery Stuffed Olives Radishes
Goose Ragout*
Wild Rice
Red Cabbage in Wine*
Individual Plum Puddings* with tiny Red Candle in each
surrounding a Melon Mold of Vanilla Ice Cream
Red and Green Mints
Coffee

TRADITIONAL CHRISTMAS DINNER
Celery Hearts
Cranshaw Melon Lime Wedges
Roast Goose Apple Stuffing
Mashed Potatoes Gravy
Brussels Sprouts with Chestnuts
Plum Pudding* Hard Sauce
Coffee

It is fortunate indeed that there are six days between Christmas, with its lavish food and drink, and the celebration of the last day of the year. Although New Year's Eve is usually considered a time for drinking freely, there are other and more charming ways of ringing the old year out and the New Year in.

A newly married couple may prefer the quiet sharing of a bottle of champagne and a jar of caviar in the living room of their own home to the confetti and confusion of a night club.

Country clubs and all manner of clubs usually hold New Year's Eve parties—they provide dance music, entertainment, and all sorts of fun. But like every other party, the best place to give a New Year's celebration is in your own home. Depending on the size of your house, an elegant and sophisticated party can be produced for a hundred people, twenty, or just eight.

Here are menus for midnight suppers—small, medium, and large. Champagne is in order with each. And a special New Year's Eve cake makes an edible decoration for any one. On a high round layer cake, simply draw the face of a clock with colored icing put through a pastry tube or bag and point both hands to twelve.

NEW YEAR'S EVE SUPPER FOR EIGHT
Foie Gras   Tina Toast*
Turkey on Frame
(carefully carved and returned to bone structure)
Thin Rye Bread   Sage Butter
Individual Cranberry Molds
Clock Cake   Coffee Ice Cream
Salted Almonds
Coffee

NEW YEAR'S EVE BUFFET SUPPER FOR TWENTY
Celery   Black Olives
Beef Maria*   Wild Rice
Endive Salad
Melon Balls in Kirsch
Clock Cake
Coffee

NEW YEAR'S EVE SUPPER FOR 100
Radish Roses   Celery Hearts
Lobster Salad
Boned Chicken in Wine   White Grapes
Watercress Salad
Hot Buttered Rolls   Spiced Crabapples
Clock Cake
Fresh Fruit Melange   Walnut Divine Squares*
Coffee

4. Once in a Lifetime

In every person's life there are especially important occasions. Two—birth and marriage—are of such import that they are celebrated every year. Since primitive times birth, marriage, and death have been observed by most civilizations with ceremonies of a religious nature. There are also lesser occasions but nonetheless important—confirmation, graduation, debut, engagement.

Close friends are sometimes asked to attend a Protestant christening. The ceremony is sometimes held in the home. Catholic christenings are always in church. After a christening, it is usual to have a reception at home. It can be small or large, simple or elaborate. Champagne is the ideal drink with which to celebrate the occasion. It may be accompanied by dainty sandwiches and wafers, or it may be followed by a luncheon.

When Catholic children take their first Communion or are confirmed, it is customary for the parents to give a celebration brunch or lunch. On Confirmation Day, Roman and Greek Catholic girls (and sometimes Episcopalians) of about twelve years of age are dressed in white with miniature wedding veils and carry little bouquets of flowers. The boys are dressed soberly, usually in dark suits.

When a Jewish girl is confirmed, she wears white but no veil. A boy wears a dark suit at his confirmation, at the age of thirteen. The ceremony, called a Bar Mitzvah, welcomes him into the religious community as a man, responsible for his own actions. It is almost always the occasion for a large and elaborate celebration. It is a gift-giving time, with such manly presents as a fountain pen or a watch.

The celebration may be a *Kiddush* after the Sabbath morning Temple ceremony, or a luncheon or evening party. In one case, I arranged an entire weekend of parties. There was a reception after the Friday evening Sabbath service at the Temple. After the Saturday Bar Mitzvah services there was a luncheon, also at the Temple, and on Saturday night there was a dinner dance at a hotel. The weekend of festivities wound up with a Sunday afternoon reception at home for neighbors and acquaintances, as well as the relatives and close friends who had attended the other parties. Punch, sandwiches, and cookies were served at the receptions.

Here is the luncheon menu:

BAR MITZVAH LUNCHEON
Ceremonial Chollah*

Gefüllte Fish   Horseradish

Filet of Prime Roast Beef   Noodle Pudding

Fresh Asparagus

Stuffed Olives   Rolls   Gherkins

Orange Water Ice*

Star of David Cake

Demitasse

The Star of David cake was a great success. To make it, make two cardboard equilateral triangles and put one over the other to form a six-pointed star. Hold them firmly together and trace the star onto another piece of cardboard for your pattern. Bake two large, shallow cakes. Place one on top of the other, and put the star pattern on top. Use a sharp knife to cut around the edge of cardboard. Brush the vertical cut edges with slightly beaten egg white to hold crumbs. Separate layers and spread with rich butter icing. Put together again and ice top and sides. Cover all with fondant. When dry, decorate with Royal Icing* and write "Congratulations to———."

Another appropriate Bar Mitzvah cake is a Bible. Follow the instructions for Book Hors d'Oeuvre (see p. 209), but use sponge or butter cake instead of bread, and cake filling and sweet icing instead of cream cheese.

The first graduation may be from grade school or even kindergarten. Parties for these and later graduations are fun to give, for after the solemn presentation of diplomas the time is right for a gay celebration. E. R. presented her husband of ten years, Sam, with a custom-made purple-lined academic gown to wear on the day he received his degree and also a surprise graduation party for him afterwards. The room was decorated with mortar boards and diplomas, and the hors d'oeuvre took on the same theme.

There were "diploma" sandwiches made from thin slices of bread rolled around a variety of spreads and then "tied" with strips of pimento. Mrs. R. used cardboard mortarboards, upside down and lined with foil, as bowls to hold nuts, olives, and such. As a final touch, she used the Open Book Hors d'Oeuvre* and instead of "Congratulations, Sam," she wrote, "Sam, we made it!"

A social debut or coming-out was once of tremedous importance in some social circles. In Victorian days it truly meant coming out into the social world. In those times, there were no dates as such until a girl, at eighteen or so, made her debut.

Now, when there is a private debut party it is small and unostentatious. It may be a tea or reception attended by close friends of the family as well as by other debutantes and young men friends. Or it can be a dinner for the young people.

In many cities there are cotillions or mass debuts—which are a great saving to families who feel they should introduce their daughters to society. Before these large debutante balls there is usually a series of small dinner parties for intimates. After the ball, may there be informal, last-minute breakfast invitations—Mother has assured her debutante daughter that she will lay in a supply of eggs and bacon and milk.

The original purpose of a debut, besides introducing the young daughter to adult society, was to "catch a man." With or without debut, with or without college, and whether or not she has a job—the average girl from eighteen on has marriage on her mind.

Some marriage ritual has been practiced by every known civilization, and wedding customs are rich in symbolism. A circle means eternity, and when the groom places a wedding ring on the bride's finger, it signifies the bond is forever. In the traditional Greek service, double rings, usually of orange blossoms, are held over the heads of the wedding couple.

The old Roman custom (still observed in Nepal) was to sprinkle wheat gently over the newly wedded couple as a symbol of fertility and abundance. In some parts of Europe, it was customary for the bride and groom to drink mead —a liquor of fermented honey—every day for thirty days after the wedding to sweeten the marriage. It was known as "honey mouth," which led to "honeymoon."

Many Jews still observe the ancient custom of the breaking of a glass—the symbol of eternal love. At the end of the ceremony, a glass wrapped in a napkin is placed on the floor and the groom stamps on it. The sound of the shattering glass is the signal for the guests to shout, *"Mazel-tov!"* "Good luck—congratulations!" When the groom breaks the glass, he is saying in effect, "I shall love you until this glass is whole again—that is, forever."

The fairy story that a handsome knight on a charging white stallion will come to rescue the young princess comes true in India. As a Hindu marriage procession progresses along the city streets, it is approached from the opposite direction by the groom on a white horse, come to meet his bride.

Beautifully decorated cakes are an essential part of all wedding celebrations today. And some form of cake—bread, crackers, buns—has always been a traditional phase of the ceremony. At the feast after a patrician Roman wedding, a "confarreation cake" was broken over the bride's head as a symbol of abundance. Early American Indian brides made cakes of meal and presented them to their braves. Ancient Anglo-Saxons had baskets of crackers for the guests at their wedding celebrations. Later, there were small, rich buns instead of crackers. These little cakes were piled in the center of the table in a high mound. By kissing over this mound the bride and groom were ensured lifelong prosperity.

The wedding cake as we know it today was invented long ago by a clever French chef. He hit on the idea of beautifying the mound of little cakes by covering them with sweet icing. Nowadays, wedding cakes are works of art, and they are expected by guests at both the simplest ceremony with just cake and wine and at the most lavish dinner.

Whether tiered or not, the cake customarily has some sort of ornament on top—a wedding bell or a bride and groom. My favorite is a small vase set on top of the cake, then iced as part of it, and filled with fresh flowers.

The cake itself can be light or dark fruitcake, pound cake or Nut Torte*. It can be covered with a shiny sugar fondant and trimmed with royal icing. A pretty way to present a wedding cake is on a mirrored plaque. The mirror should be at least six inches larger in diameter than the cake; for example, if the cake is twelve inches, the mirror should be eighteen inches. The outer edge of the mirror can be decorated with a lacy icing like that on the cake. A favorite way to decorate is to put "draperies" or garlands of icing in a different way on each tier.

It is traditional to trim the silver cake knife with a white satin bow or a small bunch of white flowers. The bride holds the knife, the groom puts his hand over hers, and they cut and eat the first slice together.

In addition to the large cake, small wedding cakes in boxes are sometimes given to the guests when they leave. Light or dark fruit-cake wrapped in parchment-lined foil is used to fill them. The boxes can be plain white paper or white moire in a small oblong shape, or little heart shapes of white satin. They are monogrammed with the initials of the bride's and groom's last names, in silver or gold, and tied with satin ribbon. Sometimes they are decked with orange blossoms or lilies of the valley. A pretty way to arrange them is in a circle around the wedding cake with long streamers from their ribbon bows hanging down from the edge of the table. Young girls adore these wedding-cake boxes. They put them under their pillows the night of the wedding and believe that they will marry whichever young swain they dream about.

From the time the bride-to-be says "Yes" until the day she murmurs "I do," there will be many festivities, much shopping, and a great deal of planning. My advice to her is, first, to figure out a workable budget with her mother and father. A wise groom-to-be will carefully work out his budget too. Here is a checklist for "Her" and one for "Him" to remind them of almost every possible cost.

Budget Guide for Bride

Entertaining
Reception to announce engagement to family and parents' friends

Reception to announce engagement to bride's and groom's friends

Party after rehearsal

Wedding

Transportation for bridal party to and from church

Canopy and runner

Flower decorations

Music—at church

Organist's fee, singer's fee

Sexton's fee

Wedding Reception

Catering—food, equipment, service

Decorations—usually floral

Music

Photography

Papeteries

Engraved invitations

Cards for the reception

At Home cards

Response cards

Announcements

Informals for thank-you notes

Postal stamps

Miscellaneous

Headdresses for bridesmaids

Gifts to bridesmaids

Accommodations for out-of-town relatives and friends (optional)

Gift from bride's parents to bride (often substantial)

Fee for professional bridal consultant

Trousseau

Bridal gown

Going-away costume

Personal wardrobe

Household linens

Budget Guide for Groom

Gifts

Engagement ring

Wedding ring
Gifts to ushers and best man
Ties, collars, gloves for ushers and best man
Wedding gift to bride (usually lasting)
Wedding Expense
Bachelor dinner
Bridal bouquet
All corsages and boutonnieres for bridal party
Minister's fee
Wedding trip
Miscellaneous
Blood-test fee
Marriage license
Personal
Clothes—for ceremony and trip
Major furnishings for new home

Some of the categories will need their own particular budget lists. For instance, the reception will include many more items than the food and wine. If the reception is held in a special party room at a hotel, there will be many hidden expenses. If it is a sizable function, there will have to be a hatcheck girl, whom the guests should not be allowed to tip. At a small hotel or a club, there are more tips to be paid than to just waiters and bar help. Any special service given by doormen and elevator operators must be recognized. In the country someone must assist in parking cars. It is a good policy to check with the police to make sure that you are violating no ordinance. The police can be helpful too.

The cost of flowers can vary tremendously. I have seen a reception where the decorations were a few bowls of daisies picked from the fields—costing nothing, but looking charming. And I have seen a Christmas wedding reception at a fashionable hotel where the decorative motif was an elaborate arrangement of masses and masses of red and pink poinsettia plants. The amount of this flower bill was enough to keep a family of four in comfort for an entire year.

Start out by making a list of all your probable expenses. If the total comes below the budget, extras can be added; or if it soars above, you can juggle and whittle down certain items. Each wedding is planned differently, and costs vary accordingly. For instance, the bride's budget guide includes expenses of a church wedding, which can be eliminated if the ceremony is held at home. If there are no attendants, another expense can be cut. An immense guest list may be cut in half to keep the original idea of an elaborate dinner. Or the decision may be the reverse—keeping the large guest list and making the reception a simple one.

Ideas of what is essential for weddings vary greatly. Every friend and acquaintance may be asked to a large church wedding, with only an intimate few attending a reception at home. Or the ceremony may be performed before the immediate family at home or in the small chapel of a church, with *everyone* invited to a large reception in a hotel or club.

Pre-Wedding Planning

Before giving menu ideas for specific wedding receptions, let's go back to the beginning—when the maiden said "Yes"—and chart plans and parties in sequence.

If the parents of the bride and the groom live in the same community but don't know each other, it is up to the girl's mother to invite the groom's family to dinner. A telephone call or an informal note will do. Sometimes the menu for such a small dinner party seems difficult to plan. What are the future in-laws like? Do they stand on formality? Do they have food idiosyncrasies or religious taboos? Do they like cocktails before dinner? One? More?

The best way is to act naturally—no pretense in what you serve or how you act. If you have no regular help, don't hire someone for the occasion unless she is familiar with your home and your manner of serving. An understated dinner is best. Chicken is a safe bet for the main course, and there should be wine or champagne to toast the couple.

INFORMAL DINNER FOR THE GROOM'S FAMILY
Hot Caraway Cheese Puffs*   Champagne
Sectioned Fresh Fruit
Broiled Chicken
Brown Rice
Broccoli   Lemon Butter
Rolls

Plum Cake
Coffee

Before the announcement of the engagement is sent to the society editor of the local papers, or to any out-of-town papers in cities or towns where either side of the family has recently lived, personal notes must be written to close relatives who live in other communities. Also before any public announcement, it is customary to give two announcement parties—one for the young friends of the couple, the other for adult friends of the two families.

INFORMAL ENGAGEMENT ANNOUNCEMENT PARTY FOR 50 YOUNG PEOPLE
Krunch Platter
Celery, Olives, Carrot Sticks, Radishes
Barbecued Franks   Steak Balls
Simple Sandwiches
Double Heart Cake
Coffee

ENGAGEMENT ANNOUNCEMENT PARTY FOR 75 ADULT FRIENDS AND RELATIVES
Hot Fiesole Bouchées*   Asparagus Cheese Rolls*
Fresh Shrimp Garden*
Porcupine Platter*
Baked Ham Cubes   Breast of Turkey Fingers
Egg Salad Fingers
Minced Tongue Triangles
Individual Heart-shaped Cakes
Salted Nuts   Pink and White Mints
Coffee

Announcements and Invitations for the Wedding and Reception

As soon as the engagement has been announced and before the announcements and invitations are ordered, list-making must start. The groom and his family should make their list as early as possible so that the bride can combine them with hers. The guest lists should be alphabetical so that it will be a simple matter to spot duplications. Invitations should also be sent to the groom's parents and to members of the wedding party, as they may want to keep them for mementoes. The full list should be broken down into three categories: announcements with "At Home" cards to be enclosed; invitations to the wedding: invitations to the wedding with a reception card to be enclosed.

The invitations and announcements should be engraved, and there must be two envelopes for each. The inside one is not sealed; it has the title and only the last name of the person or persons but no address. The stationer can supply the envelopes ahead, if time is short, so that they can be addressed in advance.

Invitations should be sent four weeks before the wedding; consequently they should be ordered at least six weeks before the date. Announcements may be ordered at the same time, and the envelopes addressed and stamped, but not mailed until after the marriage ceremony. It is best to have them mailed the day after the wedding so that their arrival coincides with newspaper notices of the wedding.

Every word in a formal engraved invitation must be written out. The only abbreviations permitted are "Mr.," "Mrs.," "Dr.," etc. Any good caterer, stationer, or jeweler who has an engraving service will have many samples of invitations or announcements to show you. He will be able to advise you about the proper procedure in every case.

For example, the bride's parents may be divorced; her mother may be a widow or her father a widower; the bride may be an orphan, or a widow, or a divorcee; it may be a double wedding of twin sisters. The stationer can be helpful in any of these instances.

Here are examples of the traditional wording for an invitation to a church wedding, a reception invitation enclosure card, a separate reception invitation, an announcement of the wedding, and an "At Home" enclosure card.

Invitation to a Church Wedding

Mr. and Mrs. Catesby White
request the honor of your presence
at

the marriage of their daughter
Jane Marjorie
to
Mr. John Wilder Cross
on Tuesday, the twenty-eighth of June
One thousand nine hundred and sixty-eight
at half after four o'clock
Church of the Heavenly Rest
New York City

Invitation to the Reception—Enclosure Card

The invitation to the reception, which is to be enclosed
with the invitation, should be engraved on the same stock and
should be approximately half the size.

Mr. and Mrs. Catesby White
request the pleasure of your company
at a reception
following the ceremony
at
The Carriage Club
Ten Park Avenue

R.S.V.P.
685 East End Avenue

A Separate Reception Invitation

When the wedding ceremony is intimate and small and
the reception is large, the invitation may be engraved on the
same sort of double sheet customarily used for the wedding
invitation.

Mr. and Mrs. Catesby White
request the pleasure of your company
at the wedding reception of their daughter
Jane Marjorie
and
Mr. John Wilder Cross
on Tuesday, the twenty-eighth of June
One thousand nine hundred and sixty-eight
at half after five o'clock
at

The Carriage Club
Ten Park Avenue

R.S.V.P.
685 East End Avenue

The Announcement of the Wedding

Mr. and Mrs. Catesby White
have the honor of announcing
the marriage of their daughter
Jane Marjorie
to
Mr. John Wilder Cross
on Tuesday, the twenty-eighth of June
One thousand nine hundred and sixty-eight
Church of the Heavenly Rest
New York City

"At Home" Enclosure Cards

The "At Home" card customarily enclosed in the announcement of the wedding is of the same paper stock as the announcement and is smaller than the reception card.

At Home
after the first of August
10 East Tenth Street
New York, New York

Invitations to Informal Weddings

When the wedding is small and informal and is held in a small chapel or at home, an engraved invitation is not necessary—and might even seem pretentious. An informal note written by the mother of the bride on conservative note paper is all that is necessary.

The note can be very short, putting down only the important facts.

Dear Aunt May,

Jane is being married on Tuesday, June 28th, at 4:30 (in the garden, if weather permits).

We're eager for you to meet her fiancé, John Cross.
Please come and plan to stay for a buffet afterward.

It is perfectly correct for the invitation to the small ceremony or reception, or both, to be phoned, because the people who would be asked to such an occasion would obviously
be only close friends or relatives.

Parties Before the Wedding

Once the engagement is announced, the invitations are
out, and the bride and groom have selected their attendants,
a round of festivities starts. There are dinners and cocktail
parties for the couple, and there are showers for the bride,
given by the bridesmaids.

If there are to be a number of out-of-town guests, relatives plan their party-giving for a few days before the
wedding so that the visitors will have a gay time and so
that the immediate families will not have to be concerned
about their welfare during the last-minute arrangements.

Often, relatives and friends who have large apartments or
homes offer to put up one or more of the visiting firemen.
This is a great relief to the bride's parents because they don't
have to arrange hotel accommodations or worry about inter-
mediate meals not taken care of by the parties.

The bachelor dinner usually is held two or three evenings
before the wedding. The groom may give this party—his
swan song to freedom and bachelorhood—but usually his
friends or ushers give it for him. The ideal place for this
party is a man's club or a private dining room at a hotel or
country club. It is sometimes held in the apartment of the
groom or one of his ushers.

Sometimes the guests make a present to the groom. This
could be a silver tray or a cigarette box with each of their
signatures engraved on it. One of the traditions for this type
of party is for the men to drink a toast to the bride-to-be
from fragile, stemmed wine glasses, then toss them into the
fireplace. The original idea for this custom was that glasses
used in a toast to the queen could never be used for a less
important occasion.

The food for a bachelor dinner, like the jokes and the singing, is hearty and he-man.

BACHELOR DINNER (AT A CLUB OR HOTEL)
Onion Soup
T-bone Steak
Baked Potatoes
Fresh Asparagus   Hollandaise
Hard Rolls
Apple Pie   Vanilla Ice Cream
Coffee
Brandy   Cigars

The wedding rehearsal is usually held the afternoon or evening before the wedding, and afterward a supper party is given by a close relative or by the mother of the bride. It is usually a very simple buffet which ends at an early hour because of the big day ahead. Unless the wedding and reception are to be at home, this buffet may be given at the house of the bride. The party can be just for the bridal party, but frequently close friends and relatives are included —especially if they are out-of-town guests.

BUFFET SUPPER (AFTER THE REHEARSAL)
Celery   Olives
Baked Ham   Pineapple Slices
Scalloped Potatoes
Green Salad
Buttered Rolls
Apple Turnovers*
Coffee

If the bride has an elaborate trousseau, she often gives a small tea to display it. This can be given during the week of the wedding, when a lot of wedding presents have arrived. It is a nice way to repay the friends who have given her showers.

Bridal Showers

A bridal shower should always be given by close friends, not by relatives. (It seems less obvious that way.)

Even so, some brides frown on them. They feel that having to give shower gifts in addition to wedding presents may be a strain on their friends' budgets. This can be avoided if a maximum price is set for each gift, or if the hostess indicates that the gifts are to be kitchen gadgets or other small inexpensive items. In any event, the cost of a shower gift should never be anything like that of a wedding gift, even if the friends are well-to-do.

Themes for shower gifts can be both imaginative and practical. They could be tin pans from a variety store, or cutlery for the kitchen drawer, or pots and pans in a particular color. Or the guests could be asked to bring one piece of silver or one glass in a pattern that the bride has chosen.

The popular decorative theme for a shower is an umbrella. A Japanese paper parasol, an old umbrella decorated with ribbons and flowers, or a handsome new one that the hostess is giving the bride-to-be—all are useful. Any of them may be opened, rested on its side on the floor or on a table, and filled to overflowing with the shower gifts.

Small paper umbrellas filled with nuts or candy make attractive place cards if the party is a sit-down luncheon, or they can decorate a flower centerpiece. Here are three menus for luncheon showers:

BRIDAL SHOWER LUNCHEON
(FOR HOT WEATHER)
Lump Crab Meat Salad in Avocado Half
Small Buttered Rolls
Jellied Fruit Molds in Heart Shape
Orange Pecan Cookies*
Iced Tea   Iced Coffee

BRIDAL SHOWER LUNCHEON
(FOR COLD WEATHER)
Scallops and Shrimp Gumbo
Rice
Brown Bread Sandwiches   Cucumber Sticks
Nut Torte Heart Cake
Coffee

AFTERNOON BRIDAL SHOWER
Heart-shaped Chicken Salad Sandwiches
Fruit Punch
Raspberry Ice
Brownies

The Wedding Reception

A reception after the wedding is a joyous event. It can be an intimate dinner for the wedding party and the immediate family or a function for two hundred or more guests.

At a large formal reception there is always a receiving line. The mother of the bride, as hostess, is first to greet the guests. Next to her stand, in this order, the groom's father, his mother, the bride's father. Next stand the bride, the groom, the maid of honor, and the bridesmaids. It is not obligatory for the fathers, however, to be in the line. Greetings are congratulatory, but conversation is so unimportant that it is not even heard in the midst of the starry-eyed excitement. There are kisses galore—everyone wants to kiss the bride.

After all of the guests have passed through it, the receiving line disperses. If there is music and dancing, the groom has the first dance with his new bride. Her next dancing companion is usually her father-in-law, while the groom is spinning his new mother-in-law around the floor. Then the bride dances with her father, and the groom with his mother. Before either of them dances with other guests, the bride dances in turn with the best man and ushers, and the groom with the maid of honor and bridesmaids.

When the reception is a buffet breakfast or supper, there is sometimes a special table for the bridal party, beautifully decorated with flowers and ribbons and the wedding cake. Even though the rest of the party is buffet, this table is served. While I've arranged it many times, I always have disliked the idea. It makes the rest of the guests seem second class.

Soon after the ceremony of cutting the cake, the bride and groom start to leave. But first the bride throws her bouquet (preferably from a balcony or staircase) to the outstretched hands of her attendants. The theory is that the person who catches it will be the next to be wed. The guests are supposed to remain at the reception until the bride and groom have left.

Here are some of the menus I have served for various types of receptions with different numbers of guests:

INTIMATE WEDDING DINNER FOR 12
Champagne
Lobster Bouchées*
Fresh Fruit Cup Imperial
Broiled Filet Mignon   Small Roasted Potatoes
Fresh Broccoli with Lemon Butter
Broiled Tomatoes Amandine
Endive and Watercress Salad   French Brie   Melba Toast
Ice Cream Wedding Bells
Nut Torte Wedding Cake
Heart Mints   Salted Almonds
Demitasse

ELEGANT AFTERNOON WEDDING RECEPTION FOR 25
Champagne
Fresh Beluga Caviar (served in silver bowl in crushed ice with chopped egg yolks, chopped egg whites, and chopped onions in side dishes nearby)
Hot Toast Fingers
Fruit Cake Wedding Cake*

WEDDING BREAKFAST FOR 30 (HIGH NOON)
Champagne
Olives   Celery Curls   Carrot Sticks
Spiced Watermelon Rind
Old-fashioned Pressed Chicken*
Watercress Fingers   Mushroom Cornucopias
Fresh Fruits in Kirsch
Wedding Cake
Salted Nuts   Mints
Coffee

AFTERNOON COCKTAIL WEDDING RECEPTION FOR 50
Champagne
Fiesole Bouchées*   Asparagus Cheese Rolls*

Fresh Shrimp Garden*
Porcupine Platter*
Assorted Small Sandwiches
Wedding Cake
Salted Nuts   Mints
Coffee

AFTERNOON WEDDING RECEPTION FOR 75
(at Country Home on the Terrace)
Sauterne Punch
Crab Salad Puffs*
Sliced Turkey Squares   Watercress Rolls
Ice Cream Hearts
Wedding Cake
Salted Nuts   Heart Mints
Coffee

AFTERNOON WEDDING RECEPTION FOR 200
Champagne
Lobster Newberg   Pastry Crescents
Chicken Salad Garnished with Toasted Almonds and
Bunches of White Seedless Grapes
Small Finger Rolls   Spiced Cantaloupe
Four-tiered Wedding Cake
Molded Ices
Coffee

This reception for 200 turned out to be a most fabulous wedding reception—but the setting sounds far from fabulous. It was a garage! The bride's family had a small, exquisite private house in Manhattan's East 60's. The living room was large enough for the thirty guests invited to the ceremony, but the list for the reception came to a round 200. This fine little townhouse had a garage (once a carriage house) at street level which was a full twenty-two by eighty feet.

The family decided that the large reception would be at their home rather than at a hotel ballroom. Transforming the garage into a reception room was like building a stage set, but the result was charming. White satin wall-coverings were fastened with fresh white flowers and green leaves. White doves on wires hung from the ceiling. There was plenty of space for all the guests, the long buffet, and an orchestra. The four-tiered wedding cake stood on a white ruffled table, and the bride and groom used a silver-hilted sword to cut it.

Anniversaries

Although each anniversary and birthday is an occasion, certain ones seem more important than others. They are milestones in life and are wonderful reasons for giving a party. The most important anniversaries are the first, fifth, tenth, twenty-fifth—and most impressive of all—the fiftieth, or golden.

Any anniversary, however, is a good excuse for a party. The symbols for each give a ready-made theme for decorations and for gifts. The various themes spur the imagination of the guests, and presents are often unusual or amusing. All of this adds to the fun of the party. Here are the original symbols for each year, but they can be expanded to include reasonable facsimiles in synthetic and plastics.

Wedding Anniversary Symbols

1st	paper	13th	lace
2nd	cotton	14th	ivory
3rd	leather	15th	crystal or glass
4th	linen	20th	china
5th	wood	25th	silver
6th	iron	30th	pearls
7th	wool, copper, or brass	35th	coral or jade
8th	bronze, or electrical appliances	40th	ruby or garnet
		45th	sapphire
9th	pottery	50th	gold
10th	tin or aluminum	55th	emerald or turquoise
11th	steel	60th	diamond
12th	silk	75th	diamond

The food and drinks served at an anniversary party are the same as at any other function of the same character—cocktail, reception, buffet supper or dinner. Exceptions are the silver and golden anniversaries, which should resemble one of the types of wedding receptions.

The decorations and serving utensils are what set these

parties apart from the others. A few decorative ideas for the most important may help you plan your own party. Anniversary parties where the guests bring presents are usually given by friends of the couple. A hostess who entertains on her own anniversary day usually tells her friends not to bring gifts.

First Anniversary—Paper

This can be a picnic type of buffet, using paper plates, napkins, and cups and plastic spoons and forks. The centerpiece for the buffet could be an arrangement of paper flowers, and there could be paper favors—hats and snappers —just like those at a child's party.

Fifth Anniversary—Wood

The centerpiece for this party could be a fruit and flower arrangement in a large wooden salad bowl. The food on the buffet table could be served from wooden cutting boards and bowls, and a bread board could be used as a tray to pass the drinks. If you have no individual wooden plates or small salad bowls, paper plates are available that have the look of wood veneer. And wooden-handled cutlery would complete the theme.

Tenth Anniversary—Tin

For a tenth anniversary celebration, a seated dinner party would be the thing. At first glance the dining table might have a formal, luxurious air, but a closer look would reveal that all the silvery gleam was tin—straight from the variety store or the kitchen.

The centerpiece, a triumph of flowers, tin, and candles, would be made from an angel-food baking pan, with flowers massed around the tube. A funnel, its tube resting in that of the cake pan, would act as a holder for a silvery candle. A circle of funnels with small candles in their necks set around the large pan would add to the glowing effect. Cookie cutters in the shape of girls and boys would be ideal placecard holders, with the name cards tied to the handles. Large molds would make handsome serving dishes and platters;

small ones could be used for salted nuts, olives, and relishes; and pie tins for dinner plates. Kitchen cutlery, of course, would be the only suitable flatware.

Twenty-fifth Anniversary—Silver

The twenty-fifth is such an important anniversary that it should be treated with the lavishness of a wedding reception. Here is one that I arranged. It was truly lovely and all twenty-five guests were duly impressed.

The invitations were handwritten in silver ink on lumarith (clear plastic) oblongs. The buffet table was covered with silver glitter cloth secured from a millinery supply house (a wonderful source for decorative props). For the centerpiece, I sprayed some fruit and leaves with just enough silver to give a frosted effect. Interspersed were some real fruit and flowers, a silvered pineapple, natural red bananas and pears, shapely bunches of black grapes with just a frost of silver, and fresh white flowers with silvered leaves. There were corsages for the women and boutonnieres for the men which the florist had frosted lightly with silver. Here is the menu for that memorable buffet.

25th ANNIVERSARY BUFFET FOR 25
Lobster Newburg
Pastry Points
Southern Fried Chicken
Fluffy Rice
Tossed Green Salad
Anniversary Cake
Coffee

Just as at a wedding reception there was champagne. The anniversary cake had a white icing and was decorated with silver *dragées* and silver leaves.

The Golden Wedding—Fiftieth Anniversary

A fiftieth wedding anniversary is so rare that it may be celebrated in a grand manner. It is the ultimate in "Once in a Lifetime Occasions" and should be honored by the attendance of many—young as well as old—acquaintances as well as friends and relatives.

This is the way I arranged one golden wedding. The buffet table was large because the guest list was one hundred. The table was covered with a white linen cloth, and the dramatic flower centerpiece was composed of calla lilies and yellow snapdragons. Small cabaret tables, each seating four, were covered with yellow linen cloths hanging to the floor. These were topped with circles of stunning gold paper that looked like kidskin. On each of these tables was a small stemmed vase containing yellow freesia and mimosa with ivy trailing onto the table. The glasses and china had gold rims and the cutlery was gold-finished.

It was a lavish cocktail buffet. And, because there were so many guests, there had to be extra serving tables, in addition to the main buffet. For instance, the champagne punch bowl had its own table, and so did the Pot of Gold presentation of pick-up shellfish. This was a large oblong roasting pan (you might borrow one from a bakery). The outside was covered with gold foil; it was filled with chopped ice, and tilted slightly by resting the back on gold-foil-covered tin cans. Around the edges of the ice were large green and gold leaves. Imbedded in the ice were glass containers of tartar and cocktail sauces; and, surrounding these dips were toothpicked shrimp, sautéed scallops, crab salad in clam shells, huge stuffed olives, hearts of celery, carrot sticks, and radish roses. Around the base of the pan were masses of green kale sprayed lightly with gold and a border of calla lilies and mimosa.

Trays of assorted sandwiches and hot foods filled the main buffet table—the hot hors d'oeuvre and chafing dish at one end, the sandwiches and coffee at the other. The five-tiered anniversary cake had a place of honor on a separate round table decorated like the others. It was cut in much the same manner as the couple had cut their wedding cake fifty years before. This time they used a gold-hilted sword, and the cake was trimmed with gold *dragées* and leaves and white orange blossoms.

Here is the menu for this particular Golden Wedding:

GOLDEN WEDDING RECEPTION FOR 100

Champagne
Hot Hors d'Oeuvre

Trader Horns*   Steak Kebabs Teriyaki*
Fiesole Bouchées*   Asparagus Cheese Rolls*

Pot of Gold Shellfish Presentation
Turkey in Golden Cream
(in Chafing Dish)
Assorted Small Sandwiches
Golden Wedding Bell Ices
Five-tiered 50th Anniversary Cake
Coffee

Almonds   Golden Yellow Mints

Each Year—Birthdays for Everybody

The first milestone in a girl's life is the day she turns sixteen: for a boy it comes when he reaches twenty-one. After that there is a period when both prefer to keep their ages private, to be celebrated only with relatives or close friends.

The next meaningful birthday for a man is his fiftieth. And as everybody knows, although women enjoy birthday parties, most of them prefer to keep the number of candles for their cake a secret.

A notable exception to this attitude was expressed by a charming, elegant woman I knew who was about to celebrate her ninetieth birthday. She was slim, stately, and proud of her age. For her party she decided to wear lavender and old lace. As she said: "It suits me, and I have always wanted to wear the rosepoint from my great-grandmother's wedding veil."

So, naturally, the theme of the party we planned for her was lavender and lace. It was a tea, held early in summer when the lilacs and wisteria made perfect decorations. We served grape juice and tea punch. There were cream cheese and grape jelly sandwiches, and as at all birthday celebrations, the cake was the thing—and this one was lace trimmed. To do it, we simply placed a large ten-inch lace-paper doily over a ten-inch round unfrosted cake. We then shook a generous amount of powdered sugar over the cake, making sure that every bit of it was covered. Next step was to remove the doily very very carefully—and there it was, an exquisite lace-topped confection!

For this ninetieth birthday party, we could have had at least two other kinds of cake with charm and novelty. For the first one, we could bake two large round cakes (sponge or pound) and carve the numerals "9" from one and "0" from the other. The cut-out figures would then be brushed over with egg white to hold the crumbs, iced in the usual way, and set carefully on a large frosted board. Or our nonagenarian's party might have had a typical round cake—layer, angel food, or pound—decorated according to personal preference and set on a mirror or on a round, iced board. The cake would be surrounded by ninety candles, set into individual frosting holders and fastened to the mirror or board.

Both these ideas can easily be adapted for birthday children of any age, even without a birthday board. This is a large round wooden platter with the center hollowed out for a cake and around the rim, twenty-one holes for candles. Although you can buy these at gift shops, a wood-working husband can make one from a piece of plywood. My board, a gift beautifully painted by the artist donor, has seen lots of service, for birthdays are celebrations at our house. We also have a music-box cake holder which revolves as it plays "Happy Birthday." This is most useful when, sometimes with no notice, we discover a birthday child in our midst. Whatever dessert is on hand becomes the birthday cake and revolves to music on the stand.

When She Is Sweet Sixteen

This milestone in a girl's life is a very important one to celebrate. She is about to become an adult, so everything about the party should be handled in quite an adult way, except the cake, of course. It could be a fairly formal dinner party or buffet supper for eight girls and eight boys—all in party regalia—with dancing afterwards. Or it could be an afternoon party just for girls. In either case, it is nice to weave the party around a color scheme—both food and decorations—with the cake as the *pièce de résistance*.

For a birthday dinner I once arranged, green and white

were the colors. The large three-layer square cake was iced in green with white decorations with sixteen white candles in *graduated* heights marching diagonally across the cake. The cake was placed in the center of the table on a large round mirror. Surrounding the cake, on the mirror, were as many gardenias as there were girls. Later, each took one flower to pin on her dress. Sugar lumps with the guests' initials iced on them in green were the place cards. The dessert was pistachio ice cream.

For another party, the colors were pink and white. The large round cake was baked in a pan with a ring center, and it was iced in pink with white decorations. A small vase of sweetheart roses stood in the center hole. The pink punch was colored with grenadine and had fresh strawberries and a big block of strawberry sherbet floating in it.

When He Becomes Twenty-one

The young man has reached the "age of decision" when he is allowed to vote, to drink at a bar, and do other such manly things. Usually a party for such a young man is a family affair, as he would be wary that his friends might consider it childish to have any great to-do for the occasion.

The cake I once made for a large family celebration was dramatic and appropriately man-size. I baked several two-inch-high cakes in large shallow pans. When they cooled, I cut out the figures "2" and "1" (which I covered with butter icing to hold the crumbs). The cakes were then placed side by side on a large wooden board. Now both the board and cakes were iced in white and decorated with red icing. Twenty-one red-icing roses, each holding a white candle, bordered the board.

His Fiftieth Birthday

The wife of a man about to reach his fiftieth birthday asked me to arrange a surprise party for him. She wanted a cake that would be spectacular and different. I began with a two-tiered cake iced in white. Against the tall, slim candle which I had placed in the center of the top tier I rested a blow-up of one of his baby pictures; on the bottom tier was a variety of smaller baby pictures, each resting against small candles. All were framed with curlicues of icing and gold beads.

Birthday Parties for Children

When a child is one year old, and particularly if he is the first baby, the mother often gives a party. It may be no more than a small cake with a candle as a surprise for her husband. Other than this, most parties for children between the ages of one and five are simple and impromptu.

Since a fifth birthday is a special one, careful plans must be made. First of all, each small guest will be much happier if he is given a gift of his own to play with at the party; otherwise he may insist on taking the gift he brought for the birthday child. It is also a good idea to ask a few mothers to come and help supervise games.

Since five-year-olds are usually too impatient to wait for the party food, the sooner it is served the better. A simple and easy birthday cake is an oblong of sponge cake (see basic sponge cake, p. 179), pre-cut into squares and dusted with powdered sugar (to make it look whole). A candle could be placed in each square, and when the wishes are made and the candles blown or clapped out, each child is given a portion.

Another birthday "cake" idea is to group individual ice cream cups in a circle and a candle in each. Small children love individual things—their own paper cup or basket of candy, a funny paper cap, a paper puller.

Until the children are a little older, the decorations need not be especially ornate or unusual. When they reach seven or eight, however, originality is needed to invent decorations, food, and games that have a surprise element.

At one seven-year-old's birthday party there was a giant mock firecracker in the center of the party table filled with tiny toys for each guest. The maypole motif is always effective, especially if there is a small favor tied to each ribbon streamer. Another way to give each child a small gift is to put the toys in a large round cake pan, each with a long ribbon tied to it. Make tiny slashes in a large piece of glossy white paper and pull the ribbons through. Now, cover the pan with the paper, with the ribbons on top, and secure the paper to the bottom of the pan with Scotch tape. If the paper is handled carefully, you will have a reasonable facsimile of a cake. The ribbons are then pulled out far enough so one of them reaches each child's place at the table.

The circus theme is always successful for children's birthday parties. It has endless possibilities; a party with pink lemonade and animal crackers; a costume party with the children dressed as clowns, bareback riders, or trained animals; a blindfold game can involve pinning on a clown's cap instead of a donkey's tail. This easy-to-make circus cake is a natural.

Ice a round cake in white and parade a line of red-iced animal crackers around the edge. Stand a long peppermint stick in the center of the cake and put a "big top" on it. The tent topping is made from a square of glossy gift-wrapping paper—either red or red and white striped. Fold the square in half, then in half again, and again. The folded paper should form a triangle. Now cut off the bottom in a semi-circle. When you open it up, it becomes a circle. Push the top of the peppermint stick through the circle, and there is the tent.

The circus cake can be converted into a carousel cake by putting a double row of animal crackers around the edge of the cake with a small peppermint stick between each pair of animals. Put the entire cake on top of a revolving musical cake holder and let it go round and round.

The color scheme and decor for any birthday party can stem from the birthstones and the flowers designated for each month. They are:

Month	Birth Stone	Flower
January	Garnet	Carnation or Snowdrop
February	Amethyst	Violet or Primrose
March	Aquamarine	Daffodil
April	Diamond	Daisy
May	Emerald	Lily of the Valley
June	Pearl	Rose
July	Ruby	Larkspur
August	Carnelian	Poppy
September	Sapphire	Aster
October	Opal	Cosmos
November	Topaz	Chrysanthemum
December	Turquoise	Holly

5. Dream Up a "Different" Party

Many hosts and hostesses don't want to give *just* a party. They want their parties to be gay, charming, and exciting, but most of all, different. There must be a central theme. To such imaginative people, a party, whether large and spectacular or small and offbeat, becomes virtually a dream party because they have dreamed up a theme that is highly original.

I have been involved in many such theme parties for both personal or business entertaining. Whether the "dreamer" had just a nucleus of an idea or had mapped out most of the details, it was always a fun assignment. Sometimes, it meant research in libraries and museums before the right props could be rented. But it was always a challenge, and therefore exciting.

Here are a few of the theme parties I have arranged. Some were expensive and some were not; some had many guests, some had few; but whether large or small, elaborate or simple, each one was a "spectacular" in its own way.

A Roman Bacchanal

The time is the twentieth century. The place is the Long Island estate of an industrial tycoon. But for one evening, time and place were unimportant. The hundred and fifty guests were transported back one thousand nine hundred years—to the Roman Empire and a party that Lucullus could have given.

The hostess dreamed up the original idea. Then she and I spent hours studying Gibbon's *Decline and Fall of the Roman Empire*, Seneca, and others. We wanted the Roman bacchanal to be as authentic as possible—and it was. Even the guests got into the act by wearing togas. The married

119

women had fillets (headbands) of gold braid, and the men were presented with crowns of green leaves.

The invitations were written on parchment scrolls. The party was held on the lawn under a huge pink tent which became the atrium, or main room, in the home of a wealthy Roman. The decorations and props included plaster busts of Nero, statues of household gods, and gladiators' hats. Huge bunches of fresh purple grapes were used everywhere. There was an authentic Roman chariot with oysters on the half shell on a bed of crushed ice, a pink marble tub filled with ice and overflowing with shellfish pick-ups, celery, olives, and more grapes. Besides the dinner, there was also a table for midnight snacks which had a cloth-of-gold covering. It was decorated with golden goblets brimming over with still more purple grapes. The late snack consisted of an abundance of cakes, pastries, and coffee.

ROMAN BACCHANAL DINNER

Hot Hors d'Oeuvre
Apicius Maize Balls   Tivoli Treats
Barbarian Spare Ribs   Wild Plum Sauce
Chilled Hors d'Oeuvre
(Chariot's Choice)
Ostia Oysters   Sicilian Shrimp   Crabflake Shells
Heart of Celery   Carrot Sticks
Radish Roses
Colossal Stuffed Olives   Jumbo Ripe Olives
Oriental Chestnuts
Nightingales' Tongues   Frankish Fantasies
Spiced Plums   Cicero Chutnut   Pickled Figs
Breast of Chicken Caesar
Lucullan Kugel
Gallic String Beans   Carrots of Thebes
Salad of the Appian Way   Gorgonzola
Garlic Bread   Cassius Pumpernickel
Roman Ice Creams
Sweetmeats from the Tiber
Coffee

Part of the fun of a theme party is not only dreaming up dishes appropriate to the occasion, but writing the menu in the same vein. Most dishes on the Roman Bacchanal menu are easily understandable, but two of them need a bit of explaining.

The Nightingales' Tongues consist of honeydew melon, peeled and cut into small wedges, with a thin slice of tongue rolled around each section. A toothpick holds it together.

The Frankish Fantasies are Italian breadsticks broken into two-inch pieces. Around each is wound, in barber-pole style, a flat filet of anchovy from which the oil has been drained. The ends of the anchovy are anchored with soft butter. When the Fantasies are put into the refrigerator, the butter will harden.

A Far Eastern Fantasy

Another tent party I enjoyed arranging was at the country home of a collector of Oriental art. His large, modern, uncluttered house made a striking background for the museum pieces in his collection.

To introduce the theme of the party, we reproduced charming Japanese prints on the outside fold of the invitations.

When the guests arrived, they were ushered through the house to the garden and over a Japanese bridge to the Oriental tent. The tent, of Oriental gold fabric, seated 200 guests, with ample room for the orchestra and for the dance floor. The walls were hung with some of the host's Japanese prints and a collection of elegant antique kimonos. The dining tables were covered with yellow cloth. The centerpieces were pineapples, used as candleholders, surrounded with exotic greens and yellow and white Fuji mums. The hors d'oeuvre cart at the entrance to the tent was decorated with coolie hats and unusual vegetables discovered in New York's Chinatown—white suede-like eggplant, crinkly greens, and two-foot-long string beans. In the wagon a bed of chopped ice held shrimp on bamboo skewers, bowls of soy sauce, hot Chinese mustard, raw cherry tomatoes, and turnip matchsticks.

FAR EASTERN FANTASY DINNER

Shrimp and Vegetable Cart
Barbecued Spare Ribs   Wild Plum Sauce

Chicken Soup with Chinese Egg Threads*
Almond Chicken with Pineapple and Water Chestnuts
Fluffy Rice   Snow Peas
Half Cantaloupe
filled with Hawaiian Coconut Custard
garnished with Whipped Cream and Chopped Ginger
Jasmine Tea

Pearls and Plumes for a Venetian Dinner

The home where a Venetian party was given was an elegant duplex apartment on New York City's upper East Side. It was decorated in baroque style opulent enough to make a lovely setting for this party.

The guests were greeted and given cocktails and appetizers on the upper floor in a room with black and white zebra walls. This cocktail interval in a setting of stark modernity gave extra impact to the dinner setting.

As the sixty guests walked down the circular staircase into the dining area, the ten tables (each set for six) they saw were a dazzle of gold and plumes and pearls. Each table was covered with white floor-length cloths topped with gold net. The centerpieces were finger bowls filled with glass marbles in which were thrust white curled ostrich plumes decorated with pearls and arranged in various lengths to make a graceful bouquet.

This is the menu chosen to suit the formal setting:

FORMAL VENETIAN DINNER
Antipasto Platters
Nova Scotia Salmon on Thin Pumpernickel
Smoked Sturgeon on Tissue Rye
Fresh Beluga Caviar
Hot Toast   Chopped Egg   Chopped Onion
Lemon Wedges   Hot Shrimp Marinara   Pastry Crescents
Celery Hearts   Salted Almonds   Jumbo Ripe Olives
Radish Roses   Spiced Watermelon Rind
Consommé Marco Polo
Veal Milanese   Baked Lasagna
Tiny Belgian Carrots
Tossed Green Salad   French Dressing
Finger Rolls

Rings of Orange Ice Lido with Brandied Whole Apricots
Walnut Divine Squares*   Chocolate Leaves
Coffee

Party themes can be suggested by any number of things—
the decor or your house, your avocation, or the hobby of a
friend. You may get an idea from current events in the newspapers, or from a movie or play which has become a great
hit. The idea may come from a trip you have just taken or
that someone is about to take. This last situation sparked off
a party which was great fun.

Around-the-World Party

The Joneses' friends, the Johnsons, were going on a
trip around the world. They decided to give the travelers a
pretend "food trip" party. They secured the itinerary and
proceeded this way.

The invitations said: "Let's sail with Mary and Dick Johnson around the world. The ship departs Friday, May third, at
four bells, from Pier 9, 126 Hawthorn Street. All aboard,
that's coming aboard, report to Captain (and Mrs.) J. Jones."

Itinerary in hand, the Joneses asked my advice.

They wanted twenty-eight guests. The Joneses' enormous
dining room could accommodate seven tables for four people
each, as well as a sizable buffet table. Each table was decorated to represent one of the countries the Johnsons would
visit. The buffet table held one of the specialties from each
country. Their first stop, since they were leaving from San
Francisco, was to be the Hawaiian Islands. Then on to China
and Japan, India, Turkey, Italy, France and Holland.

It was really like giving seven parties instead of one, and
it was fun arranging each table appropriately. The Hawaiian
table was obvious—a yellow tablecloth with a tropical fruit
arrangement in the center. We used a pineapple with a candle
on top, but could have had a coconut or a bunch of bananas
up-ended. On this table there was a lei for each guest.

Our Chinese table had a deep blue cloth with a blue bowl
of water lilies in the center. The guest prizes at this table
were embroidered Chinese slippers, which everyone immediately put on.

The cover for the Indian table was madras, and the centerpiece of exotic fruit was in an Indian brass bowl. The favors were small brass ash trays.

The Turkish table was covered in red felt and had a red fez filled with fruit as a centerpiece. There was a fez for each of the four guests.

The Italian and French tables looked quite similar. Each was covered with a red checked tablecloth. Each had a grape arrangement for a centerpiece, and pretty wine glasses as gifts for the guests.

The Holland table was covered with a pale blue cloth, and the centerpiece was a wooden shoe filled with tulips. There was a miniature pair of sabots at each place.

AROUND-THE-WORLD BUFFET SUPPER
Hawaii and Japan
Steak Teriyaki*   Soy Sauce
Italy
Mini-Pizza*
India
Shrimp Curry   Chutney
China
Rice   Kumquats
France
Small Napoleons*
Holland
Edam Cheese   Crackers
Turkey
Turkish Paste
Demitasse

The idea of the Around-the-World party may give you ideas for any number of smaller parties where the food and the decor concentrate on just one country. It could be an Arabian Nights motif with gaudy decorations and costumes. The setting could be a French sidewalk cafe with little cafe tables and chairs on your terrace; or a German beergarden, with loud, thumping music and steins of beer. Perhaps a Hawaiian party with native hula dancers or an Alaskan one— to honor our two newest states.

Alaskan Gold Rush Party

This Alaskan party was an inexpensive way to entertain a large group informally. We fixed up a three-car garage to look like an old-fashioned frontier saloon. We installed a beat-up old bar, and put lots of glasses on the storage shelves behind it. We found a player piano and an abundance of old ragtime music rolls. Red-checked cloth covered the table, and ancient kitchen chairs from a thrift shop were set around the dance floor. We had a large keg of beer on the bar; this and frankfurters on rolls were refreshment enough. The host, as bartender, was in shirt-sleeves, with a white butcher's apron over his colorful suspenders. His hair was parted in the middle, and a great false mustache was pasted on his upper lip. The men came as sheriffs, bandits, and prospectors and the women as dance-hall girls of the 1890's, all spangled and plumed. Posters of bad men "Wanted Dead or Alive" gave the final authentic touch.

Convention Hall—or Political Rally

Variations on the political theme have always turned out well in parties I have arranged when the object was to entertain a large group in an informal way. The "convention hall" can be a tent or a barn—or an actual hall. The invitations can be in the form of ballots, with the place for the R.S.V.P. to be marked by an X.

The walls of the "hall" are draped with red, white, and blue bunting. At one such party, we had made an elephant and a donkey out of wire, then covered them with green leaves, red carnations, and blue bachelor buttons. They were placed, as greeters, at the entrance. Each table was named for a state, which was indicated by printed placards on sticks. These were held erect between pots of red geraniums.

One convention party was a surprise birthday party for the husband of the hostess. We decided to make him the candidate for election, and had large campaign buttons made saying "Vote for B.B." At each place one of these buttons pinned a corner of the red terry napkin to the navy blue satin tablecloth.

Many of the dishes on the menu were identified by the states of their origin. This is the menu we dreamed up:

CONVENTION DINNER MENU
Roll-Out-the-Barrel Appetizers
(served on a barrel)
Louisiana Shrimp   Maine Lobster
New York Clams
Florida Lemon Wedges   Cocktail Sauce
Colorado Celery   Pennsylvania Cauliflower Sections
Carrot Sticks   Black Olives
*   *   *

Vote-getting Dinner
Mock Maryland Creamed Crab
Roast Vermont Turkey*
Baked Idaho Potatoes   Texas Onions*
Mississippi Vegetable Casserole
California Baked Oranges*
Coffee

If a theme party is what you want, anything in the whole wide world can give you the germ of an idea. Use your imagination and ingenuity to adapt reports in the newspaper or ancient history; literary classics or modern art; old jingles or new hit songs. The theme for a party may concern an important event in your own life or in someone else's— you've bought a new house, or you're building one, or you've sold one.

A house-warming party is given either by the new owners or by their friends. A tree or bush party is an old custom. The idea is to celebrate the partial building of a new house when the roof or just the rafters are up. A tree or bush is put on the top of the house—to bless it. And the guests, who include all the workmen as well as friends, drink many toasts to bless it further.

A "house chilling" party was given by a couple who had sold their large house in the country to move to an apartment in the city. The furniture had been moved, and the house was empty except for sixty guests, a small orchestra, and rented tables with paper covers. There was no cutlery— only finger foods were served. The house was far from dreary, and the party far from chilly. There was plenty to drink (from paper cups) and plenty to eat (on paper plates).

Two struggling young actors in New York's Greenwich Village once gave a rent party. They lived in a cold-water flat and were about to be ousted. Their friends came through with dollars as well as food and beverages.

The ditty about Dick Whittington going to London Town gave one hostess a gimmick for an informal supper party. She packed individual suppers in bandanna kerchiefs and tied them to hobo sticks.

Another hostess was inspired to give a costume party she called a Shakespeare Festival. She used a quotation from Antony and Cleopatra on her invitation:

> Come, thou monarch of the vine,
> Plumpy Bacchus with pink eyne!
> In thy fate our cares be drown'd,
> With thy grapes our hairs be crown'd.
> Cup us, 'till the world go round.

The guests were asked to dress as their favorite Shakespearean characters. The drinks were served in silver goblets, and the food was the solid English type—roast beef, Yorkshire pudding, English Trifle,* and so on.

6. Parties in the Great Outdoors

Despite all of the ultramodern, pushbutton, colorful, and streamlined kitchen equipment in almost every new American home, cooking outdoors has become a country-wide habit. But it is no longer limited to people who live in the country or suburbs. City dwellers have also climbed onto the barbecue bandwagon. Even on the tiniest apartment terrace, with the aid of charcoal and a safe little grill, city cooks can come up with a steak that's as tasty (black on the outside, red within) as their country cousins can produce with their custom-built stone or brick pit.

There is something tantalizing about the smell of food being cooked outdoors: fresh-caught trout sizzling over a pinewood fire beside any stream, baked beans and franks steaming over heated stones, the sweetish scent of marsh-mallows turning golden and gooey on a Campfire Girl's willow stick, the exotic scent that comes from the dripping of marinated shish kebab, or the bastings of soy sauce on spare ribs.

With the growth of outdoor cooking, men have been lured back into the cooking act. For a long time, males (except for professional chefs and frontiersmen) were kept away from the frying pans. Now it is the husband who mans the grill, even if he does nothing but broil the steak. Some men become gourmets, jealous of their own special barbecue recipes.

The All-American Cook-out—Barbecues

The word "barbecue" is derived from the Haitian *barbacoa*, which means "framework of sticks." Originally, such a raised framework was used for smoking, drying, and broiling meat.

128

Way back, a barbecue meant the outdoor roasting of a hog or steer and involved a gathering of many people. They were either invited guests or people who just came running from all over the countryside when they smelled the enticing aromas.

Now, it can be a steak for two on a small charcoal grill in the backyard, a roast on the spit of a custom-built outdoor fireplace for a crowd, or that all-American favorite—hot dogs roasted over a makeshift barbecue pit at a picnic.

Purists like their meat to stew (or broil) in its own juices. However, to most people, barbecuing means that the meat must first marinate for a lengthy period in an oily or spicy sauce and then must be slathered with the sauce while broiling. The dictionary defines "barbecue sauce" as: "highly seasoned . . . made chiefly of vinegar, vegetables, sugar, and spices."

Moonlight Barbecue on a California Hillside

One of the most spectacular settings for a barbecue I've ever seen was the terrace of a house perched high up on a hillside opposite the Mount Wilson Observatory in California. The guests arrived at dusk. The hills across the valley were an artist's palette of pink, mauve, and gray. Overhead were a crescent moon and winking stars.

The color scheme was coral and burgundy. A burgundy-colored cloth—a seersucker bedspread which the hostess had dyed—covered the large terrace table. The centerpiece was of massed coral hibiscus from her garden, and the table was lighted with candles in burgundy-colored hurricane lamps.

The menu was simple but most satisfying. The hostess believed in few courses, but plenty of each. We had steak, which was precut into serving portions—that practical California custom—so that each guest had his cooked just as desired.

CALIFORNIA BARBECUE
Avocado Salad
Charcoal-broiled Steak
Fresh Broccoli   Sliced Tomatoes
Toasted Rolls

Peach Dumplings*
Coffee

Barbecue Party—Family Style

When a large number of guests are coming, and especially if it is a party that includes children, hot dogs are a happy answer to the food question. Here is a way to grill them that insures thorough toasting of the meat and the rolls together. Stacks of them can be prepared in advance. Split hot dog rolls lengthwise, but only part way through so that the back crust forms a hinge when the roll is flattened out. Spread it with barbecue sauce. Cut hot dogs the same way and place on rolls. Now they are ready for the toasting racks. When they have been grilled on both sides, each guest can garnish his own with more barbecue sauce, mustard, pickle relish, or onion slices. Here is the appetite-satisfying menu to accompany the hot dogs:

FAMILY BARBECUE PARTY #1
Spliced Hot Dog Rolls
Barbecue Sauce*   Mustard   Pickle Relish   Sliced Onions
Grilled Corn on Cob
Plenty of Melted Butter
Marshmallows
with plenty of sticks to roast your own
Soft Drinks   Beer

Always a good bet for a family barbecue party are hamburgers. As a change from the usual chopped sirloin or chopped top round, try using chopped lamb or boiled ham. Season the lamb as you would beef, with crushed garlic or garlic salt, salt, and pepper, but add a bit of rosemary or marjoram. Season the ground boiled ham with brown sugar and fruit juice. A tasty addition to a ham hamburger is to grill it with a pineapple slice on one side.

Whatever type of hamburger you make, allow about half a pound per person. Broil two minutes on each side for rare; four minutes for medium; five minutes on each side for well done.

FAMILY BARBECUE PARTY #2
Grilled Ham Hamburgers
Toasted Hamburger Rolls
Dill Pickles   Scallions
Marinated Sliced Tomatoes
French Fries in Individual Foil Packages
Little Horns*
Milk   Coffee

Chicken is another favorite choice for a family barbecue. Cut small broilers in quarters and marinate them for an hour or more in Annabel's Barbecue Sauce. Drain. Broil with frequent basting of the sauce.

FAMILY BARBECUE #3
Barbecued Chicken Annabel*
Potato Salad
Pickled Beets   Cole Slaw
Vanilla Ice Cream
and
Raspberry Sherbet
(half and half)
Iced Tea

Barbecue—Mideastern Influence

Cooking a combination of foods on a skewer has become extremely popular. The original Turkish shish kebab was made from tender cubes of lamb which had been marinated from twelve to twenty-four hours in vinegar, spices, and oil. Now any combination of almost any kind of meat or fish, with vegetables or fruit firm enough to stay whole during cooking, can be threaded onto a skewer and cubed.

The meat, whether beef or lamb, should be a tender cut and should be cut into 2-inch pieces. Marinate them in garlic-flavored French dressing for an hour or more before cooking time. Make enough marinade to brush onto the vegetables each time the skewers are turned during the cooking process.

A fun way to have a shish kebab party is to give the guests skewers and let them thread their own—then cook their choices. There could be a table near the barbecue pit with an array of uncooked vegetables on individual platters, as well as the marinated meat.

SHISH KEBAB BARBECUE PARTY #1
Lamb Shish Kebab
Small Solid Onions (or wedges)　　Cherry Tomatoes
Eggplant Chunks　Mushroom Caps　Green Pepper Squares
Hot Garlic Bread
Melon Pick-ups　　Spice Cookies*
Coffee

For this party the bread could be either French or Italian, sliced part way through, spread with garlic butter, and wrapped in aluminum foil. It will heat through on the back of the grill while the rest of the food is cooking.

For a fish kebab, only firm fish such as swordfish steak or scallops should be used. The steak should be cut into inch-and-a-half-thick cubes. Fish or scallops should marinate for an hour or more in oil and lemon juice—half and half. Strips of bacon may be wound around the fish cubes to keep the fish from drying out or breaking. Orange sections or large pineapple chunks could be interspersed on the skewer for variety.

SHISH KEBAB BARBECUE PARTY #2
Fish Kebabs
Potato Puffs in Individual Aluminum Foil
Sliced Cucumber with Sour Cream and Dill
Hot Garlic Bread
Marble Coffee Cake in Pick-up Squares*
Coffee

Hawaiian Barbecue

Hawaiian, Polynesian, and some Far Eastern foods are very much alike, as is the cooking equipment. The hibachi, which is used both indoors and outdoors, has such a close resemblance to the barbecue grill that a manufacturer of iron implements in Alabama now makes facsimiles of Oriental hibachis—at a compatible price. Hawaii has given us a delightful way of eating outdoors. A *luau* (the name of the young, tender leaves of the taro plant—similar to spinach) is a feast which should by rights be served on a *lanai*—back porch to you.

The food for a *luau* may be cooked on any charcoal grill, but a hibachi will add an Oriental atmosphere. Use a profusion of flowers for decoration—even scatter blossoms and leaves on the floor of your *lanai*. Present each guest on arrival with a lei, but don't allow the impulse for authenticity to make you stretch your budget to use orchids. A chain of daisies woven into a long necklace can be just as effective.

In planning a *luau*, always keep in mind the sweet-and-sour contrast which prevails in Pacific Islands and Far Eastern foods. Should you be elegant enough to include finger bowls, be sure to float a flower in the tepid water along with a lemon slice.

To many people, spare ribs seem indigenous to Texas. But they were probably an important food in China centuries before Sam Houston. The ingredients for a Chinese spare-rib marinade are a far cry from the liquid smoke, tomato paste, and hot pepper used on the range, and the taste, of course, is completely different. To marinate ribs for four people with enough sauce left over for basting during the cooking period, combine: 2 cups soy sauce, 1 cup pineapple juice, half cup sherry, 2 tablespoons brown sugar, 1 clove crushed garlic, and half a teaspoon of ground ginger.

HAWAIIAN LUAU
Oriental Spare Ribs
Sweet Potatoes Baked in Aluminum Foil
Hibachi-broiled Bananas
(served on large green leaves)
Salad of Shredded Chinese Cabbage   Boiled Dressing
Chilled Curried Pineapple
Hot Green Tea

Clambake—New England Style

Perhaps the earliest kind of American cookout is the clambake. It is typically New England, and started so long ago that no one knows just when. Even though it is called a "bake," it is actually steam cookery.

An authentic clambake starts many hours ahead of the

party. If it is to be a noon meal, clambakers must rise at dawn to select a beach location well back from the highwater mark so that there is no chance of being waterlogged. Here they dig a large pit, gather driftwood, and build a roaring fire. Large rocks have to be found and towed, and seaweed must be fetched—plenty of it. Meanwhile the fire must be watched and fed with more wood until there is a sizable steady flame. Now the rocks are added and heated until they are white-hot and spit a furious sizzle to a splash of water. The fire can now be raked away from the pit, and the hot rocks covered with a six-inch layer of wet seaweed.

Most of my clambake biases come from a small place in Maine that I visit often. There Captain Jones, a clambake master from way back, is in charge. Others may use chickens, baked potatoes, or crabs, but not he. It is a pleasure to watch his assured way at the pit. Over the wet seaweed goes a heavy iron grate (stronger than the usual chicken wire) on twelve-inch legs; next a few hardshell clams for extra flavor and a topping of more wet seaweed. (For fifty people he uses ten bushels or more of clams.) The next layer is lobster —one hundred of them, each about one and a half pounds. Never, never, have I seen more than one lobster per guest served anywhere else. Now more seaweed and seventy-five ears of fresh corn, the outer husks and silk removed, are added and covered with wet seaweed. For the top layer, he places individual cheesecloth bags with about ten steamer (softshell) clams and one egg in each. Now comes the topping—any leftover corn husks and more seaweed. A final bucket of sea water, and the tarp goes on top, snugly weighted down with rocks.

For about an hour the guests have leisurely drinks inside the clubhouse or stand outside to sniff the aroma. At last, after looking at sample clams and eggs, Captain Jones says "Ready," and the guests line up. Each person gets an oblong paper tray with two lobsters, one ear of corn, and the cheese-cloth bag of clams and an egg; at the next table he is given potato chips, rolls, melted butter in little plastic containers, and paper napkins. Inside the club, places are set at long tables, with more paper napkins (we need them) and nut-crackers for cracking the lobster claws. A keg of beer and a coffee urn are nearby.

Some people dress up their clambakes with cole slaw,

potato salad, garlic bread, or Indian pudding. Even water-melon, however, is too much after one of Captain Jones' superb feasts.

As you can gather, the traditional New England clambake requires hard work and lots of time; no one in his right mind would attempt one without a master to direct. With less time and effort, however, it is possible to simulate a seaside clambake far from the water.

A backyard clambake has much the same menu as the traditional one, but the equipment is different. Use a large galvanized pot with a tight-fitting lid; an old-fashioned wash boiler is perfect. If your outdoor grill is not sturdy enough to support such a vessel when it is weighted down with food, a fire-pit can be devised with concrete blocks. However, it should be built by someone who knows about drafts and such, so that a wood fire can be kept roaring.

With the basic equipment arranged, you're ready to go. The whole process should take less than two hours—forty minutes or so for firebuilding and preparing, and about an hour for steaming. First, start the fire and husk the corn. Soak the husks in salted water—this takes the place of seaweed. Put a four-inch layer of the wet husks in the bottom of the boiler; the rest are to be put between the layers of food. Add one quart of water and cover the pot. When it boils, put the rest of the food in layers with the corn husks in between and on top. When you hear the hiss of steam again, count about forty minutes to ready. It is a good idea to have a few clams and an egg or two as Captain Jones does for a test sample.

BACKYARD CLAMBAKE FOR 12

Layers in the Wash Boiler
12 2-pound lobsters
18 ears of corn
(about half of the clambakers will take seconds)
120 softshell clams
12 eggs (optional)
On the Tables
Rolls   Potato Chips   Hot Melted Butter   Nutcrackers
Paper Napkins
Big wastebaskets lined with plastic bags
for easy garbage removal

Picnics—Plain and Fancy

To many barbecue enthusiasts, picnics have become obsolete. Should they happen to ask friends to a picnic on the beach, the party is more likely than not to have the aroma of a barbecue.

However, there are still many people who like the idea of an honest-to-goodness picnic—whether it's dressed up and fancy, or as plain and old-fashioned as Aunt Hattie. The nostalgia is not for the ants on the tablecloth or the sand in the sandwiches, but for the good old childhood days when a grade school or Sunday School picnic was a real outing.

Picnics can be as impromptu as two little girls hastily deciding to make peanut butter and jelly sandwiches to eat under the old apple tree. Or they can be such bacchanalian, woodland delights as Manet liked to paint in the 1800's, with a bottle of wine, a loaf of French bread, a hunk of cheese, and thou!

Picnics can also be served as carefully as a meal at home. A portable table set up in the woods and covered with a red checked cloth, the special service in a fancy picnic hamper, and the final touch of a chafing dish to flambé the dessert certainly are not lacking in elegance.

Midday or early summer afternoon, when the sun was high overhead, used to be considered *the* time for a picnic. Actually, a picnic at any time of the year is fun. There are many gay picnics before football games when there's frost in the air. A supper picnic has even become a tradition before the American Shakespeare Festival plays at Stratford, Connecticut, where permanent picnic tables have been set up.

With apologies to the fourth Earl of Sandwich, the two pieces of bread with something in between, which he created, are not necessary accouterments to a picnic. There was nary a one served at a picnic-on-the-dunes party I once arranged. The food, in fact, was more like that usually served at a cocktail buffet—only the serving and the background were different.

The host and hostess had a summer home on Fire Island, a narrow strip of land in the Atlantic off Long Island. Because no cars are permitted on the island, the cottagers use toy-like wagons to cart their provisions or the luggage of their guests to and fro.

The little wagons intrigued me. They could be decorative as well as utilitarian. So, using my principle of *making the most of what is available,* I turned the little Island wagons into serving carts.

In all the parties I have arranged, the most satisfactory serving prop is something on wheels. The revival of the tea cart proves this to anyone who owns one. It can be wheeled around to the guests. And should it be a slightly offbeat cart, disguised with the decorations and the food it holds, it gives the party an added oomph! I have used such unlikely wheeled props as wheelbarrows, supermarket baskets, pushcarts, and baby carriages. Once, I hung a basket on the handlebars of a child's tricycle and filled it with snacks. Until the party became too crowded, the son of the house rode around through the gathering, ringing his tricycle bell to promote his wares.

The very first time it occurred to me to serve food on wheels was for a party at the Empire State Building in honor of a famous political figure. The hosts wanted to invite a multitude of people and at the same time keep costs at a minimum (a usual problem). My object was to figure out a novel way of presenting inexpensive bar bites and cocktails.

My "free-wheeling" idea came on the way home after discussing the party. For the first time, I *really* noticed the four-wheeled cart my newsdealer used for delivering the morning papers. I asked the newsdealer if I could rent the cart from noon until midnight on the day of the party. He was delighted to have anything to do with the party.

In those days, before "contact" paper, I covered the cart with navy blue corrugated cardboard, which was also used to make separate compartments within the cart, as in an egg box. These were later filled with various types of bar foods—cheese popcorn, potato chips, peanuts, bacon rind, corn chips, peanut curls. The cart was wheeled about by a uniformed bellhop. Because of the novelty of the presentation, no one seemed to be critical of the fare.

Let's get back to the little wagons on Fire Island on that brilliant summer afternoon on the dunes fronting the summer house of my clients. First, there were twin wagons, roped together with a sailor's knot—one with glasses and ice cubes, the other with the liquor. The rest of the wagons were decorated with fishnet and seashells and had a base of crushed ice (plenty of it, because the sun was strong).

Each food cart was also decked with an assortment of edibles—celery hearts, spinach leaves, carrot sticks, radish roses, and huge ripe olives. One cart held crab meat in little clamshells (eaten ice-cream-cone style without forks; shells tossed into the sea). In another cart was a giant clamshell filled with tooth-picked lobster chunks and resting on ice covered with spinach leaves. Also on this cool green bed were eggs, cut my favorite way (short and plump, not lengthwise) and bedeviled with anchovy paste.

The guests were free to roam around, but for their comfort, there were many low-slung beach chairs placed in pairs with cinder blocks between to act as tables and to hold sand-weighted and flower-filled shells.

Weather is always a tremendous factor when giving a picnic because, as any dictionary says, a picnic means eating outdoors. It is always well, therefore, as in planning *any* outside function (wedding, garden party, or terrace barbecue), to make provisions for what to do and where to go if it rains.

Once I was one of a group of summer cottagers on the Connecticut shore. During the season we planned many get-togethers on weekends. It became a cooperative thing, as none of the cottages was large enough to hold all the neighbors as well as the visiting weekenders. Therefore, we used an informal clubhouse—the concrete bulkhead nearby. We had large evening picnic parties for a hundred or so, and we all chipped in by bringing our own specialties. Or sometimes, if someone was there during the week, he would plan the whole thing and we would share the expense.

If the weather was bad, we always had an ace in the hole—we would make a fast switch to a nearby barn. The emergency and the rushing gave the picnic added excitement.

So don't let the weather worry you. Rain or shine, summer or winter, almost *any* time is the time for an informal picnic. For instance, a pleasant kickoff to any fall or winter football game is the traditional pre-game picnic. That's when, no matter how chilly the air, the fun and sustenance of an outdoor feast provide inner warmth to the most cold-blooded spectator.

A novel serving table is the tailgate of a station wagon.

Often, two or more people plan a cooperative spread. They park their cars next to each other. The gate of one wagon is set up like a bar—complete with liquor, large ice-cube container, fizz water, soft drinks, and paper cups. The food is laid out buffet-style in thermos containers on the other tailgate with serving and eating utensils on the side, plenty of paper napkins, of course—and a good-sized receptacle for all the rubbish.

HOT FOOTBALL PICNIC FOR COLD DAY
Cheer Leader Bouillon
(Hot beef bouillon with sherry)
Home Team Casserole
(Hot baked beans topped with hot dogs)
Gridiron Rolls
(Hot rolls with butter-mustard spread in foil)
Touchdown Snacks
(Dill pickles, carrot sticks, celery stalks)
Coffee

7. Special Parties for Special People

Some basic principles apply to all successful entertaining, but there are also specific ingredients, rules, and hints that apply only to certain people. For example, the advice I give a young bride about entertaining would be no more helpful to the suburban mother than it would be to a bachelor —their needs and problems are different.

This chapter will include hints for hosts and hostesses of various ages, financial and social levels, and geographical locations, starting with the suburban mother.

Entertaining in Country Homes

Social life is much the same in the suburbs, in the country, and in a small city. It is community living—with P.T.A. meetings, local charity drives, and various church and school functions.

Within these comparatively small areas, circles of friends develop. Each family takes its turn at entertaining, with exactly the same group of friends in attendance.

As anyone who has lived in the suburbs or country knows, this procedure would become a bit tiresome if it weren't for the ingenuity of each host and hostess. There is a compulsion to be original. Many suburban parties are gayer and more entertaining than some elaborately planned city ones.

The suburban hostess is always interested in theme parties. If she can't dream up her own ideas, she makes a habit of clipping them from the women's magazines. Sometimes it is not a complete party idea. It might be just a color picture in a magazine of a festive dinner party which sparks her on to her own ideas for props.

One suburban housewife I know was intrigued with just such a picture. The tablecloth was lace with a red underlining on which the silver candelabra looked exquisite. She kept this clipping in her future-party-idea scrapbook and later duplicated it for a formal dinner party by using her grandmother's hand-crocheted lace bedspread over a big red beach towel.

Because partying plays such an important role in small community living, some women collect entertaining ideas and props as others do antique glass or mustache cups. I remember a hostess in Rochester who kept her wonderful assortment of props in a large closet specially built for them. She had collected many little figures, small houses, tiny cars and railroad trains, miniature animals, trees, shells, various sizes and shapes of mirrors for lakes, and even white sand for desert. With her old epergnes, many different candlesticks, linens, china, and abundant colored glass, she created unusual centerpieces keyed to the theme of each party.

Weekend Guests Mean Party Planning

Most suburban and country entertaining takes place on weekends. This is fortunate, not only for the early-to-rise commuting husbands, but for the hostess as well. If each woman in her particular clique does the same, entertainment of the out-of-towners becomes a cinch. It is pretty obvious that if you have entertained Mary's friends, the Browns from Chicago, a few weekends ago, she will wine and dine your friends, the Smiths from Philadelphia, this coming weekend.

Even with built-in suburban cooperation, weekend guests can be a problem without planning. With weekend guests at a summer cottage, the planning has to be more exact. But first, a few hints about how to make guests happy.

When the guests arrive at your home, show them their rooms immediately; give them a brisk drink of coffee or something else (depending on arrival time); sympathize with them about the horrible traffic (if they are an hour or so late); and under no circumstances say, "The dinner is absolutely burned to a crisp" or "We were due at the whatsanames at *least* an hour ago." The best bet is to keep on an even keel for a happy weekend.

One good thing for a hostess to remember is that, even if the guests are your dearest and nearest friends, they are on new and perhaps unfamiliar territory and should be told what is going to happen. For instance, if they arrive after lunch, they could be told: "There are no real plans until seven, when people are dropping by for drinks. Then we are going to the Browns for supper. It won't be dressy—just any summer things you've brought. . . . Would you like an ironing board? . . . The Lanes, whom you know, are coming for drinks. Also the Wilsons. Now, until then, do what you want —the canoe is down at the dock. Or you could swim, or rest. Go ahead and do whatever your heart desires—I have a few chores to do myself."

The main objective for a weekend party is to keep it flexible. It should not be regimented, except for parties and meals. Guests should have the privilege and time to find their own particular way of relaxation, whether beachcombing, reading a mystery in a hammock, or acquiring a deep tan. Practically any guest would give a withering look if the hostess should say, "Anyone for tennis?"—or badminton, or croquet? Guests have become more self-sufficient—which is extremely helpful to a knowing hostess.

Here are two ways to plan for weekend guests. The first is yours completely. The second puts the entertaining of your friends in the act.

Weekend Guests—(Plan #1)

It is Friday morning. You and your husband have spent the week at your beach cottage, and you have asked two couples to join you for the weekend. They will arrive in time for dinner tonight. On Thursday you did the house cleaning. So now you sit at the desk to work out the menu for the entire weekend. Naturally, you want as little confusion and work as possible. Therefore, you decided to do on Friday any baking that your menus call for. Also, your market list must be complete so there will be no need for shopping after Friday, except for fresh fruit, vegetables, or fish.

You have no maid, so you decide to dispense with a first course to minimize dish washing and jumping up and down from the table. You will have simple hors d'oeuvre instead. Because the guests are driving, and may be detained by traffic, you plan the Friday night dinner with *food that can stand*.

To simplify Saturday's cooking, you tell the guests to sleep as late as they wish. When they arise, you will give them coffee and fruit juice—then, perhaps they will take a dip in the ocean before a late breakfast. This avoids the necessity of lunch. But, of course, there will be a large bowl of fruit, cheese, and crackers on the table for anyone who wants in-between snacks. In the refrigerator are tomatoes and the meat left over from Friday's dinner for do-it-yourself sandwiches. Anyway, Saturday dinner will be early because you have tickets for the show at the local playhouse.

FRIDAY NIGHT DINNER

In the Living Room
Lobster Salad Spread   Crackers
(this is part of the lobster you
prepared ahead for Saturday's menu)
Cocktails
Potted Brisket of Beef
Instant Mashed Potatoes   Young Green Boiled Cabbage
Blueberry Pie

SATURDAY

Eye Opener
Coffee
Pineapple and Apricot Nectar

Breakfast
Pan-fried Fish with Crisp Bacon
Biscuits
Honey   Butter
Coffee

Pre-Dinner
Onion Dip*   Crackers
Cocktails

Dinner
Lobster Thermidor*
Corn on Cob   Baked Fresh Tomatoes

Cantaloupe with Fresh Berries
Coffee

SUNDAY

Breakfast
Coffee
Orange Juice
Scrambled Eggs   Canadian Bacon
Toast
Glazed Breakfast Buns*
(from the freezer)
Coffee

EARLY AFTERNOON DINNER

Clam Juice
(on the "deck")
Herb-broiled Chicken
Rice with Giblet Gravy   Tomato Mystery Pudding*
Corn Relish
Hot Rolls
Peach Pie*
Iced Tea

COLD SUPPER BUFFET

Cold Sliced Brisket of Beef
Hot Potato Pancakes (from the freezer)
Sliced Cucumbers   Sliced Tomatoes
French Dressing
Fresh Fruit   Iced Coffee

Weekend Guests—(Plan #2)

It is Friday morning; you have just taken your husband
to the commuter's special, and you are about to plan the
weekend menus and your shopping list.

You have asked two couples, who are coming on the same
train as your husband. You must meet them at 6:30, so you
want to plan something for dinner that can be cooked quickly

and easily when you return. You decide to give the children their dinners before you leave.

Saturday's menus are no problem, as you have been making plans for this big weekend many days ahead. You have arranged for the children to spend Saturday night with friends.

Therefore there will be no bother about dinner, as you and three of your friends have planned a progressive supper. The party will start at your house with hors d'oeuvre and cocktails, then it will progress to the next house for the main course and salad. Dessert and coffee will be served at the third house. Then everyone will go to the fourth house, where there is a piano—for after-dinner drinks, dancing, singing, and a midnight snack.

Everything has been carefully planned, and the four of you have chipped in to hire a bartender-butler, who will progress with the party to assist each hostess. He will have an alarm clock set to go off at the exact time the guests should move on to the next house.

What follows is the weekend menu plan of the first hostess and also the progressive supper menu.

FRIDAY NIGHT DINNER

In the Living Room
Cecily's Mystery Dip*   Melba Toast
Pickled Shrimp   Cocktail Sauce
Cocktails

At the Dining Table
Cold Boiled Lobster   Herbed Mayonnaise
Corn on Cob
Valley Salad*   French Dressing
Spanish Bundt*
Coffee

SATURDAY

Breakfast
Coffee
Blueberries and Cream

Crisp Bacon
French Toast   Tangerine Marmalade
Coffee

LUNCH BY THE POOL

Do-it-yourself Sandwiches
Sliced Bread   Mayonnaise   Butter
Cold Ham
Tomatoes   Cucumbers   Scallions
Iced Tea

As the progressive supper party starts at the house of our hostess with hors d'oeuvre, she far-sightedly cooked extra lobsters on Friday night. Hostess Number Two planned her main dish so that it would keep in a low-temperature oven while she attended the first part of the party. The salad hostess left the sliced alligator pears, tomato wedges, and chopped cucumber marinating in French dressing—all ready to be tossed into the salad greens.

PROGRESSIVE SUPPER PARTY

House #1
Hot Tawny Pippets*
Lobster Salad in Clamshells
Celery   Radishes   Black Olives
Tartar Steak in Onion Cups*
Cocktails

House #2
Chicken Curry
Rice
Chutney   Chopped Peanuts   Grated Coconut
Crumbled Bacon
Buttered Green Peas
Hot Buttered Rolls
Imperial Salad*   Cheese Sticks

House #3
Chocolate Mousse*

Parachute Cookies
Demitasse

House #4
Cordials   Tall Drinks
Cheese   Cold Roast Beef   Pumpernickel
Mustard   Catsup
Coffee

After such a full and late Saturday evening, our hostess felt that everyone would want to sleep late on Sunday— especially as the children were away. She took steaming coffee to each guest's room at about 11:30 A.M. When they were dressed, she gave them more coffee. At 12:30 she served the first meal of the day—brunch.

SUNDAY BRUNCH

Bloody Marys
Pancakes Nata Lee   Sour Cream   Wild Strawberry Preserves
Buttered Toast   Sweet Munster Cheese
Fresh Grapefruit
Coffee

SUNDAY SUPPER BUFFET

Fried Chicken (from the freezer)
Cole Slaw   Broiled Tomatoes
Corn on Cob
Hot Buttered Rolls   Dill Pickles
Open Plum Cake*
Iced Coffee

When the suburban hostess is not planning parties for her weekend guests, her local friends, and friends of friends, she is thinking of ways to entertain her own and other people's children.

Parties for Youngsters

Children love nothing more than make-believe. Masters of the unreal, small fry have a wonderful capacity for throwing themselves into the illusion or the stage setting created for them. But no matter how attractive and original the idea is, a very young child will lose interest unless a definite party program is previously worked out.

Children have very short attention spans, so new diversions should be presented periodically. Usually, parties for four-to-six-year-olds should be small and last no more than an hour.

Too much excitement makes some children noisy and quarrelsome. A quieting influence at a children's party, and a treat they love, is a story-book reader. She must be able to dramatize the stories she reads so that the little ones are entranced and really believe in the princess in distress and the fiery dragon.

A continuation of the storytelling could be group reciting of Mother Goose rhymes. This could come just before the party food—little ditties that deal with food, as so many do: "sing for my supper . . . ," "pulled out a plum," "the duchess bakes a cake . . . ," "Simple Simon met a pieman . . ."

The food can be as simple as Simon—milk or lemonade served with individual boxes of animal crackers, and perhaps a bunch of lollypops to take home. Or sandwiches and cookies, both cut in animal shapes with cookie cutters, or ice cream cones dipped in chocolate chips.

A wonderful thing about a child's party was once pointed out by a veteran partygiver who had no children of her own and was always nervous about parties she gave for children of friends. When one party was over, she gave a sigh of relief, then gave a delighted laugh. "You know," she said, "compared with an adult cocktail party, giving a kid's party is a cinch! You never have to worry about *if* they are coming, or if they really *want* to come. There are no stragglers among the kids. They arrive on time (three came half an hour ahead), they gobble the food. Then they leave with their prizes. It's all over and done with in no time at all. And there are no hangers-on!"

Of course, she put as much thought and planning into the children's party as for an adult function, and she got expert advice from the mothers about what food and play to provide. There were new divertissements every few minutes, and each

new game involved not one but several prizes so that each
child had more than one trinket to take home.

Children of about seven need less direction, but a party
program must still be worked out for them. Seven-to-twelve-
year-olds like to be consulted about party ideas, and they
are apt to give candid observations. However, they may criti-
cize rather than volunteer constructive ideas, so it is good to
have alternate suggestions.

Here are a few party ideas for the seven-to-twelve age
group.

Carnival Party

Your living room or your front or back lawn can be the
site of a gay carnival. Plenty of colored crepe paper is needed.
The doorway to the living room can be made to look like the
entrance to a carnival tent by using four-foot-long strips of
varicolored crepe paper. Make an imaginary half-circle on
the ceiling over the doorway. Use Scotch tape to attach the
strips of paper at equidistant points along the ceiling semi-
circle.

The living room itself can become a carnival tent. Use
two-or-three-inch rolls of colored crepe paper. Attach one
end of each roll to the center of the ceiling with tape. Now,
unwind each roll and, leaving it slack, attach each to the wall
at a height of five feet, and let the ends hang down like
streamers.

If the party is outside, individual booths or tents can be
set up the same way. One pole can be pushed into the ground,
and ends of narrow crepe paper taped to the top. Next, a
half-circle can be drawn in back of the pole and the other
ends of the strips can be anchored to the ground with small
sticks.

Each tent could be a booth for various types of carnival
party food—candied apples, hot dogs, lemonade, popcorn,
ice cream. They could also be the base for such games as a
"shooting gallery" (suction darts and dartboard); fishing for
prizes in a large aquarium with magnets on a string; and
"hit the doll and win a prize"—attach a rag doll to a large
empty picture frame and supply soft balls for throwing.

American Indian Party

An American Indian party naturally would be given outdoors with wigwams set up on the lawn or yard. They can be made with three sturdy dowels pushed into the ground to form a triangle, with the tops tied together. For the covering, large sheets of heavy wrapping paper are cut into semicircles. The center of the straight edge is attached to the top of the criss-crossed poles with strips of adhesive tape.

In front of the wigwam you can have a campfire, around which there could be a weenie-roast "powwow." The campfire in front of another might be for a marshmallow powwow.

Western Party

The Indian party can easily be transformed into a Wild West show. The young guests could wear cowboy and cowgirl outfits. A rodeo might be devised using hobby horses as the bucking broncos. There could be a lassoing contest. An archery set would not only be a fun game, but would be a colorful addition to the decorative scheme.

Teen-agers Like to Plan Their Own Parties

The wise mother of teen-agers relaxes and lets the crowd take over. Teen-agers generally know what they want—and what they don't want is to have their parents running their parties. This is particularly true of girls. After all, it's usually the women in the family who give the parties. Though they think they know exactly what kind of parties they want, most girls in the early teens cannot plan and carry out all the details of party giving. This is where the diplomatic mother can help. If she helps work out her daughter's good ideas, and if she soft-pedals the bad ones, the teen-ager's first party can be a great success, both as a party and a confidence builder for the young hostess. All coaching and suggestions should be done before the party or behind the scenes, never before guests.

The usual teen-age formula is lots of food and soft drinks,

and plenty of action. The menu choice is usually simple but hearty. If they decide on hamburgers or hot dogs, have any or all of these on the side: sliced onions, tomatoes, relish, cole slaw, ketchup, mustard, chili sauce, pickles. And they like to doctor their own, and often cook their own. This is as true at an outdoor barbecue grill as at a kitchen party with such fascinating paraphernalia as an electric sandwich toaster, a built-in griddle on the stove, an electric French fryer and an electric blender, for floats and such.

When the party menu consists of prepared-ahead food, many teen-age girls like to prepare the edibles, decorate and set the table, and even do the shopping without the assistance of an adult. However, if the party is large and the quantity of sandwiches seems overwhelming, a mother's helping hand will be welcome. Teen-agers will also tolerate the mother and father greeting the guests. But once everyone has arrived, the parents are expected to become invisible.

The only time parents are asked to join a party is if it turns into a stunt night. Then the mothers and fathers of some of the guests, who may be playing bridge with the family of the hostess, are invited to be judges and award prizes for the best dancing, singing, comic, or magic act.

A record player or a rented juke box is almost a must for any teen-age indoor party. Unless, of course, it should be a TV supper to watch a special program.

Almost any outdoor adult party is fun for teen-agers. Picnics, barbecues, even clambakes are just fine. And this group loves treasure and scavenger hunts.

An all-girl gathering popular in many parts of the country is an all-night slumber or pajama party. The girls arrive with overnight bags at about six. They are provided with an ample supply of sandwiches and soft drinks. (For one such party of ten girls, there were a hundred tuna-fish sandwiches and five dozen bottles of cola.) The party is usually held in the living room, and there is ready access to the kitchen. The hostess has begged or borrowed all the records she could get her hands on, and the family tries to disregard the repetitive and monotonous drone of the current singing or guitar favorites. Blankets are spread on the floor, just in case someone becomes weary before dawn.

The Entertaining Bachelors

It used to be that the single male animal expected, received, and accepted party invitations galore—with never a thought in his head about reciprocating. He did his duty by being an extra man. Sometimes he sent flowers. That was it.

Hostesses still feel that unattached men are valuable party requisites. But after asking one particular man to her social function time after time with no return invitation from him, a hostess is apt to forego the pleasure of his company.

Frequently, young city bachelors feel they cannot repay hospitality unless it is in kind. This is untrue. A wealthy hostess who has given an elaborate dinner party certainly does not expect a junior executive in an advertising agency to give an equally elaborate dinner at the Plaza. She would be delighted to be asked to a small cocktail party at his flat in Greenwich Village.

Even a young bachelor can organize a small party. There are good-looking glasses at the variety store, and ice cubes are available at almost every delicatessen where he can also buy cocktail snacks, beer, soft drinks, and mixes.

If the young man has a kitchenette, he should learn a few tricks about cooking. But before he catches onto culinary art, he can entertain a group for supper with a little effort. Frozen TV dinners can be satisfying, and many delicatessens have individual pot pies that only need to be heated. And for hot weather entertaining these shops have a fine assortment of cold meats, potato salad, cole slaw, and so on.

A young actor in an off-Broadway show once decided that cooking on a hot plate in his cold-water flat fit into his budget better than eating at the cheapest cafeteria. He started his cooking experiment with canned spaghetti. He then graduated to cooking the raw spaghetti himself, using a canned sauce. He has now developed into a spaghetti gourmet, insisting on *al dente,* and through trial and error, he has devised a repertoire of sauces. Friends love to visit him after the show for good food, good talk, and raffia-covered bottles of red Italian wine—which the guests contribute.

A young host actually needs only one delicious dish for his entertaining needs. Once he has accomplished this, the chances are he will expand his specialties.

The Entertaining Bachelor Girls

A career girl has much more desire to entertain than her bachelor counterpart. She entertains for the pure love of company. She also wants to build a social group and be asked to parties in return. Arranging a party is fun for the female. But she may have qualms about entertaining that would never occur to a man. She is more apt to be a perfectionist—everything must be just so.

Having enough time is the problem for the career girl who wants her party to be perfection. She may also be limited by the space of her apartment, or by the fact that she is a beginner in party giving. But, I believe that this female bachelor needs, more than anything, a formula to save *time*.

A career girl I know lived in an efficiency apartment—one large room, a dressing room, and a small kitchen. She asked me about giving a cocktail party for eight friends. She could not afford any outside service.

A career girl, like a bride, often has ideas that are far too ambitious. She wants to entertain in the manner to which her parents have accustomed her. Even though she may have rebelled from the type of life her parents led, she cannot help having absorbed many food ideas from it.

But, if a career girl is smart, she'll put away nostalgia for mother's hot cheese balls and decide to serve something that fits into her new way of life. Because time, and her job, is of the essence, she often pays more for foods that are already prepared.

Here is the plan I gave my career-girl friend. She now considers it a breeze—something that she can produce with one hand behind her back. I told her how to cut preparing and shopping time to a minimum.

CAREER GIRL COCKTAIL PARTY FOR EIGHT

Scotch   Rye   Gin
Soda   Cola   Tonic
Barbecued Franks (sauce p. 251)
Onion Dip   Melba Toast
Chopped Liver   Pumpernickel
Crunch Platter
Celery   Carrot Sticks   Olives   Gherkins
Salted Nuts

How to Plan the Party

I told her to check her supplies and make her market list. The first list, staples, can all be bought at leisure. The second part of the list are foods that must be purchased the day before the party.

Market List for Staples

Horseradish—8 oz. bottle
Ketchup—14 oz. bottle
Olives
Gherkins
Worcestershire sauce
Melba toast
Dried onion soup
Salted nuts—canned or raw shelled pecans
Paper cocktail napkins
Fancy paper towels
Toothpicks
Beverages: 2 qts. club soda, 1 qt. ginger ale, 6 colas, 3 tonics, alcoholic beverages (2 scotch, 1 rye, 1 gin.)

Market List for Perishables (bought the day before the party)

Fresh flowers
1 lb. cocktail frankfurters
½ pt. sour cream
1 lb. chopped chicken liver
1 small pumpernickel, sliced thin
1 bunch carrots
1 bunch celery hearts
¼ lb. butter

In many cities, cocktail frankfurters (twenty to thirty per pound) must be ordered in advance. I like the taste of the spices in kosher-style franks, but if our career girl wants to simplify her preparations, she can buy canned Vienna sausages.

Checklist—Night Before the Party

Double-check market lists, food and dish supplies against menu.

Arrange flowers, put in cool place.

Scrape carrots and clean celery. Refrigerate.

Make barbecue sauce and leave in pot.

Make onion dip. Place in covered bowl in refrigerator.

Survey room. Put away unnecessary clutter.

Move all furniture nearer the wall.

Cover chest of drawers for a bar.

Arrange liquor, glasses, napkins, and other bar supplies on bar.

Plan buffet table. Put cloth on table and arrange empty bowls and platters which will hold the different foods, and also any serving implements needed.

This is what I call a dry run. It is a dress rehearsal, so she can discover if she has forgotten any props. For instance, she may realize that she will need two or three butter spreaders next to the chopped liver. And unless she has bought salted nuts, she can roast and salt the pecans.

The Night of the Party

On the way home from work, our career girl picks up a bag of ice cubes from the delicatessen or the automatic machine at the corner. She has allowed herself thirty minutes' preparation time before the guests are to arrive. This is what she does:

1. Empties ice cubes into bucket. If it won't hold them all, she puts the rest into a bowl in the refrigerator.

2. Cuts frankfurters apart and puts into the sauce to heat. When sauce boils, turns down heat and lets simmer for twenty minutes.

3. Slivers carrots into long, slim strips. Cuts each heart of celery into eight lengthwise sections. Puts into bowl of ice water until ready to serve.

4. Drains olives and gherkins and places on serving platter. (After carrots and celery have crisped, puts them on same platter.)

5. Arranges dip in pretty bowl. Places melba toast on plate nearby.

6. Mounds liver onto platter. Shapes it with a knife into a peak and then puts it into the refrigerator until the guests arrive.

7. Places bread on serving dish or a board and puts on table.

8. Puts barbecued franks into chafing dish or candle warmer and sets on table.

Next, our confident career girl powders her nose, combs her hair, squares her shoulders, and goes to the door to meet her first guests.

When Three Is Not a Crowd

Now that the entertaining ice is broken with a successful cocktail party for eight, our career girl feels confident enough to explore other fields of food endeavor. Her mind skips gaily to the time when she'll have a foursome for Sunday brunch, or even for supper or dinner. But let us move to this level gradually.

Three is a nice round number for supper or dinner—if they are all females, that is. But if her special man is one of the threesome, it can seem a crowd. An evening meal for three (the hostess and two close friends or business associates) can be informal and simple. Preparations for such a gathering, even on a workday evening, can be as simple as stopping by the delicatessen on the way home and picking up packages of frozen food—individual frozen dinners, or packages of frozen chop suey, fried rice, egg rolls, or other Chinese delicacies that can be warmed up and divided on plates later.

Eventually, our bachelor girl will try out new recipes that she has clipped from the paper and let her friends be the guinea pigs. This experimenting is leading up to entertaining not only a foursome but to cooking dinner for a favorite male.

When Three Is a Crowd

Cooking the first meal for a special man can be a nerve-racking experience—unless it is handled with uncommon sense. The old saw about the way to a man's heart being through his stomach is easily debunked if he is not served the type of food he likes.

The best way to a man's heart is through your own head. Listening is your best tool. Stay tuned to his station and learn his likes and dislikes. There is not a man in the world who is not flattered by attentive interest.

Before you ask him for dinner, he has probably taken you out to dinner. By what he has ordered, and by a casual discussion of various dishes on the menu, much can be learned about his food preferences. A chance remark may tell you that he is allergic to lobster; or he may compare the restaurant's apple pie to the kind his mother used to bake.

Should you be an uncertain food detective, here are a few male likes and dislikes arrived at by polling a cross section of bachelors.

Male Food "Likes"

Simple foods
A short menu—not a great variety
Thick soups
Steak
Roast beef
Pot roast
Potatoes—mashed, boiled, baked
    (some were against French fries)
Gravy
Pie—especially apple and blueberry

Male Food "Dislikes"

Exotic foods
Fancy, decorated foods
Rich sauces
Dainty foods

Jellied consommé
Gelatins and aspics
Salads
Mayonnaise
Green vegetables
Buffets without tables—when plate has to be balanced on knees

Of course, there are exceptions. Some of the huskiest men are gourmets at heart, and like exploring unusual and exotic foods. So you can't depend on these lists as a bible—you still have to study your man and use your head.

In any case, serve him the foods you can cook well. Even if it is only scrambled eggs, and you can make them better than anything else, build your meal around them.

The Entertaining Bride

Modern brides frequently have had little or no training in the fundamentals of day-to-day homemaking and have to learn the simple facts by trial and error.

Some brides are so afraid of making an awkward mistake that they don't even try to learn. This, of course, is silly. The newer the groom, the more understanding and sympathetic he will be if the steak is burned to a crisp or the baked potatoes are not done through. But if at the end of a year she has made no earnest cooking effort, he will not be amused if he hears her say to a friend, "My dear, I can't tell a string bean from a soy bean."

Some young brides don't want their lack of knowledge to show, so they throw up a smoke screen. Until they learn how much they *can or cannot* do, parties may be too ambitious.

One wealthy bride I know planned a series of small backyard barbecues. Informality was the keynote. But even with a husband to barbecue the steaks for the eight guests, and a maid, she complained that her first party was far from smooth. "It took so long for everything to get served," she wailed.

Informal dining was a new experience to this girl. She couldn't visualize a table set without bread-and-butter plates (she wanted to use the silver ones she received as a wedding present). So she instructed the maid to pass everything, even the rolls. Since the first party was so hectic, she readily agreed to my suggestion—a plate of hot garlic bread covered with a napkin at each end of the table so that the guests could help themselves. She even allowed the guests to serve themselves from two salad bowls placed near the bread. These two informalities made all the difference in the world. Since then she has been giving smooth-running parties.

Another over-ambitious bride used to wear herself out trying to produce multicourse dinners in a two-room apartment. The attempted grandeur of the dinner was nullified by the anxiety of the hostess that everything be right and by the constant clearing of the table for still another course. And just imagine the shambles of dishes in the kitchen afterward!

Far better to have a simple meal where everybody is relaxed than a pretentious one that causes tension. When the new bride is a novice at entertaining, she should strive for simplicity. She should eliminate extraneous niceties. She should plan ahead so the serving will seem effortless. And, most of all, she should do one or more dry runs on every dish on the menu.

Here is an easy menu for newlyweds. The main part of the meal is all-in-one, yet more impressive than a casserole. It is substantial, and dressy enough for any small dinner party. A boned leg of lamb is a cinch for the young husband to carve; the butcher will bone it for you. The lamb should be roasted in a 350-degree oven thirty minutes per pound. The vegetables are cooked around the roast. Allow forty-five minutes to cook small, peeled potatoes and small, whole carrots. Small, whole, unpeeled zucchini will take about thirty minutes.

At serving time, place the lamb on a large hot platter with the vegetables surrounding it. Then, instead of salad, decorate the platter with fresh, crisp watercress. The pie can be baked in the morning.

NEWLYWED DINNER PARTY FOR SIX

Boned Leg of Lamb	Tomato Juice	Mint Jelly
Pan-roasted Potatoes	Carrots	Zucchini
	Watercress	

Garlic Bread
Lemon Pie Heavenly Cloud*
Coffee

Sizable Parties—Small Inner Space

To the shopper for an apartment in a new city building, four and a half rooms sound spacious. But not to anyone who has had a floor-through in a brownstone or to someone moving from a large suburban home. The typical four-and-a-half consists of two bedrooms (baths are not counted as rooms), a kitchen or kitchenette, and a living room. The half-room is usually an adjunct to the living room —the short end of an "L" to be used as a dining area.

Once I was called by a charming and seasoned hostess who had recently moved from a country home to just such an apartment. She had given all manner of parties for all numbers of people at her previous home. She had had a staff of servants; there were never any difficulties about space and she never had a caterer.

In her new environment, this sophisticated and talented hostess was stymied. She wanted to entertain thirty-five people at once. She was fully aware that she could not entertain with her former graciousness.

Together we worked out a formula for a cocktail buffet. First, I suggested professional tricks for making more room. One of her bedrooms was furnished like a study, so we decided to turn this into the bar room. The formica-topped chest of drawers became the bar, and the desk with the same type of top was just right for some platters of finger foods.

In the living room, all large chairs and other pieces of furniture were pushed as close to the wall as possible. All small gimcracks, breakables, small ash trays and clutter were removed from mantels, tables, and shelves. They were replaced by large ashtrays at strategic points.

The apartment did not seem in the least denuded. It looked neat, and the thirty-five people would be decoration enough. The flowers for the occasion were low-slung masses of color—no long-stemmed beauties for people to catch their sleeves on and tip over.

The long, narrow table for the buffet was pushed close to the living room windows. Enough stack stools and folding snack tables were rented so the guests would have a place to perch and have something to put the plates on—other than laps or knees.

Young Mother—Small Children

Joan is the busiest young woman I know. She and her husband have three children—aged five, three, and eighteen months, a dog, and a cat. The family of five lives in a six-room ranch house. Joan does a fine job of keeping everybody well fed and happy and the house spic-and-span with a cleaning woman only once a week. It is a lively household.

In spite of her many modern appliances—washer, dryer, dishwasher, and garbage disposal—Joan's on the go from morning to night. Her work is literally never done. Since the tykes must be tucked in before the grown-ups can relax, company in this house is generally limited to two or four guests for late dinner. Of necessity, Joan has learned to serve food that needs no last-minute care.

Wednesday is usually company night, because that's the day the cleaning woman comes. And that's when the pots and pans sparkle and the house shines. Joan loves cooking dishes with a foreign flavor. Her Wednesday company dinner might well be chicken cacciatore, cooked slowly on Tuesday night while she does the ironing.

SUBURBAN COMPANY DINNER
Pineapple Juice
Chicken Cacciatore*   String Beans
Bulgur Wheat
Tossed Salad   French Dressing
Jennie's Winthrop Pudding*
Coffee

This kind of meal has a big advantage for busy Joan. The chicken can be heated and ready for the children's dinner. At the same time, she cooks enough bulgur wheat and green beans for them and for the party dinner, too. The wheat is kept hot in the double boiler, just as rice would be. After the children have been served their beans, the rest are tossed into the stew pot to be bathed in the mouth-watering gravy of the cacciatore.

8. Pleasure and Business

Parties are my business. And an important phase of my work is to produce business parties which in turn will stimulate business.

The purpose of a party given by a business concern is to *sell*—either a specific product or the good will of the company itself. Therefore the Internal Revenue Service considers it a legitimately deductible expense. Almost any party given in one's home is partly deductible, if it can be proven that some of the guests were asked for business reasons (see p. 303).

Parties—Good-will Builders

Many business parties have the aspect of purely social functions. There is no word of business injected into the gay conversations with the guests. Of course, each member of the firm is alerted about which V.I.P.'s have accepted and is briefed on how to handle them. But this is the soft sell. The keynote is hospitality—to cement business friendships.

Usually such parties are pegged to a national holiday, the anniversary of a company, or a move to new offices. These are all logical reasons to give a party, and disguise the basic reason—to gain prospects and influence customers. I have handled good-will parties for advertising agencies, news services, banks, and law firms.

There is an ethical code among professional people about not publicizing their wares. Therefore the party I planned in the sumptuous new suite of a large firm of real estate lawyers had the air of a huge private party. More than 500 of their best customers and prospects had been invited.

The suite was large, but, with so many people, the trick

was to keep the traffic flowing. When they entered, there was a pretty girl at the reception desk to see that everyone signed the guest book. Nearby were three others, who saw that their hats and coats were checked in a small adjoining office serving as a cloakroom. From here the guests were ushered by a junior member of the firm to the next office, where there was a good-sized bar and where the law partners were stationed to greet their customers. The guests were then taken or directed to the largest office in the suite—the library—from which the other offices opened. The desks had been moved against the walls, and at one end was a buffet table where three chefs carved turkey, ham, and roast beef. The table also held pickles, various types of sliced bread, condiments, and coffee. There was no room for sitting at tables, but the guests did not seem to mind. And there was room enough for another bar here—so that no one had to return to the first bar.

The party was a tremendous success. I doubt if any single member of that law firm could estimate in dollars and cents just how much the party paid off, but they are completely aware that building good will pays long-term dividends.

Even companies with products to sell sometimes would rather promote the company name than a specific item. They have noted that members of the press frequently heave a tremendous sigh of relief when they arrive at a party and find that nothing is being touted. They relax, enjoy themselves, and make a mental note to plug this darling, non-commercial company at the earliest opportunity.

Parties to Promote a Product

The star at a business party can be practically anything that is created, designed, dreamed up, produced, or manufactured today. It can be a new type of lemon juice, hot dog, or frozen cake. It can be a dishwasher, refrigerator, or stove. It can be a new lipstick or fabric color. The star may also be collective—a complete line of new hats, dresses, suits, and coats, or a new play or movie, a newly published novel, an exhibit in an art gallery.

Every star-born party I arrange is a challenge. Each one has a personality of its own, which I attempt to dramatize

—even in a small way. For instance, a publishing house decided to give a party to promote a new book, a serious novel. The tone of the party was far from jazzy. The company was staid, and the guests were intellectuals—writers, friends of the author, book reviewers.

The party was to be held in an oak-paneled room—sedate as can be. But the guests were amused by the huge hors d'oeuvre book. The name of the author and the title written on the open pages added a gay note to the somber surroundings. The thing about this party that impressed me most was the way the handsome young editors acted as hosts. They outdid the most cordial and experienced hostess I've ever encountered. Evidently, they had been well groomed for the job; as each reviewer arrived, an editor was right there to see that he was well taken care of.

No gimmicks are needed in catering the opening of an art show. The drama is on the walls, and the food and drink are extremely simple. Depending on the importance of the artist (or the price tags on his works), the fare is variable—from champagne to wine punch to plain iced tea. Sometimes there are simple sandwiches.

The excitement of a party after the opening of a new play is such that special decorations are lost on the guests. However, on one such occasion when the play had a ballet scene in its midst, I hung miniature ballet slippers among the flowers in the centerpiece. A few people noticed them despite the discussions about the new show—and crunching of celery and sipping of champagne.

The business parties that have been the most demanding in ideas, and therefore the most fun, have been those given by food and fashion companies. More hot dogs than oil paintings are turned out each year. More hats and dresses are manufactured than books and plays. So food, fashion, and cosmetic concerns give more and merrier promotional parties.

One reason food and fashion promoters ask the advice of a party consultant is that they want their parties to be highly original, and they know that a professional party giver would never duplicate an idea for another group of food or fashion editors.

There are physical aspects that a party planner should remember. For instance, I have watched the ladies and gentlemen of the press for many years, and I have learned from their habits. They are usually burdened with briefcases or notebooks. Sometimes they sit on the impedimenta to get it out of the way; often they use the floor. They should have a convenient place on which to make their notes, to have an ash tray, and to set down their drink or plate when a particularly exciting fashion comes down the runway.

When the party is in a manufacturer's own showroom, the buyers' writing tables are usually large enough to hold almost anything except a luncheon plate. This fact made me devise the idea of box lunches (see Index). Guests can hold the boxes in their laps and use the tables for making notes, resting an ash tray, etc. Sometimes even the tables must be removed to make extra chair space. Then box lunches are the most practical solution.

Box lunches have an added advantage which I had never dreamed of—they are taken home by guests who can't finish them or who have another luncheon date later on.

The manufacturer of double-container insulated carrying bags asked me to devise a luncheon party. This is how it worked: one hundred food editors were notified that a hot lunch would be sent to their offices the day before Thanksgiving. Each insulated bag was filled with a hot turkey leg, baked potato, roll, and mince pie. The cold section held butter and salad. This gimmick convinced the editors about the qualities of the product—and they also had a bag to use for picnics in the future.

Fashion and beauty editors and buyers have become so jaded with the avalanches of parties thrown at them that it sometimes becomes difficult to dream up a party that will capture their interest. One time I arranged a boat party for out-of-town fashion editors (at least two hundred of them from all parts of the United States). It was then an unusual thing—it was held on the boat that circles Manhattan Island. Now it is no longer interesting because *it has been done*.

A party extra which has been used over and over again, and is still successful both for business and personal parties, is to have a graphologist or palm reader tell the guests all about their past and future. When the entertainer is a handwriting expert, it is smart to use the company's business stationery for the guests' handwriting sample and analysis. (They take it home and keep it!)

Whenever I am called in to discuss a business press party, I try to learn everything I can about the company and the product they wish to promote before I even think of the menu.

I could, of course, reach into my bag of tricks and pull out an idea. But to be individual, the theme for each party should stem from the company or its product—a promotional slogan, a color, even the name of the company.

For a dress company, the luncheon menu was Bouillabaisse à la Marseille waterfront, French chef, copper kettle, and all. A sportswear manufacturer keyed a new collection to the theme "Falling in Love with X. Co." After the press review, a mammoth heart-shaped hors d'oeuvre cake on a mirror was wheeled into the showroom. When it had been fully admired, it was cut and served with the cocktails and highballs.

When food editors were asked to the opening of the Domino Sugar Bowl Kitchen for a Christmas buffet, one of the refreshments was Domino's Sugarbowl Punch, their own tested recipe. When the same food editors were asked to a luncheon given by X Meat Company, it was my job to create all the fantasies I could, using frankfurters, bolognas, and other kinds of their smoked meats and cheeses. The results were zany, but fun. On one wall was a roly-poly Santa Claus made of the largest frankfurters in the world and dressed in a red costume. On display we had small character dolls made of regular size franks—a cowboy, a dachshund, a dancer with a ballet skirt of overlapping bologna slices. There was a birthday cake made of a round flat cheese with a hot dog stuck in the middle to look like a candle; and there were checkerboards using alternate squares of sliced meat and cheese.

One of my greatest challenges was a brunch that a famous designer asked me to handle. He had invited a hundred editors of women's service and homemaking magazines to see new designs in furniture inspired by his visit to St. Croix in the Virgin Islands. He wanted the decor to be reminiscent of the Caribbean Isles; the food, too, but it must be hot, he emphasized—and there was no stove, refrigerator, or sink in his plush showroom!

The question of native decorations was readily solved at New York City's public market at 116th Street, which sells tropical fruit from the West Indies. The host had prepared a large mirror-topped table which he had flounced with a gay coral-and-black checked cloth. For a background we used stands of green bananas and plantains. Then there were baskets filled with papayas, yams, choyotes, coconuts, green peppers, and those fascinating angoustipepinos (which look like long red salamis). For further decoration, there were yellow fans and native straw hats. Small round tables were covered with the same fabric as the buffet. Here is the menu:

VIRGIN ISLAND BRUNCH
Glasses of Papaya Juice
(in beds of crushed ice with green leaves)
Langousta à la St. Croix
Tiny Pastry Crescents
Celestial Coconut Cake
Coffee

It is always a delight to work with one public relations woman and her clients. She is extremely imaginative. Unlike many creative people, she is quick to accept the brain children of others. To introduce their new fragrance, called *Muguet de Bois,* one of her clients, Coty, gave a luncheon for beauty editors. Each guest was presented with a charming wicker hamper with a bunch of lilies of the valley tied to the top. The baskets were filled with a box lunch. I was fortunate in being able to match the package design of the new product to both napkins and plates.

MUGUET DE BOIS BASKET LUNCHEON
Giant Strawberries with Stems
(placed on plate in circle around powdered sugar)
Sandwich of Paté-spread Rye Bread with Sliced Turkey
Bedeviled Egg   Spring Salad
Nut Cake   Cookies
Salted Nuts   Lily of the Valley Mints

Cellophane wraps kept everything fresh, and coffee was served to the guests after lunch as they sat in the Coty showroom, which had been transformed to look like a dell in the French woods.

Another of her clients with whom I always enjoy working

is such a creative designer that she spurs you on to do original things. One party for the fashion press was for her presentation of a new collection of what she called "4-D Hats." This too was a picnic lunch—in pink baskets that were as prettily decorated with ribbons and flowers as Easter hats.

To carry out the 4-D theme, all the food was arranged in fours. The contents of the basket was in four layers. We had made a four-layer cake—gold, green, lavender, and pink. I found cigarettes in the key colors and attached them to little silver-foil ash trays with Scotch tape.

4-D BASKET LUNCHEON
Top Layer
Vegetable Kebab
(Raw mushroom cap, radish, pickled onion, green pea pod threaded on hand-carved wooden spear)

2nd Layer
Tiny Fried Chicken Legs

3rd Layer
Spring Salad
(Wrapped in foil of the key colors)

4th Layer
4-D Cake

When I was planning one party with Miss Daché, she remembered a prop which she had stored in the basement and hadn't used for years. It was a wooden camel on a roller platform and made a dramatic and applause-making entrance. At the end of the millinery show, Miss Daché gave the cue, "How Dry I Am." The camel was rolled in, festooned with feathers and flowers and colored candles. On top of the panniered sides were trays of appetizers.

This was an exciting prop, but my personal delight came in watching Miss Daché's expression when she saw the surprise I had devised for her. Rolling behind the camel was a cart on which was a hat that *I* had designed. The crown was a large satiny purple eggplant. The brim was made of overlapping slices in pink bologna, with an accent of green leaves.

This millinery masterpiece was trimmed with plumes of endive, quills of scallions, and rosettes of radishes and black olives. Before anyone could nibble a smidgen of the decorations, pictures were taken. It was a very photogenic hat and was reproduced in many newspapers. Do you think this bothered designer Daché? Not in the least. After all, it was mentioned that the vegetable hat was part of her press review. Although purely a gag, "Lilly Daché" appeared in print—and it was spelled correctly. That is what publicity means.

Business Parties—to Make a Buck

Fund raising is said to be the fourth largest industry in the United States. Of course, many of the millions collected by such worthy causes as the Red Cross, Community Chest, hospital funds, federations, and many others are solicited by direct mail, personal calls, telephone, etc.

There are other means toward the same end. In large cities there are theater benefits—the "house" is bought out for a night by a single group. The charity take then comes from the price of the tickets, plus varying deductible amounts tacked onto the regular cost of admission. Another method of fund raising also used in large cities is a series of grand charity balls, starting in October and winding up in the late spring.

But the concern of this book is neither socialite functions nor those run by professional fund raisers. We will discuss smaller causes that are important to a community, and we will try to suggest devices for making a dollar.

The main problem with amateur fund raising is that almost everyone volunteers. But when the crucial time comes, many of them suddenly have a sick child, a toothache, or some other crisis. So the burden falls onto the shoulders of a few stalwarts. Even then, there is no one person who has been designated to make all final decisions. Even the chairman of the committee, no matter how strong her character, hesitates to say "Yes!" or "No!" without consulting the other members.

My advice to any group intent on a charity drive is to appoint a chairman who understands the work and is willing to do it. Give her full responsibility. Then allow her to appoint her own committee of the people she is sure will really work along with her.

Whether the project is a church-building party and the idea is to sell bricks at the annual congregation dinner; or a strawberry social to make the money for the raising of the roof; or a covered-dish supper to stir up enough cash to burn the mortgage of the schoolhouse—the problem of organizing volunteer help is always the same. Someone has to be in charge to be sure there is enough of Mrs. Dilly's peach cobbler and not too much of Mrs. Lacy's baked beans. The chairman of the committee must be a diplomat as well as a worker and manager.

A covered-dish supper usually turns out to be somewhat of a surprise—and a very good one. Even without suggestions, the variety is almost always endless.

A church dinner is somewhat different from a bring-your-own supper. The dinner has to be planned per head. Sometimes tickets for a church dinner are sold ahead of time with a deadline for purchasing. No one without a ticket is allowed to enter the dining room. This is the best way to run such a dinner: it's easier for everyone.

However, some church dinners are planned with expandable dishes which can accommodate any late-comer with his two dollars-or-so to pay. If many have not paid in advance, it is obvious that the dinner has not been promoted effectively. At such times the hard-working committee can never tell whether there will be a mess of stew left over or if the latecomers will have a watered-down variety.

CHURCH DINNER FOR A DEFINITE NUMBER OF PEOPLE

Cantaloupe (or Grapefruit)

Baked Breast of Chicken   Mushroom Gravy

Baked Sweet Potatoes

Green String Beans

Apple Pie   Cheddar Cheese

Coffee

CHURCH DINNER FOR A VARIABLE NUMBER OF PEOPLE

Tomato Juice   Crackers

Cathedral Fricassee*   Rice
Peas
Blueberry Pie
Coffee

This is a stretchy menu. All the foods can be divided into smaller portions—in case you have planned on one hundred, and a hundred and thirty-five show up. Extra cans of tomato juice will help; and also such emergency provisions as canned meat balls and minute rice. Such circumstances do give the committee members gray hairs. Again, a strong-minded person *must* be in charge.

There has been a trend lately to raise money by giving parties in borrowed settings. New York City's Gracie Mansion has been loaned from time to time to worthy organizations. The committee asks a professional to arrange a tea or cocktail party. A special speaker is sometimes engaged. Admission is charged, and the organization nets the difference between intake and expenses.

Sometimes the night before the official opening of a special exhibit or art show is devoted to charity. For instance, invitations were once sent to a preview of a display of A.I.D. room settings. The twenty-dollar charge included supper, which was donated by a prominent restaurant. Since there were virtually no expenses, the Herald-Tribune Fresh Air Fund benefited handsomely.

Each year, the fashion industry puts on what is called "The Party of the Year," given for the benefit of the Costume Institute of the Metropolitan Museum. It is one of the most elegant events of the New York winter season, and is attended by everybody who is anybody on Seventh Avenue, top-flight store executives, and fashion editors. Each pays a hundred dollars to see a fashion show (usually old costumes from the museum), dance, and eat supper. But the original hundred dollars is just the beginning. Volunteer helpers are constantly coming around with extras, such as tickets for the ten-, twenty-five-, and hundred-dollar grab bags. The beautifully wrapped and mysterious packages are filled with donated merchandise that is worth at least twice the price of the ticket. Since most of the work is done by volunteers, and the merchandise donated, there is always a good amount left for the Costume Institute even after the supper, orchestra, and ballroom have been paid for.

Tours of ancient homes and beautiful gardens have long been a source of revenue and are becoming popular as an almost effortless way to raise funds for garden clubs, historical societies, and any number of other causes.

In the spring, garden-club groups have a series of tours which are attended by garden enthusiasts from all over the country. When these people go home, they give a full report to their local clubs about what they have seen. The price of the tour usually includes the inspection of from six to eight gardens in a particular area; for instance, penthouse gardens on Park Avenue or backyard gardens in Greenwich Village. The hostesses sometimes serve punch and cookies. But there are no costs to the cause except printing the programs and tickets, and perhaps a prize for the most popular garden. This type of fund raising has expanded to include tours of kitchens, and homes of famous people.

Business Parties—Intraoffice

Perhaps the most important business parties are those held in the office. To many workers—executives as well as underlings—the place where they work is almost as important as their home. After all, subtracting commuting time, they spend almost the same number of hours in each.

Perhaps because of this, top management frequently plans group parties on holidays and special occasions to cement the family-like relationship. Management also arranges celebrations to honor employees who have stood by for ten, twenty, or even thirty years. Usually a fountain pen, watch, or medal is presented to the "star" of the occasion.

But the best parties given within an office are the personal ones which have nothing to do with the management. Sometimes they are held during lunch; but more often they occur after the shop has closed. The reasons for such parties can be quite varied—a secretary has just become engaged, a bookkeeper may be getting married, the office boy could be leaving for the Armed Forces, or the office manager is about to have a baby. All of these occasions can be impetus for a gay and friendly party. They are given in the home away from home and therefore can be casual and informal.

The decorations and the presents need not be elaborate, and the food and beverages can be sandwiches from the local delicatessen and soft drinks or coffee from the office machine.

But the very best within-the-office party is the one where the employees decide to give some sort of party for their boss. He seems to be a formidable fellow, but they have decided to break through his ice by celebrating his birthday or arrival-at-the-company anniversary.

Many companies, both large and small, have found it a great convenience to have a fully-equipped kitchen adjacent to the conference or board room. This facility has proved to be such an asset that some companies have a cook working every day of the week to serve lunch to varying numbers of people on short notice. This is an informal and hospitable way to entertain clients on home ground. It is also a time saver, when an all-day meeting is in progress, not to make a lengthy break by going to a restaurant for lunch. It is an extremely useful device for an important policy-making staff meeting, a small and informal discussion group, or a meeting of the board of directors.

BOARD OF DIRECTORS LUNCHEON FOR 12

Fresh Fruit Cup
Celery   Olives
Prime Ribs of Beef
Browned Potatoes   Watercress Garnish
String Beans Amandine*
Hard Rolls   Butter
Coffee Ice Cream
Old Dutch Cookies*
Coffee

The office kitchen can also be useful for informal breakfast gatherings—fruit juice, coffee, Danish pastries. Or for teas and cocktail parties in the late afternoon.

Part Two

NATA LEE'S PARTY RECIPES

Introduction to Part Two

Throughout the book there have been menu suggestions for all types of parties, many of which include one or more of my tried and true recipes. Some of them have been handed down to me from my grandmother. A few of them have been given to me by friends and customers. But almost all of them have been worked over and improved by me.

This is my personal cookbook. And my hope is that the hostess who tries the recipes will enjoy them and then make them truly her own by personal innovations.

This section has enough recipes for a yearful of parties. But it is intended only as a party supplement to your day-by-day, cover-everything cookbook. However, there are many recipes here which you may wish to use in your everyday menus. For, after all, an enthusiastic cook can add zest to the menu and make an ordinary family meal party-like.

Most recipe books start with appetizers, go on to soups, and progress as an actual meal does. But I am going to start this part of the book with seven of my stand-bys—a magic seven that can be varied and multiplied into many times seven recipes.

These seven recipes are the foundation of my menu making. I met them early in my life, and I've used them over and over again in various ways, shapes, and forms for my own parties. I have used them so many times that now I can practically make them with my eyes closed. I don't have to stop and think—making them is almost automatic.

Because parties are my business, I am always on the lookout for new ideas. Often the new idea is developed from one of these basics—and the variations go on and on. As I mentioned early in the book, they are my party wardrobe, and my repertoire.

When I was going over my recipes with my editor, she asked why I used the word "about" in so many. Couldn't they be exact? My answer was: "Are all eggs alike? Do you know that for two of the very large ones that we use, you must use three of the small size to get the same volume? I used to season a certain mixture with one teaspoon of salt and no pepper, because I like it that way, until I found two kinds of critics. For one group the mixture was too salty; for the rest, too bland."

Now I also like to include the words "to taste" with any seasoning. Those words please me when I find them in another's recipe, for they mean that when I make the dish and season it to my taste, it has become *my* dish. Somehow the phrase always seems to spark ideas for me.

I am reminded of an energetic woman I met in Victoria, B.C., in her popular restaurant facing Puget Sound. When she first used the expression "finger cook," I did not know what she meant. Then she demonstrated by scooping up a tiny bit of sauce with the tip of her index finger and tasting it. Whether by finger or spoon, the cook must be guided by taste.

Another thing is relevant before you read the recipes. You know that foods vary greatly—eggs in size and viscosity, lemons in size, juiciness, and acidity, and so on. Do you know that one person's measure of one cup of flour will weigh exactly four ounces, while another's measure will weigh a fraction of an ounce over or under? It would, of course, be more accurate if Americans based recipes on weight, as much of the rest of the world does. Failing that, I must resort to "about."

Foods vary, and tastes vary, and to meet that situation I make recourse to "optional." To indicate that a substance is not essential, but that some persons like it, I have enclosed the suggested ingredient in parentheses.

So here are my treasures. Value them well by using them often!

Note: The recipes are printed in a way that I have found is extremely easy to follow. The ingredients are listed in the order of their use, on the left-hand side. Directly opposite, on the right-hand side, is the method of procedure.

SEVEN BASIC HELPERS

Basic Sponge Cake
Basic Nut Torte
Linzer Cookie Dough
Basic Butter Cake
Basic Cheese Dough
Basic Pancakes
Basic Yeast Dough

Basic Sponge Cake   *serves 8*

6 egg yolks . . . . beat well
1 c. sugar . . . . add and beat
1 lemon rind, grated . . . . add and beat
1 orange rind, grated . . . add and beat
1 c. cake flour sifted with
1 teas. double-action bak-
    ing powder . . . . fold in carefully
6 egg whites, beaten stiff. . fold in carefully

Bake in ungreased 8″ spring form 350°, 45 to 50 minutes.

Basic Sponge Cake is a quick-into-the-oven jewel. In my early days friends would ask "How do you make this?" and I'd often answer "With feathers," for it is so light that it can be fed to a baby or to a great-grandmother, to a football player or to an ulcer patient.

Use for:

    icebox cakes
    English trifle
    fresh coconut layer cake
    mocha layer cake
    little cakes
    plain loaf cake (later, stale pieces can be toasted for
        zwiebach)
    crumbs for petits fours (glacéed bites)

Basic Nut Torte   *serves 8–12*

8 egg yolks .... beat well
1 c. powdered sugar .... add; beat well
⅛ lb. (2 oz.) bitter
     chocolate .... heat together until chocolate is
                  melted,
⅛ c. milk .... stirring constantly; cool, add
½ lb. finely ground
     walnuts (1⅓ c.) ... add
8 egg whites, beaten stiff.. fold in carefully

Bake in 8″ spring form 350°, about 1 hour.

Basic Nut Torte is rich enough for dessert. This is my favorite for birthday cakes and wedding cakes. It is sturdy enough to hold in shape, even bears the weight of several tiers. Note that there is no flour in this luscious recipe. The ground nuts are used instead.

Note: For sturdiness needed in *very* large cakes (2, 3, or 4 times this recipe) to be set one on the other in tiers, add 1 tbsp. flour for each 8 eggs.

Variations: May be flavored with orange, brandy, rum, coffee. Nuts may be walnuts, almonds, hazelnuts, or brazils.

Cake may be split, filled and covered with whipped cream, Butter Cream Nata Lee, Hungarian Chocolate Icing.

Cake may be trimmed with candied cherries, ground or chopped pistachios, scraped chocolate, jelly, colored sugars.

Basic Linzer Cookie Dough   *for 10-inch cake*

¼ lb. butter .... cream
½ c. superfine sugar .... add
½ lemon rind, grated ... add
2 egg yolks .... beat; add
1 c. all-purpose flour ... add

This makes a very soft dough. It cannot be rolled, but must

be patted carefully into the pan from ¼ " to ½ " thickness, depending on its use.

Bake at 325°—time depends on use.

For many years now, I have been going steady with this basic—an old-fashioned Middle European cookie dough known as *Muerbe Teig*. I call it Linzer Cookie Dough. Do learn to use it, for you can have lots of fun with it.

Its best-known property is that, when baked, it will stay fresh for several days. I first found it a special friend when I needed a sturdy, make-ahead dessert for long country weekends. It turned out even better than expected. Use for:

cookies	cherry cake
apricot squares	plum cake
open fruit tarts	peach cake
apple cake	blueberry cake

Basic Butter Cake   *makes 24 squares 2" x 2"*

¼ lb. butter	cream until soft
1 c. sugar	add and cream
3 egg yolks, beaten	add
1 teas. vanilla	add; beat
½ c. milk	
1½ c. cake flour, sifted with	
3 teas. double-action baking powder	alternate milk and flour mixtures
3 egg whites, beaten stiff	fold in gently; put into buttered 8 x 12 x 2 pan

Bake 35 minutes, 350° oven.

Basic Butter Cake is a handy little helper. It is richer than most standard butter batters, lighter and more delicate. I could call this a feather cake, too. You might want to serve it at a P.T.A. meeting or for your child's birthday cake.

You can use this basic for any cupcakes or layer cake. You can bake it in sheets to be iced; or top it with a wonderful coffee-cake streusel.

Basic Cheese Dough   *enough for 1 batch caraway cheese puffs*

¼ lb. salt butter (cold)
¼ lb. cream cheese (cold)
1 c. all-purpose flour ... cut solids into flour with knife as for pie crust until the pieces are the size of peas and each piece of fat well coated with flour; squeeze mixture together in hand several times until it forms a cohesive ball of dough; wrap in foil; chill several hours; roll out like pie crust

Always start to bake this crust in a hot oven, 450°; baking time depends on use.

Some people make this by adding ice water, as in the usual pie dough. I think it is flakier without.

Note: When using this dough for bottom of fruit pie, be sure to cover it well with flour or egg white, or to put a thick layer of corn flakes on top of the bottom crust to absorb the fruit juices and keep bottom crust flaky.

Cheese Dough is one of the most flexible doughs I know. I use it for pie crust, for French pastry, little tarts, and apple dumplings as well as for appetizers like liver strudel and cheese puffs. There is no limit to the new things you may find to do with it. Here are some of the things I've made from it:

Sweet	*Salty*
open apple cake	liver strudel
fruit pies	cheese puffs
jam tarts	barberpole franks
apple dumplings	dillies
apple turnovers	salmon tricorns
fruit cobblers	bouchées
little horns	cheese sticks
napoleons	pastry pizza

Pancakes

```
3 whole eggs .......... beat well
½ c. flour ............ add, beat again
1 c. milk ............. add, beating more
```

This makes a very thin batter and, to my mind, or rather my palate, the thinner the batter the better.

Every country has its own version of pancakes: the French, crepes; the Hungarians, palicinta; the Germans, blintzes; the Russians, blini, and so forth. So many different ways of making pancakes! So many accompaniments and you can make them all with this basic recipe. Believe me, you do not have to have Grand Marnier to make the most delectable desserts. Use this basic recipe. Make the cakes in a 9″ skillet with plenty of butter . . . don't start them if you are going to be thrifty. The trick in making the thin dessert pancakes is to have the butter plenty hot, pour in *very little* batter, and immediately tilt the skillet with a circular motion so that the batter will entirely cover the bottom with the tissue of hot ambrosia. Keep the flame high; they taste better made quickly. Turn pancake when it starts to bubble, brown second side, remove to serving dish and quickly blanket with thick sour cream and a dusting, to taste, of sugar and cinnamon. Then dish up as food fit for a king. Indeed it will make any crown feel better to have a series of these right from the pan. These dessert pancakes, in their own way, are as delicious as the much more expensive crepe suzettes. They are not for big crowds. They are best when they are literally hot off the griddle.

Basic Yeast Dough   *makes 3 dozen small schnecken*

YEAST MIXTURE

```
½ oz. dry yeast
2 tbsp. lukewarm water
½ teas. sugar
```

½ tbs. flour . . . . mix all together in a small bowl; put aside in warm place to rise and become spongy

MILK MIXTURE

2 tbsp. butter
⅝ cup milk . . . . put together into small saucepan and scald; cool to lukewarm

EGG MIXTURE

1 egg, beaten
½ teas. salt
¼ c. sugar
2 teas. cream
1 teas. rum
grated rind of ½ orange
grated rind of ½ lemon
½ teas. vanilla . . . . use a large mixing bowl; put all of egg mixture into it and beat; add yeast mixture and milk mixture and beat smooth

2 cups flour (or more) . . add gradually; beat smooth

Knead dough on floured board until satiny and elastic; butter a big bowl, put dough into it, and flip the ball of dough upside down so that both sides are well buttered. Cover with a towel and put in warm place to let dough rise. When it has doubled in bulk, roll it out on floured board, and proceed with Schnecken (p. 265) or other yeast cakes or breads.

Yeast dough is fun; it's mysterious, unpredictable. You can never absolutely control its expansion. Yeast is a mold which grows rapidly under certain conditions. It's somewhat like an infant that needs tender, loving care.

The first yeast dough I ever tried was a disaster. I used a good recipe and made the dough exactly as instructed, until I came to "let rise." How long, I wondered? Someone said "until double in bulk," but I didn't know what that meant. Today I know a good test is to press a finger gently on the top of the dough. It makes an indentation. If it has not risen enough, the indentation stays. If it is ready to be rolled out, the dough will spring back and the finger mark will disappear.

If it has risen too long, the dough will collapse at your touch. What to do then? Just push it all down and let it rise again.

I still love to play with yeast dough, to watch it rise and to sniff the good homey smell of the growing bulk. It's fun to handle and exciting to shape.

Use for:

> schnecken
> Dutch apple cake
> Swedish tea ring
> any sweet rolls

Reduce sugar in egg mixture III to 1 tbsp. and use for any kind of bread or rolls or:

> challah (Jewish Sabbath twist)
> Bermuda bantam buns
> various appetizers

Appetizers

Platter Presentations

Porcupine Platters   *serves 40–60 people (with other things)*

Baked Ham Porcupine starts with a cold clove-studded whole baked ham. First cut a one-inch-thick slab from the bottom, then place the remainder on the platter with the round side up. To give the structure height, you may anchor it with florists' sticks against a grapefruit that has been cut flat across the bottom. Cut the slab of ham into uniform 1″ cubes. Spear a cube of ham with a toothpick and then stick it into the whole ham, just as you would stick a pin into a pincushion. Repeat until the ham is covered with cubes. The rest of the cubes can be speared, to be ready as refills. A bunch of grapes adds a charming decorative note.

Sometimes, for small parties, a pineapple is the cushion for the cubed meat.

Breast of Turkey Sticks may be served independently or around the Porcupine Ham.

> 1 breast of turkey, roasted (12-20 lb. bird, p. 230)
> 1 pt. Alaskan dressing (p. 250)
> 2 c. sliced almonds, lightly toasted

Cut the entire breast away from the bone. With a very sharp slicing knife cut the breast meat lengthwise into slices ½" thick. Cut each of these slices into sticks ½" by ½" by 2"; the grain should run the long way. Push a toothpick into one end, at an angle. Dip the other end first into the Alaskan dressing that has been poured into a shallow plate, next into a plate of toasted almonds. Arrange the sticks side by side on the serving platter.

Thinly sliced almonds may be purchased by the pound in most metropolitan markets. To toast, spread evenly on cookie sheet, broil lightly. Watch carefully, as they burn easily.

These platters have been described as food pictures.

Nova Scotia Salmon Platter   *will serve 25 or more*

1 lb. cream cheese . . . . . soften
1 unsliced pumpernickel
   or rye bread . . . . . . cut thin slices; spread with softened cheese
2 lbs. thinly sliced Nova
   Scotia salmon . . . . . put slices of the smoked fish on top of the cream cheese; press down with a spatula to smooth and help it adhere; trim irregular edges away with scissors; use small pieces to fill in empty spots

The result will be about 20 neat, open sandwiches. They may be made a day or two before your party and stacked in piles of 5 (nothing in between). Wrap in wax paper or foil and store in refrigerator. When ready to use, have ready a large silver tray.

1 eggplant ....cut bottom straight across, so it will stand upright; put it at one end of tray

1 tail of a smoked
  salmon ....anchor tail firmly to eggplant, with the caudal fin high; use florists' sticks or round toothpicks; take open sandwiches from refrigerator; cut off crusts; cut each large sandwich into two, three, or four little sandwiches; arrange these pieces in trim rows around the platter

Platter may be garnished with green leaves and a bunch of black grapes trailing from the eggplant; salmon is usually served with eighths of lemon or lime, a pepper mill, and sometimes with a topping of capers.

Ice-bowl Garden Platters

A do-it-yourself ice bowl is a dramatic serving piece. Order a ten-pound block of ice (adequate for a medium-size party). Make a hollow in the ice by placing a bowl of very hot water on top of the block. The ice melts and a slight hollow is formed. When the water in the bowl cools, refill it with more hot water until the cavity in the ice is the right size. The outside of the ice bowl may be left plain or decoratively chiseled with an icepick. The ice bowl can be made days ahead and kept in the freezer.*

* The ice bowl will melt slowly at room temperature, but for a long party, the platter for holding it must be deep enough to collect all drippings. In very hot weather, I've sometimes used a basting syringe to siphon the water from the tray. Outdoors, it can be squirted onto the lawns; indoors, it can be emptied into a container kept under the table.

When you are ready to set up this platter, place the ice bowl on a folded towel on the platter to prevent the cake of ice from slipping. As ice is translucent, the color from beneath will shine through. Placing large green leaves on top of an absorbent cloth or sponge is effective; or try spinach leaves, shredded red cabbage, or carrot shavings.

For a Shrimp Garden, allow for each person 2 or 3 shrimp depending on size. Shrimp run 8 to 24 per pound, uncooked.

Line the hollow of your ice bowl with cups of red or white cabbage or lettuce. Fill with the cooked, cleaned shrimp, which have been speared with toothpicks. For a pleasing arrangement, place the shrimp with the picks all pointing in one direction.

Use lettuce cups or cabbage as holders for the different garden foods. Nestle these natural containers on the platter against the base of the ice bowl. Any of the following make good garden-platter fillers:

bedeviled eggs	finocchio
ripe olives	radish roses
stuffed olives	raw peas in pod
carrot sticks	fresh strawberries with hulls intact
celery heart curls	sticks of other vegetables
scallions	cherry tomatoes

Variations of garden platters using the ice bowl idea can be made with other shellfish:

Crab lumps in tiny clamshells and topped with a dab of dressing.

Cold lobster chunks, toothpicked, for dipping into Celestial Fish Sauce.

Cold sautéed scallops, speared and ready for tartar sauce.

Frog legs sautéed are a delightful conversation piece. They're a natural pick-up food . . . and the ultimate in sophistication.

Alaska King Crab, cut into one-inch chunks and toothpicked.

Herring-by-the-Sea Platter   *allow 1 filet for 3 people for a cocktail party, 1 for 2 people as an appetizer*

3 filets pickled herring . . place in glass dish
½ pt. sour cream . . . . . . add
juice of 1 lemon . . . . add and stir

(if lemon is small,
use 2)

1 sweet onion, peeled ... cut into slices; add; mix cream so
that it covers all; cover tightly; let
rest in refrigerator for 2 or 3 days
before using.

Cut the filets into one-inch pieces. Put them into a stemmed
silver bowl with the sour-cream sauce. Place the bowl on a
silver platter. Around the base arrange alternate slices of
pumpernickel and unpeeled red apples (dip apple slices into
lemon juice to keep from discoloring).

Place forks or a container of toothpicks near the herring
bowl. The guest will take a piece of herring and put it onto
an apple slice, onto the bread, or onto both. A few of these
tasty open sandwiches can be made up by the hostess and
placed around the platter to point the way.

This same herring in cream sauce is good on lettuce as a
first course for a seated dinner.

Hot Appetizers—Do-It-Aheads

These do-it-aheads can be frozen; since they are served hot,
they will have that fresh-from-the-oven goodness.

Asparagus Cheese Rolls

fresh, unsliced white
bread .... cut very very thin (⅛)″ slices; trim
to 2″ x 3″ rectangle; lay each rec-
tangular slice on a damp towel and
cover with another damp towel for
a few minutes to make the bread
more pliable

¼ lb. very soft butter
½ lb. cheddar cheese,
grated
1 tbsp. prepared
mustard .... combine; spread some butter mix
on each rectangle of bread

canned asparagus tips,
    drained .... dry thoroughly by letting stand on
                    soft side of bread crusts; cut to
                    2" lengths with scissors; place a
                    piece of asparagus on one end of
                    spread rectangles

Roll up from end holding asparagus tip, place seam down on
damp towel; chill; to serve, place Asparagus Cheese Rolls
seamside-down on pan under broiler; toast, turn; toast other
side; serve hot.

There's no way of telling how much bread and asparagus
you'll need. If your asparagus is used up, open another can
to use up the cheese or grate more cheese to use up the
bread. It can be a continuous process, sandwich board to
freezer.

Trader Horns

Chinese water chestnuts,
    canned .... drain well
thin bacon—take out of
    refrigerator early so
    it is not stiff or dip
    into hot water to
    soften .... roll strip of bacon tightly around
                    water chestnut; fasten with tooth-
                    pick
brown sugar .... sprinkle on; broil until bacon is
                    crisp (sometimes picks must be re-
                    placed before serving)

Steak Teriyaki *1 lb. trimmed meat (2 lbs. gross) will serve 10–15*

boneless sirloin steak
1" thick, prime, well
    hung .... remove fat and gristle; cut into 1"
                  cubes

firm tomatoes, cut small
    (or cherry tomatoes,
    cut into halves)
green pepper, cut small
cocktail onions, drained
bamboo sticks, 6″ long .. grease heavy skillet with fat from
    steak; pan-fry cubes, stirring constantly with wooden spoon
soy sauce to taste ...... pour over steak and juices in pan;
    (instead of salt)   stir; place one steak cube onto each
    readied bamboo stick; place sticks
    (all one way to present to guests)
    on small platter and serve at once

Thread small pieces of tomato, green pepper, and onion on bamboo skewers before you cook steak.

Stuffed Mushrooms   *makes 75–100*

3 lbs. medium mush-
    rooms .... wipe with damp paper towel; remove stems and reserve
2 lbs. sausage meat ..... grill; pour off fat
mushroom stems,
    chopped
½ teas. sage
salt and pepper .... combine with sausage meat; correct seasoning

Fill caps with mixture; broil carefully for only three minutes. Mushrooms should be underdone and still firm. Serve hot.

Tawny Pippits   *makes 12 large or 24 small rolls*

2 lbs. veal for scallopini.. cut into 3″ x 5″ sections
¼ lb. Provolone cheese,
    grated
1 bunch parsley, chopped
    fine (about 1 c.)

½ teas. oregano
½ c. sour cream ....combine; place 1 teas. of mixture
                      on each piece of veal; roll up and
                      skewer with toothpick
shortening ....sauté; remove skewer; spear with
                      fresh toothpick; serve hot

Mini-Pizza   *serves 75–100 people (with other things)*

Reduce sugar in Basic Yeast Dough recipe to one tablespoon
(see p. 183).
1 batch Basic Yeast
   Dough ....roll ¼″ thick; cut into circles 2″
                      in diameter
1 lb. fresh tomatoes ....peel and dice
2-2 oz. cans anchovies ..dice
1 lb. American or Swiss
   Cheese ....dice fine

Mix tomatoes, anchovies, and cheese. Spread on each round
of dough. Let rise until light.
   Bake at 400° about 15 minutes. Serve hot.
   Mini-pizza can be frozen at any stage after the dough has
been rolled and cut. Freeze circles of dough; freeze dough
with topping; freeze partially baked Mini-pizza.

Caraway Cheese Puffs   *makes 30 puffs*

Use Basic Cheese Dough recipe (see p. 182).
1 Cheese Dough recipe ..roll out oblong, ¼″ thick
½ c. cheddar cheese,
   grated ....sprinkle over ⅔ of dough; fold ⅓
                      with no cheese over half of the
                      rest; fold again. This will give you
                      three layers of dough. Roll this ¼″
                      thick; repeat folding process, this
                      time with no cheese; refrigerate ½
                      hour; roll chilled dough into ob-
                      long ⅜″ thick; cut into strips 1″
                      x 2″.

1 egg white, beaten a
    little .... brush on strips
caraway seeds .... sprinkle on strips

Bake 450° for 12 minutes. The result is improved by chilling before baking.

Bouchées are miniature patty shells. Use Basic Cheese Dough recipe (see p. 182). Roll dough ¼″ thick. Cut all the dough into rounds with a cutter 1½″ in diameter. Cut the centers from *half* of these rounds with a small cutter, 1″ in diameter, to make rings. Brush the solid rounds with slightly-beaten egg white. Place rings on top. Press lightly together. Chill. Bake at 450° until light amber in color. Dough will puff up to make exquisite little containers. Fill with any appetizer mixture. The tiny one-inch circles that are left can be used for Tea Buttons.

Marine Mix   *enough for 50–100 bouchées, depending on size*

1½ lbs. finnan haddie ..	put in drip pan with cold water to cover; let stand a few hours or overnight; pour off water and add fresh
1 tbsp. butter	add; bake at 350° about 15 minutes until tender; drain liquid; flake fish with two forks until quite fine; put aside
2 tbsp. butter	heat in saucepan
2 tbsp. flour	add; stir constantly; cook about 5 minutes until smooth and the raw flour taste has gone
1 c. milk .... (or cream for a richer sauce)	add gradually; stir constantly over low heat; simmer for about 10 minutes; add flaked fish to sauce; cook slowly until hot; fill mixture into miniature patty shells for Marine Bouchées

To use as a breakfast or supper dish, do not flake fish, but cut it into pieces.

Lobster Thermidor Mix

1 lb. lobster meat, cut
    very fine ....add to sauce; heat

    Thermidor Sauce   *(makes 2 cups)*
1 small onion, diced
1 green pepper, diced
2 oz. butter ....sauté vegetables in butter
¼ lb. mushrooms,
    sliced ....add and sauté
½ c. ketchup
½ c. chili sauce ....add; stir; cook slowly
3 tbsp. dry white wine
½ pt. sweet cream .....add

Fiesole Mix

1 lb. raw veal cutlet, cut
    into tiny cubes
2 tbsp. butter or oil
1 onion, chopped fine
½ green pepper, chopped
    fine
¼ c. parsley, chopped
    fine ....sauté meat and vegetables in butter;
                   add seasoning: cook about 10 min-
                   utes over low heat; stir constantly
1 lb. mushrooms,
    chopped fine ......add
½ teas. oregano ....add
½ c. grated cheese .....add; stir.

Fill bouchées with hot mixture. To heat for serving, place in
350° oven about 5 minutes.

Barberpole Franks

Roll Basic Cheese Dough thin. Cut into ½″ strips. Start at

one end of cocktail frank and wind dough around it barber-pole fashion. Press to seal end. Bake in hot oven 10 minutes. Serve with mustard.

Dillies   *makes 30*

½ batch Basic Cheese
    Dough .... roll out ¼" thick
dill salt .... sprinkle on; roll up; roll out again
                     ½" thick. Cut out with small cordial glass

egg yolk, beaten .... brush rounds
dill seed .... sprinkle on top

Bake 15 minutes, 450° oven.

Little Drumsticks

A display of little chicken legs in a poultry store gave me an idea for a cocktail party when the hostess wanted something new in party foods. I called them Little Drumsticks. Plan more than one for a person. They're that good. These can be cooked, frozen and warmed up for the party.

flour
salt
pepper .... combine; place ¼ c. at a time in
                     brown paper bag
drumsticks from young
    chickens .... place two drumsticks at a time in
                     the bag; shake until chicken is well
                     coated with flour

Fry in deep fat until brown and tender, about 10 minutes. Cool. To heat for serving, place in 350° oven until heated through. Sometimes galax leaves are stapled on, to serve as holders instead of paper frills.

Salmon Tricons   *makes 24*

Follow directions for Jam Tarts, p. 274; but use following mixture instead of the preserves:

1 lb. salty smoked salmon (lox)	mash up
¼ c. sour cream	add
¼ teas. freshly ground black pepper	add

Mix all together. Use as directed.

Liver Strudel   *makes 24 small strudel*

1 batch Basic Cheese
  Dough .... roll into very thin oblong sheet; cut into 3 long strips

1 batch Chopped
  Chicken Liver
  (p. 199) .... put liver mixture through meat grinder, then into pastry bags without a tip, to produce pencil-shaped rolls; run these rolls on each of the 3 long strips; brush with pastry brush wet with cold water along one long edge; roll up from opposite side and cut into desired lengths; place seams down on baking sheet; chill; bake at 450° for 20 minutes; serve hot

The strudel may be frozen, either raw, half-baked, or fully baked.

Bermuda Bantam Buns   *makes 12*

Reduce sugar in Basic Yeast dough recipe to 1 tbsp. (see p. 183).

½ batch Yeast Dough .. roll ¼" thick; cut into 24 2" circles
1 Bermuda onion, cut fine ... sauté golden; pour egg over onions and scramble; place teas. of mixture on half of the circles, cover with other halves;
1 tbsp. butter
1 egg, beaten
salt to taste .... press edges together
milk .... brush with milk; let rise

Bake at 400° about 12 minutes. Serve hot as an appetizer. Remaining half of dough may be made up and frozen.

DIPS

Mediterranean Caviar

1 eggplant, unpeeled .... bake at 350° about 30 min. or until soft; open; mash
1 tbsp. oil (approximate)
chives, chopped
fresh dill, chopped ...... add; combine

Optional additions to the eggplant pulp are many: minced garlic, Italian red onions chopped fine; more oil; vinegar; wine; scallion leaves, cut fine with scissors. This is one of those marvelous foods that are prepared "to taste"—a challenge to any creative cook.

Clam Dip Bari

8 oz. cottage cheese
1 can minced clams (1 cup)
3 tbsp. dry Vermouth (optional)
juice of 1 lemon
1 tbsp. horseradish
clam broth .... combine; add broth gradually until mixture is consistency of mayonnaise

Eggs Lido

6 hard-cooked eggs,
    chopped
1 unpeeled red apple (the
    hard, tart kind)
    finely diced and
    sprinkled with lemon
    juice
½ c. finely chopped celery
½ green pepper, finely
    chopped
½ c. mayonnaise
1 small Italian red onion,
    finely chopped . . . . . combine all
salt . . . . to taste
pepper . . . . to taste
8 or more black olives,
    pitted and cut fine . . optional

Endive leaves, washed and crisped, are strong enough to serve as dunkers for any dip; and they're so welcome by the calorie-conscious. You'll find they go well with Eggs Lido.

Charoses

This dish symbolizes the mortar which the ancient Israelites, enslaved in Egypt, made into bricks. On Passover, each generation since the Exodus has eaten Charoses at the beginning of the Seder dinner. There are many different ways of combining the nuts, apples, and wine. Some people grind the nuts; many add a dash of cinnamon.

1 firm apple . . . . peel; cut up very fine with knife;
    put into bowl
½ c. walnuts . . . . cut with chopping knife fairly fine;
    add

¼ c. sweet Passover
    wine .... add and mix (for looser mix, add
                more wine)

Serve on small pieces of matzos.

Chopped Chicken Liver

1 med. onion, chopped
    fine
¼ green pepper, chopped
    fine
1 stalk celery, chopped
    fine
2 tbsp. chicken fat ..... sauté vegetables in fat
½ lb. chicken livers,
    diced .... add; sauté lightly; cool
2 hard-boiled eggs
    chopped .... add

Leave mixture rather rough, except for strudel. Chopped liver is ideal for sculpturing. Using either your hands or two knives, to match your party theme: a heart, a ring, a cone. One of my most successful "sculptings" has been a pineapple. Use four times the recipe given here. Make a pineapple-shaped mound; stud with slices of small stuffed olives. Push the green top of a real pineapple into the top of the mound. Serve the sculptured pineapple at one end of a platter. Surround with rows of melba toast and crackers. If the temperature is warm, lay the sculptured pineapple on its side. Be sure to put butter knives next to the platter for the guests to use as spreaders.

Tartar Steak

1 lb. ground round steak
1 teas. onion salt
1 teas. salt
dash of pepper
dash of garlic salt ...... combine; mix thoroughly

One of the important things to remember in making Tartar Steak is to have very lean, very fresh meat. Some people love it just loaded with freshly ground pepper. Others add chopped anchovies, pickles, olives or toss in the yolk of an egg. Frequently it's made or served with chopped onions. I use onion salt and serve it on onion cups.

Goose Grieben (Cracklings)

Cut the skin of a goose, duck, or chicken into 1″ pieces. Fry slowly to render fat. Remove pieces from hot fat. Place in shallow pan in 350° oven to crisp. Serve with slices of rye bread . . . and a salt shaker.

Crab Dip Bombay

2 c. crab flakes
1 c. sour cream
1 teas. curry powder
¼ c. grated coconut
salt
pepper ....combine

Crab Bombay is exquisite made with freshly grated coconut. To prepare, heat the fresh coconut in a 350° oven before cracking with a hammer. Carefully remove the milk. Peel. Grate the meat coarsely before adding. The results are guaranteed to be good. It is exotic to serve this dip from a hollowed-out pineapple or other tropical fruit. Place on a platter and surround with well-drained artichoke bottoms instead of crackers.

Onion Dip

Combine one package of dried onion soup (1½ oz.) with 1 cup sour cream. This has become an almost universal dip. But here's a new taste twist—add a dash of vermouth.

DUNKERS

There is a special requirement for dunkers: They must be strong enough to support the weight of a bite of whichever dip they are to accompany. They don't have to be bread or crackers; often we've used low-calorie greens.

Ice Cream Cones

If you want to make the cones smaller, wet edges, cut with scissors. Heat in oven. Fill with salad (use an ice cream scoop).

Tina Toast

thin sliced bread	cut slices into halves, squares, triangles or fingers
butter	use plenty—fry in *hot* pan

This is not an economy dish. Use lots of butter, or don't make Tina Toast; use crackers instead.

Onion Cups

Onions, Spanish or Bermuda	cut root and sprout ends; remove outer skin; cut lengthwise; separate into cups
Artichoke Bottoms:	canned or fresh; fresh will be firmer
Artichoke Leaves:	canned or fresh; fresh will be firmer
Endive Leaves:	washed, crisped, and dainty; fine with any dip
Hamburger Rolls:	split part way and hollow out; toast
Banana Chips	
Potato Chips	
Crackers	
Breads	of every variety

FANTASIES

For want of a better name, I call these cocktail foods "fantasies." They're neither sandwich, nor canapé, nor any other classification except delightful and amusing tidbits.

Bologna Fans

thin slices bologna ..... cut into thirds to make fans
stuffed olives .... slit part way; insert bologna slices
                          at point to resemble fan

Cheese Carrots and Apples

any soft yellow processed
      cheese .... let stand at room temperature;
                          mold with hands or butter pads
                          into carrots or apples
parsley .... garnish

Bologna Toots

thin slices of bologna ... roll into cornucopias
cream cheese
horseradish to taste ..... mix, fill the toots

Two squares of chicken wire, with four wooden spools wired at the corners to hold them apart, make a handy holder for these little toots while they rest in the refrigerator.

Salmon Flowerpots

Nova Scotia salmon
      slices .... flatten
cream cheese

chives ....mix; spread on salmon; roll up—
                         chill
parsley

Cut 1″ rolls. Stand up. Arrange sprigs of parsley as though
they were sprouting.

Pecanchovy Bon Bons

1 tbsp. anchovy paste
3 oz. cream cheese .....mix; make small balls
large pecan halves ......insert balls between nut halves; re-
                        frigerate

Dum-dums

Munster cheese or carrots
     or celery ....cut into match-stick size
pitted black olives ......put 1 stick into each olive center

A few Dum-dums stuck into an old-fashioned glass make a
nice center for a plate of fantasies.

Chicken Marbles

finely chopped chicken
     salad ....make balls walnut size
chopped pistachio nuts ..roll marbles in nuts; refrigerate

Nightingales' Tongues

honeydew melon ....peel, then cut into wedge-shaped
                        slices about 4″ x 1″
thinly sliced tongue .....wrap each slice around wedge of
                        melon; fasten with toothpick

Sesame Sticks

solid piece of tongue .... cut into strips ½″ x ½″ x 2″
mayonnaise ....spread on strips
toasted sesame seeds .... cover strips completely; refrigerate

Cream Puff Shells   *makes 100*

¼ lb. butter
1 c. water ....bring to a boil
1 c. flour ....add all at once; stir immediately
                       until mixture makes a ball; remove
                       from heat at once; cool
4 eggs ....add one at a time, beating well
                       after each; drop dots of batter as
                       big as a quarter by teaspoons or
                       through a pastry tube onto greased
                       cookie sheets; bake 450° for 10
                       min.; reduce heat to 375° for 20
                       min.

When you can no longer hear a crackling noise from a puff,
it's baked. Some people fill puffs through a hole in the bottom. You're apt to have leakage that way. Let them cool
first. Then cut the puff through the side with a sharp knife,
but not all the way through. Keep one side attached so the
top will remain hinged to the bottom.

One good filling which I use often is tuna or crab salad.
For Roquefort puffs you may use just Roquefort cheese as
the filling; however, I prefer

Cecily's Mystery Cheese

½ lb. Roquefort cheese.. put in blender
½ lb. cream cheese .... add
4 tbsp. fine cognac ..... add; mix smooth; put into crock
                          and store in refrigerator

The refrigerated mixture will keep for months. The excellence of the brandy makes all the difference in the result.

Bedeviled Eggs   *makes 12*

6 hard-cooked eggs
  (20 minutes) ...... cut in half, crosswise; remove yolks carefully and put through fine strainer; set whites aside
1 teas. salt
1 teas. dry mustard
1½ tbsp. mayonnaise ... add to yolks; mash to a smooth paste; if too stiff, add more mayonnaise

Cut thin slice off bottom of egg-white half, to make it stand straight. Fill the egg white with yolk mixture using a pastry bag or tube. Garnish with sprig of parsley.

Variations

Anchovy Eggs
1 tbsp. anchovy paste ... add to mix
  (or more, to taste)

Ham Eggs
½ teas. deviled ham ... put in bottom of each egg white

Curried Eggs
1 teas. curry powder ... add to mix

Turk in Boat
6 shrimp .... marinate in French dressing; drain, stand one shrimp up in each stuffed egg, narrow end up

Falafel

This is sold by the street vendors of Israel. It is an Oriental roll, split, filled with green salad and balls of fried ground hummus.

Green Salad

1 Boston lettuce
1 iceberg lettuce
1 bunch radishes, sliced
1 green pepper, diced
4 firm tomatoes, diced
chives, chopped .... mix

Dressing

6 tbsp. olive oil
2 tbsp. fresh lemon juice
salt
pepper
1 clove garlic
½ teas. dry mustard .... mix

Hummus Balls

2 cans chick peas ...... drain; mash
1 tbsp. oil
juice of 1 lemon
½ teas. salt
pepper to taste .... add; combine; shape into balls the
size of walnuts
vegetable shortening .... fry balls in deep fat or oil

Hamburger Rolls

These can be substituted for the Oriental Pitah, also called Lebanese bread. Split rolls part-way through. Mix green salad and dressing. Spoon into roll. Put 3 or 4 hot Hummus balls on top, push them gently onto top of salad.

LAST-MINUTE COCKTAIL QUICKIES

Always be ready for surprise guests. Keep the makings for Last-minute Quickies on hand. Naturally, what you keep on hand will depend on what you like. Here are a few suggestions:

A can of cocktail franks can become barbecued franks, at a moment's notice (for sauce, see p. 251).

In no time at all, a box of potato pancake mix can be transformed into hot delectable Pancake Pickups about the size of a silver dollar. Serve with a shaker of onion salt.

An apple and a bit of cheese on hand? Make a Cheese Apple (see p. 278).

But, if your poor cupboard is bare, and all you have in the house is tonight's dinner, use it!

If your dinner is *ground beef:*

Make miniature hamburgers; brush with soy sauce; broil, spear with picks; serve.

Make Tartar Steak; serve as a dip with crackers or onion cups; or make into balls.

Pat seasoned chopped meat about ½" thick onto a flat cookie sheet. Lay thin strips of any cheese in a criss cross pattern on the meat. Broil, then cut into squares. Serve on bread or crackers, and pass the ketchup!

If your dinner is a *slice of ham 1" thick:*

Cut the ham into cubes. Serve cold on toothpicks. Add a stuffed olive, a cube of cheese, a gherkin, or a cocktail onion to make a kebab. Or broil with pineapple chunks. Spear a ham cube and 1 or 2 pineapple chunks with a pick. Serve hot.

FORK FOODS

A wholly new food in the gourmet's world is rare. Seldom does a Burbank cross a peach with a plum to create a nectarine. We can learn to present, however, the many foods we have in different ways. If you have been serving only finger foods at your cocktail parties, why not add one of these fork foods to your next menu? They're served as simply as any other cocktail food. The fork food (unless self-contained like the next two recipes) is dished up from the buffet table onto a small plate, and a fork goes along.

Individual Cheese Souffles

2 teas. butter .... melt in skillet
2 teas. flour .... add; stir until bubbly
2 c. hot milk .... add gradually; stir till smooth; cool
4 egg yolks, beaten .... add
dash Worcestershire sauce
dash cayenne pepper
1 teas. mustard
1 teas. paprika
½ c. grated American
    cheese (sharp) ..... add, stir until smooth; cool
4 egg whites beaten stiff. . fold in

Put in ungreased, individual containers, ramekins, or custard cups placed in pan of hot water. Bake at 350° about 25-30 minutes. Serve immediately with plenty of paper napkins to protect your fingers.

Oysters Casino   *serves 8–12*

24 large oysters in shell. . scrub; open; leave on half shell;
                      place in baking pan
2 tbsp. chopped scallions
2 tbsp. chopped chives
dash of cayenne pepper
4 tbsp. melted butter
salt, pepper .... combine; put some of mix on top
                      of each oyster
6 strips crisp bacon
    (optional) .... crumble onto tops of oysters

Bake at 350° for 5 minutes or until oysters swell and begin to steam. Serve on a bed of rock salt. Yes, they can be eaten standing about; that's the idea with cocktail fork foods.

Ham and Potato Salad Torte

Pack finely diced ham salad firmly into the bottom half of an 8″ spring form (or removable bottom cake pan). Salad should be about 1½ " deep. Chill until firm. Then spoon a 1½ " layer of finely diced potato salad onto the ham salad; press firmly onto the ham. Chill at least one hour.

When ready to put on serving platter, loosen the salad from the rim of the spring form with a knife. Remove the rim. Then, holding the bottom of the form with one hand, press chopped parsley all around the sides of the salad torte. Enough will cling to make a green wall. Place torte, bottom tin and all, on a round serving platter. A dash of paprika and a sprig of parsley for the center, and your creation is ready for the table. To serve, cut like a cake.

Hors d'Oeuvre Cakes

The basis of all sandwich loaves is bread with appetizer fillings spread thickly between the layers. The outside of the cake is covered with softened cream cheese and appropriately decorated, usually with radishes, green peppers, pimentos. It's served just as you would serve any cake.

I've made hors d'oeuvre cakes in every conceivable shape . . . round, square, oval, triangle. I even fashioned one as a three-tiered wedding cake. One I remember as dramatic was made in the shape of an open book for an author's birthday party.

To Make an Open Book

Remove all the crusts from an unsliced loaf of bread. Cut the bread into 8 lengthwise slices.

Divide into 2 stacks of 4 slices each.

Fill each stack with 3 different appetizer mixtures to make a 4-layer cake.

Place the two cakes, about 1" apart, on a flat tray.

Spread softened cream cheese on 3 sides and top of each cake. Draw a fork along 3 sides of each cake to make lines which simulate the pages of a book.

Place a ribbon over the separation between the 2 cakes as a bookmark.

Decorate to suit the occasion.

SANDWICHES

Skilled sandwich making requires unsliced sandwich loaves, an extremely sharp slicing knife, and a steady hand. The filling must be soft enough to be spread without tearing the bread. For all sandwich preparation, spread a damp towel flat on the working board, and another one over the cut bread and ingredients on the board. Bread dries rapidly, so keep it under wet cover as much as possible.

Closed, Loaf and individually rolled sandwiches can be made in advance. Wrap first in foil or waxed paper, then in damp towels, and refrigerate. The paper prevents sogginess, and the dampness of the towels keeps them airtight and fresh for several days.

Closed sandwiches need not be plain. They can be colorful, cut with a knife into a variety of sizes and shapes. If you cut them in stacks, take care that your aim is straight, otherwise your stack may turn out looking like either a pyramid or a pagoda. Sizes for cocktail sandwiches have no standard. They vary with each hostess. Some like 'em big. Some little. Crusts on. Crusts off. Another moot question.

Using a standard slice of bread, here's how you can vary the cuts:

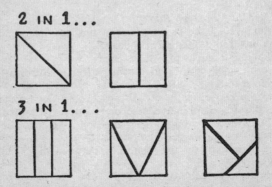

4 IN 1...

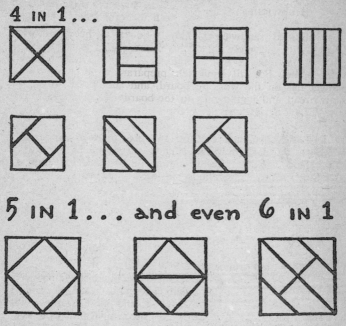

5 IN 1... and even 6 IN 1

Closed sandwiches can be colorful, novel, and made of ever available foods. Side-stacked to show the filling, they make a colorful center for a sandwich platter.

Tomato Sandwiches

fresh white bread .... cut 2 thin slices for each sandwich

mayonnaise .... spread smoothly on each slice

hard-boiled eggs, sliced .. place one slice in the center of a slice of bread

fresh tomatoes, quartered,
sliced, well drained . . place a quarter-slice in each corner of the bread, around the egg;
top with the other slice of bread;
chill; trim crusts and cut diagonally into 2 or 4 triangles

salt to taste

Loaf Sandwiches

Besides being a colorful surprise, there are other advantages to loaf sandwiches. They can be made three days
ahead and at party time the loaves can be sliced into individual fancy sandwiches, almost no last minute work.

Ribbon Sandwiches
2 thin slices white bread
3 thin slices Date-nut
Bread
cream cheese, flavored
with grated orange
rind . . . . put slices of bread together with
cream cheese; nut-bread slices make
the outside and middle; wrap, chill;
to serve, slice down into ribbons

Pinwheels

Making pinwheels is simple. Cut a thin slice of fresh
bread, lengthwise of the loaf. Spread with any soft tasty filling
and roll it up tightly like a jelly roll. Chill. When it is firm,
slice.
My particular contribution to pinwheel variations is:

Solid-center Pinwheels

fresh bread, unsliced . . . . cut bread into thin slices, lengthwise of the loaf

cream cheese, softened.. spread generously on each slice
Nova Scotia salmon,
     sliced .... make a roll of a slice of the salmon
                           that is as long as bread is wide;
                           place it at one end of the bread

green pepper, cut into
     thin strips about the
     length of the bread
     width .... place a strip on each side of the
                           salmon roll; roll up tightly; wrap;
                           chill

These little rolls are usually cut into 8 pinwheels. The con-
centration of color makes them interesting. The proportion of
filling to bread, greater than in the standard pinwheel, makes
better eating.

Date-Nut Checkerboard Sandwiches

When I give this recipe I am always reminded of the
old cookbooks where recipes began, "catch a nice young hen."
To make checkers you have to bake the date-nut bread first,
preferably a day ahead. Some of you may just go out and
buy one, loaf or canned, but for those who want to taste the
very best of its kind, here is mine:

DATE-NUT BREAD

1 lb. pitted dates
2 teas. baking soda
1½ c. boiling water .... combine; let cool
2 oz. butter .... cream
1½ c. sugar .... add; cream
2 whole eggs, beaten ... add; beat smooth
3½ c. flour .... add alternately with date mixture;
                         beat smooth
1 c. walnuts, chopped .. add
1 teas. vanilla .... add

Bake in greased loaf pan 275° from 1 to 1¼ hours. It is practical, if bread is to be used for checkers, to bake in three 1-lb. loaf pans.

TO MAKE A CHECKERBOARD

1 Date-nut bread
1 white bread, finely
    textured, unsliced
cream cheese
sweet butter .... soften; combine half and half

These intricate little sandwiches are not as difficult to make as they may look. It is precision work. Don't expect results in the beginning, for it is practice that gives you skill in this sort of thing. It is essential to use an extremely sharp knife with a broad blade.

  a. From the flat bottom of the date-nut loaf, slice a 1″ slab. From the white loaf, cut a matching slab. Put slabs together with cheese-butter mixture. Be sure to spread each slab to make it stick better. Chill.

  b. From this sandwich, cut lengthwise 1″ slabs. Spread each with cheese-butter mixture. *Put together in reverse.* Chill again.

  c. Now make a diagonal cut through the white section to form two triangular loaves. Cut a very thin slice from the bottom of the original date-nut bread (tissue-like—perhaps ⅛″ thick). Spread *both* sides with mix. Insert tween the two triangular loaves to make a diagonal line of dark in the white. Chill again.

  d. Cut four more tissue-thin slices from bottom of the date-nut bread. Trim all four sides of the checked loaf you have made, to make it as smooth as possible. Spread one outer side with mix; spread one thin slice with mix. Put together. Repeat for each of four sides. Chill again.

  e. To serve, cut slices of the loaf, about ½″ thick. Care must be taken to see that these loaves are very cold before cutting. And don't put the sandwiches out all at once, especially in hot weather, or they may come apart.

making a
CHECKERBOARD

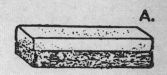

A.

B

B
end view

C
end view

D
end view

Individually Rolled Sandwiches

Cornucopia   Watercress Roll   Envelope   Mushroom Roll

Since I'm millions of sandwiches old, I've learned some practical techniques for making these pretties: thin, thin bread; very fresh bread, finely grained bread. Work with a damp towel under and over the component parts of the sandwiches. Learning how to seal is important to the sandwich maker. Softened butter is smeared on the edges to make them inseparable. When sandwich is refrigerated, always lay it on the seam. The weight of the sandwich itself will hold it closed. As the butter firms, the seam is welded.

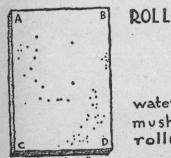

ROLL-UPS

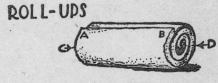

watercress &
mushroom-shaped
rolls

Roll-ups

For watercress or mushroom-shaped rolls, start with a rectangle. 2″ × 3″ is a good proportion. Make a pattern from cardboard or a piece of bread crust. It is easy to stack 5 thin slices of bread, place the pattern on top, and cut 5 squares at once. Spread each piece with a filling; roll up; chill.

Soft cream cheese squiggled through a pastry tube makes the head of the mushroom-shaped roll. Watercress sprigs may be inserted in one end or both ends of the watercress roll.

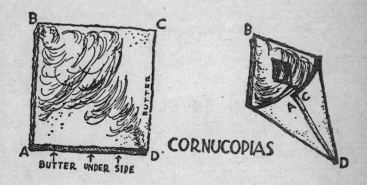

For cornucopias and envelopes, a perfect square is necessary. Make it as big or as little as you like so long as it is square.

Cornucopias

unsliced, fresh bread .... cut into very thin slices. Cut slices into squares 2″ × 2″

paté .... place filling on bread from points B to D. Spread heavily at point B and lightly at point D

very soft butter .... smear butter on two edges of the
                         bread square, under side of *A-D*
                         and top side of *C-D*

Holding point *D* stationary, gently roll *A-D* over the filling to
meet *C-D* and press the buttered edges together. Place seam
upside down on a damp towel. Cover with another damp
towel. Chill.

black olives .... cut slices of olive from the pit. Cut
                        into diamond shapes and place in
                        center of each cornucopia to gar-
                        nish

Fillings for cornucopias and envelopes can be paté, chopped
mixes, whole anchovies, or pieces of Nova Scotia salmon.

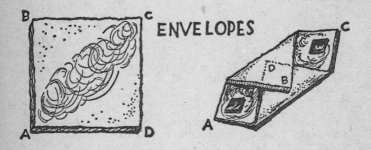

Window Sandwiches

This is my name for closed (or double, or whatever *you*
call them when you mean two pieces of bread put together
with a filling) sandwiches with a design cut out on the top
piece of bread. We do many variations on this theme.

Children's Windows

In this one, the window is filled in.

2 slices white bread
1 slice whole wheat
    bread
cream cheese
jelly .... spread one piece of white bread with the cream cheese and jelly. Cut rounds (with a cookie cutter) from the two remaining slices of bread, replace the *hole* in the white bread with a new "window" from the whole wheat bread (this white slice with the whole wheat circle makes the top of the sandwich); press firmly on to filling; chill; trim edges; serve

Any cookie cutter, of course, can be used to make the cutouts—a bird, a Christmas tree, or whatever suits the party occasion.

Flower Windows

1 slice of white bread ... cut a 2¼" round with a cookie cutter
cream cheese and
    anchovy, mixed .... spread round of bread with mix
1 slice of whole wheat
    bread .... using a liqueur glass 1¼" in diameter, cut out 3 tiny rounds from the whole wheat slice and overlap the rounds on top of the filling to form petals of a flower
green pepper strips ..... use to make the stem

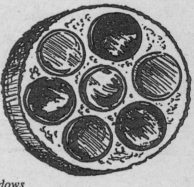

Stained-glass Windows

1 slice white bread ..... cut 2½″ round
cream cheese .... spread on
pimento and green
      pepper .... cut tiny circles, with your smallest cutter, of the red and green peppers; place them, alternating colors, in a row all around the edge of the sandwich

See-thru Windows

2 small squares white
      bread .... with cookie cutter, make a circle in one square
cream cheese and olive
      mix .... spread solid square with mix; on top of filling, place square with the window

Soups

Gazpacho   *makes 1 quart*

This Spanish vegetable soup has taken the food world by storm; it has become as popular as broiled grapefruit a few years back. Is it snob appeal that causes its popularity? Whatever the reason, this particular one is low in calories, quickly made, and tastes better than other recipes of the same name.

1 green pepper, diced
2 tomatoes, peeled, seeded
1 cucumber, peeled
½ cup celery & carrots,
    diced
4 sprigs parsley
½ teas. salt
¼ teas. pepper .... put all into blender; mix 1 minute
2 teas. lemon juice ..... add to mix in blender; mix 30 seconds more; remove from blender
2 c. canned beef
    consommé .... stir into the vegetable purée
1 tbsp. corn oil (not
    olive oil) .... stir into soup; chill; serve cold
1 clove garlic (optional)
1 onion or 4 scallions
    (optional) .... blend with vegetables

This can be served in a soup cup or as a wonderful cold appetizer in a juice class, with crushed ice, or on the rocks over ice cubes.

Bouillabaisse   *serves 6*

This wonderfully flavorful fish chowder, which I first tasted at the Marseilles waterfront, is another extremely variable dish. Because of the difference in the fish native to the Mediterranean waters, the French chowder tastes different from ours. This is a reasonable facsimile, with some shortcuts.

2 onions, chopped
1 stalk celery, diced
1 clove garlic, minced
2 tbsp. oil . . . . sauté vegetables in the oil until golden
1 can tomatoes, #2 . . . . add; cook slowly
1 tbsp. chopped parsley
salt and pepper
¼ teas. thyme
1 teas. paprika
dash cayenne
pinch saffron
1 bay leaf
¼ teas. fennel (optional)
2 c. clam juice
1 can lobster meat
1 lb. shrimp, cooked, cleaned
½ lb. scallops
1 lb. piece codfish . . . . . add; keep over very low flame; scallops and cod will cook in the soup
1 cup dry white wine . . add before serving
1 lb. small mushrooms (optional)

This is usually served with French bread sliced on the slant.

Vichyssoise

Grandma's old-fashioned potato soup has come back into style.

2 medium onions
2 leeks . . . . peel, slice thin

4 tbsp. butter .... sauté vegetables in butter, but do
                          not let them get dark; cook slowly
2 tbsp. flour .... add; stir smooth
4 large potatoes, peeled . slice tissue thin; add
2 qts. extra-strong
    chicken broth ...... add, cook slowly until potatoes are
                          soft; put all thru a very fine strain-
                          er; chill
1 pt. heavy cream ...... add; chill

    Garnishes
1) scallion shoots ...... cut snippets with scissors and put
                          some in each cup of soup
        or

2) whipped cream ...... put blob on each soup serving
   chives .... put pinch of cut chives on cream

        or

3) sour cream .... put teas. on each soup portion
   paprika .... put dash on each blob of sour
                          cream

Mushroom and Barley Soup   *serves 6*

This is a meal in itself.
8 dried mushrooms .... wash; soak for 1 hour; drain; chop
2 qts. beef stock .... strain stock; remove all fat; heat
¼ c. medium barley .... add to boiling soup
½ teas. salt .... add
1 potato, finely diced ... add
1 carrot, sliced fine .... add; add mushrooms, cover, cook
                          slowly for an hour or more; cor-
                          rect seasoning; serve

Grandmother's Double Chicken Soup
with Matzo Balls   *serves 8*

Grandma always said: "If you want a cup of *good* soup,
use a whole chicken for it." She meant, of course, that she

liked strong soup, not water. The backs of chickens make good soup, and they are much cheaper than the whole fowl that grandma used, provided you have a parts store near you.

Note: Chicken feet contain gelatin and are wonderful for soup. With the wider distribution of eviscerated poultry, however, they have become scarcer than hen's teeth.

6 lbs. fresh chicken parts,
    backs, necks, wings . . singe; wash, clean
3 qts. cold water
1 onion, peeled
celery tops
8 sprigs parsley
1 carrot, scraped
2 teas. salt . . . . put parts, vegetables, and seasoning into the cold water; cook slowly about 2 hours; strain

Matzo Balls   serves 8

2 tbsp. chicken fat . . . . . soften
3 eggs, beaten . . . . add; beat well together
1 teas. salt . . . . add; beat
1 tbsp. finely ground
    almonds . . . . add; beat
    (blanched or un-
    blanched)
a dash nutmeg   add; beat
⅓ c. matzo meal . . . . . . add slowly to make batter; *chill*
    (approximately, be-   *well;* shape into marble-sized balls
    cause eggs vary   (try out one ball in boiling water;
    in size)   if it does not hold shape, add a
                  very little bit of meal); chill again,
                  try test ball again

Drop *chilled* balls into boiling water 15 minutes before serving.

Chicken Lemon Soup

2 qts. strong chicken

broth .... bring to boil
½ c. washed rice ...... add; simmer 20 minutes

4 eggs
Juice of 2 lemons ...... beat together vigorously; gradually
add 1 c. hot broth; beat constant-
ly; combine with rest of soup;
serve at once

For an Oriental touch, add Chinese Egg Threads. Allow one
yolk for each person.

Chinese Egg Threads
1 egg yolk .... beat with fork; drop slowly into
boiling soup (preferably chicken);
serve at once

Main Dishes

Scrambled Eggs   *For each person:*

2 eggs .... beat in a bowl
1 tbsp. milk .... add
¼ teas. salt .... add
1 tbsp. butter .... heat butter; pour in eggs; reduce
heat to very low flame as soon as
mixture is poured; do not stir;
gently lift with spatula onto plate
when just set

Eggs Thermidor

For each person allow 1 or 2 hard-cooked eggs. Heat eggs
in Thermidor Sauce (see p. 194). Amount of this recipe is
enough for 6-12 eggs.

Shirred Eggs

Butter a glass pie plate. Sprinkle bread crumbs lightly in it.
Gently slip 2 whole eggs onto plate. Season with salt and
pepper; sprinkle very lightly with crumbs; bake in 325° oven
until set.

Good to make in large pans for many guests.

Creamed Chicken Mr. A.   *serves 6*

1 qt. cooked chicken	
meat	cut into cubes
3 tbsp. butter	melt
2 tbsp. flour	add; blend smooth
1 pt. strong chicken	
soup	add, blend smooth; cook about 15 min., stirring often
½ c. cream (optional) . .	add; blend smooth
dash of nutmeg	add; add chicken meat; serve

Note: I like to use roast turkey instead of chicken, because
it is so tasty and can be cut into bigger cubes.

Chicken Anita   *serves 4–5*

Chicken should be boned for buffet service with no small
tables.

2 2-lb. broilers, cut into individual serving pieces	
salt	
pepper	
flour	shake in bag, a few pieces of chicken at a time
4 tbsp. oil (or butter) . .	brown chicken in shortening until golden; put chicken into greased casserole

2 cloves garlic, chopped
   fine
1 bay leaf
6 sprigs parsley
½ teas. thyme
2 large tomatoes, peeled
   and cut up
1 leaf basil
1 c. white wine
1 jigger brandy .... add all to chicken; cover casserole, cook over low flame until
almost tender, turning pieces of
chicken several times; after 30
minutes, taste and correct seasoning

12 black olives, pitted .. add; cook 10-15 minutes longer, or
until chicken is tender

Canary Island Chicken   *serves 6*

2-2½ lb. broilers, cut up
½ c. flour .... put into bag together and shake
to coat chicken with flour; shake
off excess

¾ c. oil
2 cloves garlic, minced
1 medium onion,
   chopped .... sauté together for 5 minutes; add
chicken and sauté until golden

2 cups dry white wine .. add
hot chicken stock (from
   backs, necks, wings,
   gizzards) .... add enough barley to cover chick-
en

1 bay leaf
⅛ teas. thyme .... add
salt and pepper .... add to taste; cover; simmer over
low heat until almost tender

1 teas. saffron, dissolved
   in 2 tbsp. hot water

15 almonds, chopped ... add; simmer 15 minutes longer, or until chicken is tender; cook uncovered if sauce is too thin, to allow evaporation; serve

Optional Ingredients

½ c. bread crumbs
3 tbsp. oil .... sauté together
2 hard cooked eggs,
    chopped fine
¼ c. chopped parsley ... top chicken with rows of bread crumbs, eggs, and parsley

Chicken Cacciatore *serves 6*

There are many variations of this glorified chicken stew.

3 lb. stewing chicken cut
    up
1 onion, chopped fine
2 tbsp. oil .... brown in oil
1 can tomatoes
¼ lb. mushrooms, sliced
1 teas. salt
⅛ teas. oregano
¼ teas. thyme
1 pinch rosemary ...... add

Cook 1 hour or until tender. If you use small broilers it will take from 30 to 45 minutes to cook.

Chicken Salad *serves 8 generously*

5 c. cooked chicken
    or roast turkey .... cut into cubes
2½ c. celery, cut up ... add
1 green pepper .... cut up fine; add
1 c. Alaskan Dressing ... add; mix

This is just enough dressing to hold salad together. You may like more.

Chicken Salad Henshaw   *serves 8*

Allow one cup of salad for each portion. That's a generous eight servings to 2 quarts.

Make two packages of orange gelatin according to the manufacturer's directions. Divide the gelatin into two parts. Pour equal amounts of one half into eight individual molds, small bowls, or large cups. Set them on a tray in the refrigerator. When the gelatin is just beginning to set, tilt the molds, so that the sides get coated. Then, when the gelatin is firmly set, fill each bowl with the chicken salad. Now pour equal parts of the remaining liquid gelatin into the eight molds. Chill, set, and unmold. If you have done this carefully, the gelatin will completely enclose the chicken salad. Set each salad on a bed of shredded lettuce. Garnish with a perky bunch of watercress and several little wedge-shaped pieces of California orange.

Sculptured Salads

To sculpt salads, use your hands, or two spoons or two knives, to shape the form you desire; or if your talents do not lie in this direction, pack salad in a bowl, chill, and then dump it onto the platter.

Left-over turkey may be made into a spectacular conversation piece by making it into a salad and "sculpting" it into the shape of a pumpkin. Grated carrots may be gently patted on for color.

Old-fashioned Pressed Chicken   *serves 8–10*

4 lb. fowl, cleaned
1 onion
1 carrot
celery tops
2 teas. salt . . . . put into pan, cover with boiling water; simmer; when chicken is tender, remove, strain stock; simmer until 1 cup liquid remains

Remove skin and bone from chicken. Cut chicken into pieces, place in bread pan or a fancy mold. Correct seasoning. Add stock. Chill until firm.

To Serve: Turn out like any gelatin mold, onto large platter. Garnish with lettuce, watercress, pimento.

Roast Turkey
Mix for Basting Turkey   *for 20 lb. turkey*

¼ lb. butter
¼ c. flour
1 onion, chopped fine
1 clove garlic, chopped
    fine
½ teas. dried ginger
1 teas. salt
¼ teas. pepper
½ teas. thyme
1 teas. paprika
½ teas. majoram ......mix all together. This mix will keep in the refrigerator for 2 weeks

Optional Ingredients

bay leaf
½ teas. sage
¼ teas. mace
½ teas. dry mustard

Clean turkey well; rub a cut lemon inside the cavity; rub mix well into turkey, inside and outside, putting it more heavily on the legs and wings; roast in open pan at 350°; baste frequently, at least 6 times during roasting time; breast meat will be juicier if the bird is face down a large part of the time. If too heavy to turn, and breast and legs are getting too brown, dip clean cloth into the juices in the pan and cover them; keep cloths basted, too. Turkey is ready to eat when drumstick meat is soft to the touch, usually about 3 hours. That depends, though, on how young and tender the bird is.

Ragout of Goose with Apples   *serves 20 or more*

meat from 1 goose, raw
flour . . . . remove from bones and cut into
                                    serving pieces; shake in bag with
                                    flour to coat
¼ c. fat or butter . . . . . brown meat in fat; place meat in
                                    casserole
1 onion, cut up . . . . sauté in remaining fat
salt and pepper
pinch cinnamon
2 lbs. raw sour apples,
    peeled, sliced . . . . . . combine with onion; pour over
                                    meat in casserole; cover; bake in
                                    350° oven until tender
hot stock from bones . . . add a little at a time, as needed

Note: Left-over goose may be used for this rich stew.

Sweet and Pungent Tongue   *serves 4*

1 c. boiled beef tongue
    cut in 1-1½ " cubes. . heat in Orange Almond Sauce

Orange Almond Sauce

1 c. water
6 ginger snaps . . . . crumble cookies into water; stir
                                    until smooth; boil

½ c. brown sugar
¼ c. white vinegar
¼ c. orange juice . . . . . . add; simmer 10 minutes
½ California orange,
    skin and pulp cut
    fine
¼ lemon, cut fine

1 oz. (2 tbsp.) white
    raisins
1 oz. (2 tbsp.) blanched
    almonds .... add; simmer 20 minutes
                chopped

Sauce freezes well. I like it best with tongue or ham cubes. I've also used it with chicken, beef, veal, lamb, sweetbreads, and spare ribs.

Variations: Substitute wine vinegar, dry white wine, or vermouth for some of liquid.

Crown Roast of Lamb Rousseau

A crown is probably the most dramatic roast you can choose: It's really only 2 racks of chops. The butcher will shape it for you; he will scrape the ends of each rib to form the points of the crown, then stand up the chops, tiara-like; also he must crack the bones, so it will be easy to carve. The scraps are ground with extra meat to put into the center. Plan 2 chops a portion. Seasoning: 2 cloves garlic, juice of fresh lemon, and 1 teaspoon marjoram. Roasted small whole carrots are in the pan with the meat so that they will bathe in the meat juices. Roast about 1 hour. Remove roast from the oven and pour off fat. Mound center of crown with mashed sweet potatoes seasoned with ginger and dotted with butter. Return to oven to reheat. Five minutes before serving, brush hot melted mint jelly over the potato center and the outside and over the bare chop ends of the crown. To serve, transfer roast to a large round chop plate. Put a small hot canned apricot on each chop bone. Tuck a bunch of fresh mint into the sweet-potato center. Heaps of green peas, divided by the whole baby carrots, go around the crown. Serve it to your guests proudly, as if you were sharing the crown jewels.

Marinated Steaks

Place steaks in well-seasoned French dressing for at least an hour before grilling. Then drain and put on a foil-covered tray ready for the grill.

Veal Fiesole   *serves 25*

Note that these are very much the same ingredients as those for the Fiesole mix; the different proportions, however, allow the flavor of the meat to predominate for this supper dish.

10-12 lbs. veal for scallopini	...... cut into fork-size pieces
1 c. flour	.... put a little flour in paper bag; add handful of veal pieces; shake; remove veal; repeat to coat all veal pieces
1 lb. butter	.... use a little butter at a time, and brown veal, a few pieces at a time; put browned pieces into heavy pot
6 onions chopped fine	.. add; brown in remaining butter
3 lbs. mushrooms, washed	.... cut stem ends; slice; add
1 qt. soup stock	.... add; add more liquid if too dry
1 c. chopped parsley	... add
2 c. grated hard cheese—sharp cheddar or romano	.. add
3 teas. salt (or to taste)	.. add
2 teas. oregano (more to taste)	add; correct seasoning; simmer .... slowly until meat is tender

This dish can be made ahead and frozen; it stands reheating well. I like to serve it with green noodles, tossed salad, and fresh fruit; it makes a welcome change from the ubiquitous Beef Stroganoff or Chicken à la what-have-you.

Beef Maria   *serves 6*

2 lbs. flank steak	...... trim fat; slice ¼ ″ thick across the grain; cut into strips

4 tbsp. butter .... brown meat in butter in Dutch
                         oven

4 cloves garlic
¼ c. chopped parsley
¼ teas. thyme
½ teas. salt
2 oz. tomato purée
1 basil leaf
1 c. dry red wine ...... add all; cook slowly until meat is
                         almost tender—about 35 min., de-
                         pending on size of pieces and ten-
                         derness of meat

12 medium mushrooms,
       quartered .... add; continue cooking until mush-
                          rooms are tender (may be made
                          ahead and frozen)

½ teas. rosemary
    (optional)
½ teas. oregano
    (optional)

Our Way with Baked Ham

12-20 lb. tenderized ham
1 box whole cloves
½ lb. brown sugar
1 pt. fruit juice
    (any juice—canned or
    fresh—Maraschino
    juice very good)
1 teas. ground cloves

Make a paste of the brown sugar, ground cloves, and juice.
Remove most of fat. Score criss-cross lines on rest of fat; put
whole clove into center of each diamond. Pat brown-sugar
paste onto ham. Bake ½ hour, basting frequently with pan
juices.

Columbus Day Covered Casserole   *serves 4*

1 lb. fresh string beans.. break into 1″ pieces
3 large tomatoes ...... peel; slice

2 medium onions ...... peel; slice
3 green peppers .... slice
½ c. parsley .... chop; put all into greased casserole
¼ c. oil .... pour over all; cover; bake 250° for 3 hours or let cook slowly on asbestos pad, over lowest flame, same amount of time

1½ lbs. ground meat
salt and pepper to taste
½ teas. marjoram
 or
½ teas. oregano .... season to taste; make balls size of walnuts; after vegetables have cooked 2 hours place meat in casserole; correct seasoning; cover; bake 1 hour more

This dish may be served hot or cold. It invites variations; for example, add mushrooms, zucchini, okra, celery, etc. This is a good dish without the meat, as a vegetable casserole.

Cathedral Stew

2 onions, diced
2 tbsp. chicken or other
 fat .... cook onions in fat until golden, about 15 minutes; reserve onion

giblets (wings, necks, gizzards, hearts) from
 2 chickens—about
 2 lbs. .... brown giblets in same fat
2 c. boiling water or
 stock .... add; add reserved cooked onion
salt and pepper .... add to taste; simmer gently for 1 hour

1 lb. ground beef
1 egg, beaten

2 tbsp. cold water ..... mix together; add salt and pepper to taste, form into small balls the size of walnuts; add gently to the chicken stew; cover; simmer again for about 15 minutes (if a thicker gravy is desired, let the stew cook rapidly uncovered for a few minutes)

When I need an idea for a substantial, very thrifty main course for a luncheon for 600 men, this is what I serve, with rice and biscuits.

Baked Stuffed Fish   *serves 10–12*

STUFFING
1½ c. bread crumbs
1 egg, beaten
4 oz. butter, melted
1 onion, grated
1 teas. chopped parsley
1 teas. salt
dash of pepper
    (optional) .... add; mix well; correct seasoning
1-4 lbs. fish .... scale; clean
2 teas. salt
¼ teas. pepper .... sprinkle on fish; fill fish with the stuffing; fasten with toothpicks and lace up with cord
4 oz. butter, melted .... brush fish; bake in greased drip pan at 400° about 35 minutes, until flesh separates easily from bone; baste often with pan drippings or more butter, if needed

Eric's Potluck Broil   *serves 6*

6 slices bread, cubed ... put into greased shallow pan
2 lbs. fish filets .... placed over bread

4 oz. butter, melted with
4 oz. grated Parmesan
    cheese . . . . pour over fish; broil 12-15 minutes
                           until cooked; serve at once
dash of oregano
    (optional)

This idea works very well with bay scallops or with cooked shrimp. The amount of butter can be adjusted to the diets of your guests. It is best to broil in a glass, ceramic, or stainless-steel pan so the food can go directly from broiler to table.

Lobster Thermidor in Shell   *serves 12*

6-1½ to 2 lb. lobsters. . . cook, split; remove meat from shells very carefully to keep shells intact

Thermidor Sauce
    (p. 194) . . . . for this use, leave mushrooms in quarters; put lobster meat into sauce; correct seasoning; put into 12 lobster half shells

grated Parmesan cheese
bread crumbs . . . . sprinkle on top; heat in oven; serve; or cool thoroughly; wrap in foil; freeze

Curried Shrimp Pancakes

Use Basic Pancake recipe (p. 183); make as many pancakes as you will need, stacking them one on top of the other as they come off the pan. These can be made the day before the party, cooled, and refrigerated. When ready to heat before serving, place spoonful of Curried Shrimp on each pancake, roll up, lay carefully in well-greased casserole. Be sure that each pancake gets its share of shrimps; any extra can go on top of the pancakes.

Heat in 350° oven, 20 minutes.

Curried Shrimp   *serves 6*

4 tbsp. butter .... heat in saucepan
2 tbsp. flour .... add; stir until smooth
1 c. milk .... add; stir until smooth
½ teas. curry powder
   (more if you like it
   hot) .... add
2 lb. cooked cleansed
   shrimp .... add whole; put into pancakes; serve
                    hot

I like to leave the shrimp whole, except for pancakes, as
there is something to bite into. Of course, the Curried Shrimp
can be served without pancakes, in a casserole or chafing dish.

Mock Maryland Crab or Smoked Creamed Finnan Haddie or Marine Mix

I change the names of dishes like the French do their streets.
It is more fun that way. For a buffet dish serving 8, double
the recipe for Marine Mix given on p. 193. Flake the fish
into *large* pieces for this use. Also, add a teaspoon of nutmeg.

Grandma's Gefüllte Fish   *serves 10–12*

2½ lbs. yellow pike
1½ lbs. whitefish ..... have fish scraped clean and fileted
                        at the market

head, bones, skin of fish
2 medium onions, sliced
3 carrots, sliced
1 teas. salt
½ teas. pepper
2 potatoes, sliced ...... put to cook in 1½ qts. water in
                        large soup pot or fish kettle. This
                        makes the stock in which you will
                        cook the fish balls.

2 onions, medium
1 teas. salt
2 large eggs
2 tbsp. matzo meal
½ c. cold water
¼ teas. pepper .... grind fish filets in a grinder; add
all the other ingredients, and put
into a wooden bowl; chop with
chopping knife until fine; shape
fish into small oval balls with wet
hands and drop them at once into
boiling stock; repeat; when all balls
are made, cover pot; cook slowly
for 1 to 2 hrs. depending on size
of balls; remove the fish balls gently
when cool, put into a bowl, strain
the fish stock carefully over them,
and chill. The stock will jell.

Note: Always serve with red horseradish. Some people will
want to use more salt or pepper; others use a pinch of sugar;
still others like the fish darkened with onion *skins* in the
stock.

For Appetizers: Make the balls about the size of walnuts.
For individual portions the sizes vary from 2 inches to about
the size and shape of an Idaho potato. This filling may also
be shaped into a long loaf, to be served sliced.

Salmon Mousse   *serves 8–10*

3 lbs. fresh salmon
1 teas. salt
1 qt. boiling water ..... simmer salmon very gently in the
water for about 30 minutes; re-
move fish; reduce stock; flake fish
into large pieces

2 envelopes gelatin
¼ c. cold water .... soak gelatin in water 5 minutes

2½ c. hot fish stock
½ c. dry white wine
1 tbsp. horseradish
1 tbsp. prepared
    mustard .... add to gelatin mix; cool; strain
1 pt. heavy cream,
    whipped .... fold into cooled mixture; then fold
                    in the flaked fish; correct season-
                    ing; place whole mixture in mold;
                    chill; unmold; serve

Stuffed Filets, L. L.

For each portion, use 2 small flounder filets. Place stuffing on one piece of fish, cover with the other, fasten with toothpicks; brush fish with melted butter, bake in 350° oven for about 20 minutes. Remove picks; serve.

STUFFING, L. L.

for each portion, figure:
2 tbsp. fresh crab flakes
1 tbsp. Alaskan Dressing
1 strip crisp bacon,
    crumbled .... combine

Praying Shrimp   *serves 8*

4 lbs. extra-large shrimp,
    cooked (12 to a lb.,
    6 to a portion) ... shell, leaving tail shells on as han-
                    dles; remove veins
¼ lb. butter .... heat shrimp in butter
2 large iceberg lettuce .. shred lettuce and pile in the center
                    of each individual plate; stand
                    shrimp up all around lettuce; pour
                    Apricot Sauce over shrimp; serve
                    with more sauce, to be passed

Apricot Sauce   *Yield 2¼ cups*

¼ lb. dried apricots
3 c. water .... cook until apricots are soft; strain
1 c. vinegar
½ c. granulated sugar
2 tbsp. brown sugar
½ teas. salt .... add to strained mixture; cook 10 minutes
1 teas. arrowroot
   (or corn starch)
1 tbsp. cold water ..... blend smooth; add to sauce; cook slowly at least 5 minutes more

Vegetables

Gertie's Green Dish   *serves 8*

2 packages frozen
   French-cut string
   beans
½ teas. salt .... put into 1 c. boiling water; from time water reboils, cook 4 minutes; pour off water; put into greased casserole

1 can cream of mush-
   room soup
1 can milk .... mix and add to beans in casserole; bake in 350° oven for 5 minutes

1 package frozen
   French-fried
   onions .... mix in very lightly; bake 10 min. more

If time is of the essence, the whole deal can be done in a saucepan in about 10 minutes. It is easy to use up left-overs with variations of this idea.

Carrot Noodles   *serves 8*

4 large carrots	scrape; with vegetable scraper, shave thin slivers the length of the carrot
2 oz. butter	
½ teas. sugar	
½ teas. salt	
½ c. boiling water	add to carrot shavings and cook a very few minutes

Curried Corn Pudding   *serves 8*

4 tbsp. butter	melt
¼ c. flour	add; mix to smooth paste
1 c. milk	add slowly, stirring constantly; cook over low flame until smooth
½ pt. cream	add slowly; stir and cook slowly; cool
4 egg yolks, beaten	
1 teas. salt	
dash pepper	
2 teas. sugar	
1 tbsp. mild curry powder (or more, to taste)	add
6 ears fresh corn, kernels removed from cob, or 2 cans corn #2 (5 cups)	add
3 egg whites, beaten stiff ..	fold whites carefully into the mixture; put into well-buttered casserole; bake uncovered 1 hour at 300°

Note: If not sure of oven, it is wise to put casserole into pan of warm water like a custard. This dish can be made with kernel or cream-style corn; the results are different, but each is delicious.

Red Cabbage   *serves 8*

1 head red cabbage .... shred fine
4 tbsp. butter .... melt in heavy pot with cover; add
 shredded cabbage; stir constantly

3 tbsp. molasses
3 tart apples, peeled,
 sliced thin
1 large onion, grated
1 lemon, rind and juice
½ c. red wine
salt to taste .... add all; cook covered very slowly,
 1 to 1½ hours; stir often

Serve with roast goose or baked ham.

Baked Fresh Tomatoes   *serves 6*

6 whole firm tomatoes,
 cored .... put into well-greased casserole
½ teas. salt
dash of pepper
½ teas. basil or 6 basil
 leaves .... add
4 oz. butter .... dot over tomatoes
½ c. bread crumbs or
 toasted sesame
 seeds............. sprinkle over tomatoes

Bake at 350° 20-30 minutes, depending on size of tomatoes.

Glazed Texas Onions   *serves 8*

16 medium onions ..... parboil, drain; reserve liquid; put onions into greased casserole

3 tbsp. butter .... add
¼ c. onion liquid
1 c. orange juice
¼ c. brown sugar ...... add

Bake at 400°, 30 minutes; if not brown and bubbly, place under broiler for a few minutes. Watch carefully.

Sweet-potato Souffle   *serves 8–12*

3 lbs. sweet potatoes ... boil; peel; mash

3 oz. butter .... add

½ teas. salt
2 tbsp. white sugar
3 tbsp. brown sugar
½ teas. cinnamon
½ lemon, grated rind
    only
½ orange, rind grated
    and juice
1 or 2 tbsp. brandy
3 beaten egg yolks ..... add all
3 egg whites, beaten stiff. . fold in; pour into well-greased casserole
sliced orange
sliced almonds .... place on top for garnish; bake in 350° oven about 1 hour; if casserole is made a day ahead, bake ½ hour; then bake ½ hour more at serving time

String Beans Amandine

Brown sliced almonds in butter and pour them over freshly cooked green string beans.

Oriental Eggplant   *serves 8*

2 oz. butter
1 med. eggplant, peeled.. cut into 1" cubes
½ lb. fresh mushrooms.. slice
4 whole fresh tomatoes.. peel; quarter
1 lb. string beans ...... cut or snap into pieces
¼ teas. oregano
¼ teas. rosemary
¼ teas. thyme .... add

Place ingredients in layers in well-buttered casserole. Dot with butter. Sprinkle with spices. Cover. Bake at 350° for one hour.

Tomato Mystery Pudding   *serves 8*

10 oz. tomato purée .... put into saucepan
¼ c. boiling water ..... add; heat to boiling
¼ teas. salt
1 c. brown sugar .... add
6 slices bread .... remove crusts; break up into small pieces; place in buttered baking dish
¼ lb. butter, melted .... add to bread; add tomato purée mixture; cover; bake 1 hour at 350°. *Let stand uncovered for 5 minutes before serving* with the meat course, instead of a starchy vegetable.

Few people have ever guessed what this one is made from; the guesses are a fun conversation starter; and everyone tries to give it a new name; so far, the right one hasn't been suggested.

Spinach Soufflé Ring   *serves 8*

2 lbs. spinach, cooked .. chop very fine; cool
1 onion, grated .... add
4 egg yolks, beaten ..... add
1 c. cream .... add
salt, pepper .... season to taste
dash nutmeg .... add
4 egg whites, beaten stiff.. fold in

Bake in well-greased ring mold at 350° for 35 minutes.

Starters and Salads

Meal Starters

Meals have been greatly simplified in the last decade; they are no longer accustomed to those fancy entrées, or a must-have-fish-before-meat-for-a-formal-dinner attitude. Everyone knows of the California custom of serving salad as the opener of the meal. You will find that most of the dips may be transformed into a first course by serving them on salad greens. In fact, almost all the appetizers I have given you can be used for this purpose, either at the table or in the new way that has come to be more accepted, that is, to have the first course in the living room, or on the patio, and to start the meal with the main course.

Juice of the Sea

1 part clam juice, cold
1 part tomato juice,

cold ....mix well together, serve in chilled
                    glasses

Fresh Dill Tomato Juice

Hattie used to can the juice from her own garden
tomatoes with fresh dill; that was ambrosial. I don't have a
vegetable garden, nor do I have the time to can any juice,
but I cut snippets of fresh dill into factory-canned tomato
juice, or sometimes, a dash of dill salt, if I cannot get the
fresh herb.

Imperial Salad

I use all kinds of greens—Bibb and Boston lettuce, chic-
ory, escarole, Chinese cabbage, dandelion leaves, watercress,
and fresh spinach leaves. Mix them all or just a few. Add ripe
olives, marinated in French dressing with a clove of garlic.
    Lots of other things may be added: thinly sliced raw car-
rots, thin slices of unpeeled zucchini, or sweet pickles. And,
for flavor, chopped fresh dill or scallion tops. You can get
more hints about salad treatment from any comprehensive
cook book, but in case you are new at it, or don't know,
always wash salad greens when you bring them from the
market, put into vegetable bin, the hydrator of your refrigerator, or, if you don't have one, use a large plastic bag. Then,
when you take them from your refrigerator, they will be dry,
crisp, and ready for the salad bowl.

Valley Salad

sliced avocado
grapefruit segments
garlic croutons
spinach leaves
escarole
Chinese cabbage ....toss with dressing

Alligator Pear on the Half Shell   *serves 8*

4 alligator pears .... cut into halves, lengthwise; remove
                              pit; carefully scoop out and dice
                              flesh of pear leaving skin as con-
                              tainer
½ c. celery, cut up fine
¼ c. green pepper, cut
   up fine
Italian Dressing .... add to diced pear; pile gently into
                              shells; put each on serving plate
½ small red cabbage,
   finely shredded
escarole leaves .... garnish

Roquefort Roses

1 bunch celery, washed.. separate stalks
1 part roquefort cheese
1 part cream cheese .... fill stalks with cheese; put stalks
                              together again to resemble original
                              bunch; chill; cut into slices

large beefsteak tomato   place slice of tomato on a leaf of
lettuce leaf .... lettuce; on tomato place a slice of
                              the stuffed celery; use as starter or
                              salad

Erin Pipe Dreams   *1 cucumber serves 3–4*

1 straight cucumber,
   unpeeled .... cut into 3 or 4 parts; stand on end;
                              scoop out each part carefully, leav-
                              ing a shell; chop removed cucum-
                              ber

1 small can anchovies,
   cut up .... add to chopped cucumber

1 lemon, juice . . . . add
4 radishes, sliced thin . . add; pile into "pipe" bowls
long green pepper . . . . . . cut strips for pipe stem
watercress . . . . make a bed for pipe

Or use four-leafed clovers, if you can find them.

Cabbage Rose

Hollow out center of a young green cabbage, leaving some of the outside leaves to curl down to resemble a rose.

center of cabbage . . . . . . chop fine
½ c. celery, cut fine . . . add
unpeeled red-skinned
    apple . . . . dice; add
¼ c. seedless raisins . . . . add
1 carrot, scraped . . . . grind; add
½ c. mayonnaise . . . . . . add
juice of 1 lemon . . . . add
1 teas. celery seed . . . . . add; mix

Fill cabbage rose with the cole slaw; makes a nice decorative accent for a cold meat platter.

Sauces, Dressings, Relishes

Cocktail Sauce I

1 qt. chili sauce
¼ c. horseradish
¼ c. prepared mustard
juice of 1 lemon

dash Worcestershire
    sauce ....mix all together

Keeps well in refrigerator.

Cocktail Sauce II

1 pt. (8 oz.) ketchup
1 pt. (8 oz.) chili sauce
3 tbsp. horseradish
salt and pepper to taste
2 tbsp. mustard
½ lemon, juice
⅛ c. vinegar, white
1 onion, grated ....mix together

Keeps well in closed bottle in refrigerator.

Celestial Fish Sauce

1 pt. mayonnaise
1 teas. salt
½ teas. ground pepper
¼ c. prepared mustard
¼ c. horseradish
1 tbsp. Worcestershire
    sauce
¼ c. lemon juice ......mix all together

Keeps well in refrigerator.

Alaskan Dressing

is like a Russian dressing; it's especially tangy and so versatile
that I keep it on hand all the time to serve with many different kinds of salads as well as cocktail fare. Store in covered
container in refrigerator; keeps well.

1 pt. mayonnaise
5 tbsp. horseradish
2 tbsp. prepared mustard
¼ c. chili sauce
¼ c. ketchup
½ teas. paprika
1 teas. salt
1 small onion, grated
2 tbsp. vinegar
1 tbsp. lemon juice
⅛ teas. pepper .... mix all together

Hazel's Roquefort Dressing

⅓ part blue cheese
⅓ part French dressing
⅓ part mayonnaise .... mix well in blender for a smooth
texture; for a rough texture, add
the cheese last, and mix it in with
a fork

Serve on hearts of lettuce, cold asparagus, or sliced tomatoes.

Italian Dressing

¼ c. salad oil
4 tbsp. good sherry
½ teas. salt
dash of pepper
pinch of oregano ...... mix all together

Of course, you can use wine vinegar, in the usual way. It is
amazing, though, what a difference the wine makes. I got
this one from a friend, who told me she just got it from
someone else; I suspect it will go the rounds like a grass fire.

Barbecue Sauce   *for frankfurters*

1 bottle (14 oz.)
   ketchup

¼ c. (⅛ lb.) butter
1 tbsp. horseradish ..... heat in heavy pot; simmer about
                    15 minutes

Cook cocktail franks in sauce; drain to serve.

Annabel's Barbecue Sauce

½ c. corn oil
¾ c. chopped onion .... cook until onion is soft
¾ c. ketchup
¾ c. water
⅓ c. lemon juice
3 tbsp. sugar
3 tbsp. Worcestershire
    sauce
2 tbsp. prepared mustard
2 teas. salt
½ teas. pepper .... add all ingredients; simmer slowly
                    about 15 minutes

This amount is enough to baste and serve with two chickens.
Also recommended for hamburgers, hot dogs, etc.

Chilian Sauce   *enough for ½ c. meat*

¼ c. hot water
½ c. chili sauce
pinch of oregano .... simmer 10 minutes

Very good for heating up meat left-overs.

Cranberry Relish

1 lb. raw cranberries
1 large navel orange,
    seeds removed
1 large firm apple,
    cored .... put fruits *with skins* through grinder

1½ c. sugar
¼ c. brown sugar
dash cinnamon
    (optional) .... add and mix thoroughly

Make several days before using, because the flavors will meld and the result will be more subtle. It's good with any meats, but especially with poultry and pork. This will keep a month in your refrigerator.

Peach Mustard Relish

1 can pickled peaches
1 tbsp. dry mustard
1 teas. arrowroot ...... cook syrup from can with mustard and arrowroot until syrup is reduced to ½ cup; cut up peaches and add to syrup

1 whole orange
½ lemon .... grind or cut up fine; add and mix

Serve hot or cold with meat and listen to your guests ask, "*What* is in this?"

Corn Relish

2 c. corn niblets
1 c. cabbage
½ c. cut up celery
1 green pepper, seeded
1 red pepper, seeded
1 small onion .... grind all together; put into heavy pot

½ c. sugar
1 tbsp. salt
1 teas. celery seed
1 tbsp. dry mustard

1½ c. vinegar ....add; bring to boil; let simmer for
30 minutes; cool; may be canned

Ayarr's Curried Fruits

1 can pineapple chunks.. strain; cook juice until reduced to
one-half the amount
½ teas. curry powder
(more to taste)
1 tbsp. brown sugar .... cook in juice 10 minutes; add pineapple chunks; simmer 5 minutes for
flavor to permeate fruit; cool; serve

Make any firm fruit the same way. Peach or pear halves,
crabapples, or white cherries are good; figs or apricots will
disintegrate. A mixture of fruits, served in a glass bowl, is a
conversation piece for a large buffet party.

Of course, you can start with fresh fruits, if you like.

Desserts

Marble Coffee Cake

Divide the Basic Butter Cake recipe (p. 181) into two
parts. To one half, add 2 oz. bitter chocolate, melted over
hot water. (An easy trick for melting chocolate is to make
your own little bowl with aluminum foil by pressing a square
of foil around most of a whole orange. Put this makeshift
bowl, with the chocolate in it, on the pilot light. When the
chocolate has melted, scrape it into the batter with a bowl
scraper. Discard the foil bowl . . . so much less to wash.)

Fill a greased baking pan 8″ × 12″ × 2″ by carefully
alternating tablespoons of light and dark batters. Bake at
350° for 35 minutes. Don't give it half a chance to cool—
this is specially delicious as it comes from the oven.

Butter Cake Squares   *makes 24 squares, 2" x 2"*

For February parties:

1 recipe Basic Butter Cake (p. 181).
1 recipe Boiled Icing (p. 283); flavor with vanilla.

Bake cake in oblong pan, 8" × 12" × 2"; frost; cut into squares; put candied cherry on each square.

Walnut Coffee Cake

1 recipe Basic Butter
    Cake (p. 181) ..... pour batter into greased pan 8" × 12" × 2"

Topping

¼ c. chopped walnuts
2 tbsp. sugar
1 tbsp. cinnamon ...... mix all together; sprinkle over batter; bake in 350° oven, 35 minutes

This is my favorite for boxed lunches.

Spanish Bundt

1 recipe Basic Butter
    Cake (p. 181)
LEAVE OUT VANILLA
1 tbsp. cinnamon ...... add cinnamon; bake cake in a high ring mold sometimes called a Turk's Head; when cool, sprinkle with Vanilla Powdered Sugar

Vanilla Powdered Sugar

Put powdered sugar in a glass jar with 3 or 4 pieces of vanilla bean, cut about 1" long with a scissors. Close jar tightly. Use sugar after a week.

High Hat Cake   *serves 8*

1 recipe Basic Butter
    Cake (p. 181)
4 oz. bitter chocolate ... melt and add to recipe before egg
                      whites

Bake in 1 low 9″ layer for brim and 4 low 6″ layers for
crown.
· With green coloring tint Boiled Icing (see p. 283) a pastel
green. Put layers together with icing and use to frost the outside, so the cake, when done, will look like a hat with a tall
crown. If you want to make it more realistic, tint a small part
of the icing dark green and put it around the base of the
crown as a ribbon.

Easel Cake   *serves 12–24*

3 10″ cake layers ...... put together with your favorite fill-
                      ing and icing; place on large round
                      tray

1 piece cardboard ...... cut into shape of a heart

1 10″ layer only 1″
    high .... using cardboard pattern, cut cake
                      into heart shape; use pattern for a
                      firm bottom for cake; ice bottom
                      first and let dry; ice top and sides
                      of heart cake; decorate appropri-
                      ately with red; inscribe "Be My
                      Valentine"

1 small easel or card-
    board fold .... stand easel on top of 10″ layer
                      cake; push into icing for firmness;
                      carefully prop the heart-shaped
                      "valentine" against it as you would
                      a painting

Easel cakes may be made for many occasions and need not, of course, be heart-shaped.

Fresh Coconut Layer Cake   *serves 10*

1 recipe Basic Butter
    Cake (p. 181) ......bake in three 9″ layers
1 recipe Boiled Icing
    (p. 283) ....use for filling and icing
1 fresh coconut ....grate on coarse grater; interesting
                      if unpeeled and grated; if used
                      peeled, the cake is called a "Snow-
                      ball"

Note: To open coconut: place coconut (the dry, brown kind sold in our markets as fresh) in 325° oven for 15–20 minutes. Cool until you can handle it; wrap in towel and tap it with a hammer. Have a bowl ready to catch the milk, which should be refrigerated. Discard brown husk. Peel brown skin (if you want an all-white cake). Refrigerate coconut until you are ready to grate it.

Mocha Layer Cake   *serves 10*

1 recipe Basic Sponge
    Cake (p. 179)
1 teas. mocha ....add mocha; bake in three 9″ layers
1 pt. heavy cream,
    whipped
4 tbsp. mocha essence
2 tbsp. powdered sugar ..combine; use for filling and icing
walnut halves ....garnish top of cake with border of
                      nuts

Plain Sponge Loaf   *serves 20*

1 recipe Basic Sponge
    Cake (p. 179) .....bake in loaf pan; leave unfrosted
                      for those who like a plain cake;
                      slice as needed; keep well wrapped
                      in foil

Challah—*Sabbath Twist—more cake than bread.*
Yield, 1 large twist

1 recipe Basic Yeast
 Dough (p. 183)
REDUCE SUGAR IN
 RECIPE TO 1
 TBSP. ....divide dough into 3 parts; braid
  dough, pinching each end to make
  a point

1 egg yolk, beaten ......brush on twist
poppy seeds ....sprinkle on; let rise until light; bake
  at 350° for about 45 minutes

Orange Walnut Torte

1 recipe Basic Nut Torte
 (p. 180)
OMIT CHOCOLATE
 AND MILK
1 grated rind of orange
2 tbsp. good brandy ...add for flavoring; proceed as usual

ICING AND FILLING

½ batch Mocha Butter
 Cream Icing
 (p. 282)
OMIT CHOCOLATE
AND MOCHA
ESSENCE
1 grated rind of orange
2 tbsp. brandy ....add for flavoring; proceed to spread
  layers and frost cake; keep in re-
  frigerator until serving

Swedish Tea Ring

recipe Basic Yeast
 Dough (p. 183) ....proceed as for Schnecken (p. 265)
  until you have the dough rolled

out, spread with the filling, and
rolled up like a jelly roll; make 1
or 2 rings of the filled dough,
pinch edges together to form complete circle; make slashes with
knife or scissors in outside of
dough; turn filled dough up to show
filling; let rise until light; bake at
350° 35–40 minutes

GLAZE

1 c. confectioners sugar
4 tbsp. milk
a few drops of lemon
    juice . . . . mix all together to a very thin
    state; brush on rings as they come
    hot from oven

Dark Fruit Cake   *makes 10" cake; weight 10 lbs.*

2 lbs. raisins
1 lb. currants
½ lb. citron
¼ lb. orange peel
¼ lb. lemon peel
½ lb. figs
½ lb. dates
¼ lb. candied cherries
½ lb. blanched
    almonds . . . . cut up; store in glass jar
½ c. brandy . . . . pour over fruits and nuts (can be
    prepared weeks in advance)
½ lb. butter . . . . cream
1 c. sugar
6 eggs, beaten
½ c. grape jelly
½ c. sour milk
1 c. honey
½ c. brandy . . . . add
2 c. flour

1½ teas. salt
2 teas. nutmeg
2 teas. cinnamon
1 teas. allspice
¼ teas. ground cloves
¾ teas. baking soda
1 teas. baking powder .. sift together; add to butter-sugar-
egg mixture, then add fruits and
beat batter very well; put in well-
greased pans; cover with well-
greased paper; bake in 275° oven,
for about 3 hours; store finished
cake in tin with open box of brown
sugar (if kept long, an occasional
drizzle of brandy will keep cake
moist)

Cheese Torte   *serves 12–15*

CRUST

1 box zwiebach .... grind fine
½ c. sugar
1 teas. cinnamon
2 oz. butter, melted .... add and mix thoroughly. Grease a
10-inch spring form and line pan
with mixture, saving enough for
the top

FILLING

6 egg yolks .... beat very light
1 c. sugar
2½ c. heavy cream
grated rind and strained
  juice of 1 lemon
1 lb. cream cheese
1½ lb. pot cheese ..... add; put through a fine strainer
6 egg whites, beaten stiff .. fold in; carefully fill lined 10″
spring form; put rest of crust on
top; bake in low oven, 300° 80–90

minutes; DO NOT MOVE, but
leave it in oven to cool; serve the
next day with a sprinkling of
pistachio nuts on top

This makes a particularly good dessert after a vegetable,
fruit, or fish meal.

Dutch Apple Cake (2)   *one cake serves 6*

1 batch Basic Yeast
  Dough (p. 183) ... pat dough into 2 greased drip pans
                     or glass baking dishes approximate-
                     ly 8 × 12 × 2
8 sour apples .... peel; quarter; slice thin; press slices
                     into dough in even rows
4 tbsp. sugar
4 tbsp. brown sugar
1 teas. cinnamon
2 tbsp. butter
juice of 1 lemon .... sprinkle all on top of apples; let
                     rise in warm place until light; bake
                     at 375° about ½ hour, until apples
                     are tender and dough a golden
                     brown

Freeze the second cake. Serve Dutch Apple Cake hot or cold,
with or without whipped cream.

Chocolate Roll   *serves 8*

5 egg yolks .... beat well
½ c. superfine sugar ... add and beat
⅓ c. cocoa .... add and beat
1 teas. baking powder .. add
5 egg whites, beaten stiff.. fold gently into mixture; continue
                     folding motion until egg white is
                     completely blended in

Line 12″ x 15″ pan with well-greased paper. (Use unsalted
fat or sweet butter.) Smooth batter into pan; bake at 350°

for 20 minutes. Have ready a large cake rack; on it a large sheet of paper (or a clean towel) with superfine sugar sprinkled on it. Put cake sheet upside down onto sugared paper. Let stand for ½ minute, until the steam has escaped; then roll up quickly into the paper or towel. If the edges on the long sides have already stiffened, you may have to trim them with a sharp knife to get the cake to roll. Roll should be quite loose; when cool, unroll the cake, spread it with filling, re-roll, cover top with the cream filling; mark with fork to resemble a log; decorate with sprinkle of coarsely chopped pistachio nuts.

WHIPPED CREAM FILLING

1 pt. heavy cream,
    whipped
2 tbsp. confectioners
    sugar .... combine
1 teas. vanilla or brandy . . add

Walnut Roll   *serves 8*

6 egg yolks .... beat very light
½ cup sugar .... add and beat
1 cup finely ground
    walnuts .... add
1 teaspoon baking
    powder .... add
6 egg whites, beaten stiff . . fold in carefully; bake in shallow pan 10″ × 13″, lined, well greased, and floured; 15–18 minutes in 350° oven; turn out on brown paper dusted with powdered sugar; roll up; fill as desired with
1 pt. whipped cream or
    1 qt. ice cream .... if ice cream can be bought in a cylindrical container, it can be pushed out in one long sphere that just fits the roll

Natsapple Cake   *serves 8*

Pat 1 batch Basic Linzer Cookie Dough (p. 180) carefully into 10″ spring form, making the sides about 1½″ high. Fill with filling. Cover. Bake at 325° for about 1 hour, or until dough is delicately brown. Uncover during last half of baking time.

FILLING

1 qt. very stiff apple
    sauce or peeled,
    sliced apples
(sweeten and flavor to
    taste)
½ c. seedless raisins ... mix together

Open Peach or Plum Cake   *serves 8*

1 recipe Basic Linzer
    Cookie Dough
    (p. 180) .... pat into 10″ glass pie plate
10 large peaches or
    plums, peeled ...... cut even slices and lay them on
                                dough
2 tbsp. sugar
½ teas. cinnamon
juice of ½ lemon ...... sprinkle on fruit; cover with foil; bake for 1 hour at 325°; uncover last 30 minutes

Lemon Ice Box Cake

2 dozen Lady Fingers ... line bottom and sides of 7″ spring form with split lady fingers, rounded sides toward the pan, set close together
1 recipe Lemon Pie
    Filling (p. 273) .... put a layer of filling, then a layer of
OMIT EGG WHITE   more lady fingers; end with lady fingers on top like spokes of wheel
Refrigerate at least six hours before serving. May be served with whipped cream.

Hazelnut Torte   *serves 8–10*

9 egg yolks .... beat light
1½ c. powdered sugar
2¼ c. ground hazelnuts
½ c. bread crumbs
1 teas. baking powder
1 teas. vanilla
pinch of salt .... add
9 egg whites, beaten stiff .. fold in; put into greased and floured
                          8″ spring form; bake at 350° one
                          hour; cool; split into 3 layers (or
                          bake in 3 8″ layer tins with re-
                          movable bottoms); spread with fill-
                          ing; cover with whipped-cream
                          icing

FILLING

2 egg yolks
¾ c. ground hazelnuts
½ c. granulated sugar
½ c. milk
½ teas. cinnamon
½ teas. vanilla .... cook in double boiler until thick;
                          cool
2 teas. rum .... add; spread between layers

ICING

1 pt. heavy cream,
    whipped
1 tbsp. powdered sugar
1 tbsp. rum .... mix all together

English Trifle Cake   *serves 8*

SPONGE CAKE

1 recipe Basic Sponge
    Cake (p. 179) ..... split cooled cake into 3 layers;
                          place one layer on serving plate

strawberry preserves .... spread thickly onto bottom layer; gently cover that with next layer

custard cream .... spoon over second layer; gently cover with last layer

1 pt. heavy cream,
  whipped .... cover top and sides of cake with the cream, sugared and flavored with brandy or rum; keep in refrigerator until serving time

CUSTARD CREAM

6 yolks, beaten .... place in double boiler

½ c. sugar .... add and stir

½ c. flour .... add and beat very well, until blended

1 pt. milk, warmed ..... add slowly to egg mixture; stir smooth

2 inches vanilla bean ... add; cook in double boiler, stirring often; when thick, remove vanilla bean, cool

Schnecken *makes 3 dozen small buns*

1 batch Basic Yeast
  Dough (p. 183) .... let rise until double its bulk; roll out onto floured table to a rectangle approximately 24" × 48"

FILLING

6 oz. butter, beaten soft . spread with spatula all over the thin dough

⅛ cup sugar

1 teas. cinnamon
  more or less, to taste

¼ c. currants

¼ c. raisins

¼ c. chopped pecans .. sprinkle each, in turn, over the buttered dough

Roll up as for jelly roll. Cut into 3 dozen small pieces. Put into prepared muffin tins. Let rise again, at least 1 hour, in warm place. Bake at 350° for 30 minutes. While still warm, turn syrup-covered cakes out onto a baking tray.

TO PREPARE MUFFIN TINS

¾ lbs. brown sugar
⅜ c. cold water
1 tbsp. butter
large pecans .... let come to boil; put 1 tablespoon syrup and 1 or 2 pecans into each muffin tin; (may be prepared ahead, placed on sheets, and stacked)

Walnut Divine Squares *makes 60 small squares*

DOUGH

¼ lb. butter
¼ c. sugar
¾ c. flour
½ teas. salt
2 eggs
½ teas. baking powder
½ teas. vanilla .... cream ingredients together until soft and smooth

Pat in thin layer over bottom of lightly greased and floured 8″ × 12″ × 1″ pan. Bake in moderate oven (350°) about 10 minutes.

FILLING

2 eggs .... beat well
10 oz. brown sugar
4 level tbsp. flour
½ teas. baking powder
½ cup shredded coconut
1 c. chopped walnuts
½ teas. vanilla .... mix and add

Spread over baked bottom layer as it comes from oven. Return to moderate oven (350°) and bake for 15 minutes longer.

FROSTING

2 tbsp. butter	cream
1½ c. confectioners sugar	add
2 tbsp. strained orange juice	add little by little
1 teas. strained lemon juice	beat until smooth, spread over cooled baked filling
½ c. coarsely chopped walnuts	sprinkle on top of frosting; cut cake into small squares

Glazed Buns *yield 36 buns*

Follow Schnecken recipe (p. 265) exactly, but do not put rolls into the muffin pans. Instead, put them into 2 drip pans approximately 12″ × 8″ × 2″. Let rise again, until light; bake at 350° for about 30–35 minutes. While warm, turn out onto shallow pan. Brush with glaze and serve hot.

GLAZE

1 c. confectioners sugar	
4 tbsp. milk	
a few drops of lemon juice	mix together to a very thin state

Tea Buttons *makes 80*

1 recipe Basic Cheese
    Dough (p. 182)
2 egg whites, slightly
    beaten
sugar
cinnamon

Roll dough ¼″ thick. Cut out with 1″ round cutter or liqueur glass. Put on cookie sheet. Smear with slightly beaten egg white. Sprinkle with sugar and cinnamon. Bake at 400° about 10 minutes or until brown.

Chocolate Wafers   *makes 40 or more, depending on thickness*

½ lb. almond paste
⅔ c. confectioners sugar
⅓ c. flour
2 egg whites . . . . form into a smooth dough; chill

Roll out thin. Cut with cookie cutter. (Professionals use a metal stencil and spread the dough on with a spatula.) Bake at 350° to a delicate light brown. For the icing, use dipping chocolate; melt over hot water, put on roughly with a knife or spatula. A sprinkle of chopped pistachio nuts is always pretty on the chocolate.

Chocolate Nut Torte Squares   *makes 40 squares 2″ × 2″*

1 recipe Basic Nut
    Torte (p. 180) . . . . . bake in pan 12 x 8 x 1
1 recipe Hungarian
    Chocolate Icing
    (p. 282) . . . . smooth with spatula over sheet of cooled cake; when cool, mark out squares for cutting; put a nut in the center of each square (when cutting, use a knife dipped into hot water to avoid tearing the tender cake)

Apricot Linzer Squares   *makes 60 squares 1½″ x 1½″*

1 recipe Linzer Cookie
    Dough (p. 180)
apricot preserves

squeeze of lemon ......pat two-thirds of dough thinly onto shallow pan 10″ × 15″; bake at 325° to pale golden; while hot, spread with preserves; with an icing tube, put a criss-cross of the balance of the dough onto the preserves; bake at 350° until light brown; cut hot or cold into small squares

Old Dutch Cookies *makes approximately 200*

1 lb. butter ....cream very soft
1 lb. brown sugar ......add and cream
2 egg yolks, beaten .....add and mix
5 c. flour (scant) ......add and beat
egg whites

Divide dough into 6 equal parts; pat thin onto 6 cookie tins 10″ × 15″; roll smooth with sides of a floured high-ball glass. With a ruler and knife, mark out guide lines for cutting the cookies later into squares 2″ × 2″. Beat egg whites with a fork; dump onto cookie sheet; smear with hand; pour what is loose onto the next cookie sheet of dough. You may have to add an extra egg white, depending on the size of the eggs. When all are marked out and smeared with what will be the shine on your cookie, place a split blanched almond diagonally in the center of each square.

Bake two trays in oven at a time, at 350° about 15 minutes. Cut on guide lines *while warm.*

Caution: In removing cookies from the baking sheet with a shovel (pancake turner) be sure that you place them on a flat surface to cool; otherwise they might crinkle.

Linzer Cookies *makes about 75*

2 batches Basic Linzer
  Dough (p. 180) ....pat smoothly onto 2 baking sheets; bake to pale brown in medium oven, 350°
seedless raspberry jelly .. spread onto lightly baked dough while warm

MERINGUE

6 egg whites, beaten stiff
    (4 from dough,
    plus 2)
¼ c. sugar
1½ c. finely ground
    almonds ....combine; spread smoothly over
                           jelly-covered dough; bake again
                           about 10 minutes

While warm, make lengthwise cuts with a knife; then diagonal cuts to form diamonds.

Parachute Cookies   *makes 75*

I call these "Parachutes" because they are such quick drop cookies.

¼ lb. butter, softened
⅓ c. sugar
1 egg, beaten
¾ cup flour
½ teas. vanilla ....combine all and beat well

Drop teaspoons of batter onto greased cookie sheet. Bake at 350°. Garnishes before baking: walnut, raisin, candied orange peel, candied cherry. Garnishes after baking: dipping chocolate or chocolate icing put through a tube and run back and forth on the sheet of cookies, so that the result is chocolate lines.

Dough for Children's Cookies   *makes 50 or more*

¼ lb. butter
1 c. sugar
4 eggs, beaten
½ teas. salt
1 teas. vanilla
3 c. flour
1 teas. baking powder ..cream

Chill well; roll to ¼ ″ thickness. Cut out with cutters. Brush with beaten egg white. Sprinkle with colored sugars. Bake until light in color, 350° about 20 minutes

Orange Pecan Slices   *makes about 100*

½ lb. butter .... cream
2 c. brown sugar (13
    oz.) .... add and mix
2 eggs, beaten
3 oranges, grated rind
    only
2 teas. cinnamon
3½ c. flour, sifted with
2 teas. baking soda .... add and mix
2 c. broken pecans ..... add and mix

Shape into long oblongs, about 2″ wide. Wrap in foil, chill in refrigerator. When ready to bake, slice individual cookies thinly from the loaf; put on a cookie sheet; bake at 350° for about 15 minutes.

Loaves of cookie dough may be kept in refrigerator for a month; slice and bake as needed.

Spice Cookies   *makes 100 or more, depending on size*

½ lb. vegetable
    shortening, softened
1½ c. sugar
3 eggs
1 teas. cinnamon
1 teas. allspice
1 teas. cloves
1 teas. salt
½ c. molasses
3½ c. flour
1 teas. baking soda..... combine all and beat smooth; put
                        through tube, or drop by spoonfuls
                        onto greased cookie sheet

1 egg, beaten .... brush on cookies

raisins or pecan halves .. to decorate, put raisin or nut in
center of each cookie; bake at
350° for about 12 minutes; remove from pan while hot

Cherry Upside-down Pie   *serves 6*

2 cans sour red cherries,
drained .... put into well-buttered 9″ glass plate
(covers bottom scantily)
½ to 1 c. sugar, depend-
ing on tartness of
cherries .... add
cinnamon to taste ...... sprinkle over cherries
lemon to taste .... squeeze over cherries
1 recipe Basic Cheese
Dough (p. 182) .... roll out a round bigger than the
pie plate with the cherries; tuck
extra dough under itself and press
to pie plate to seal; prick top for
steam escape

Bake at 450° for 15 minutes, then turn down to 400° for
15 to 20 minutes more, until dough is browned. Turn out
upside down by inverting cake plate over pie plate, and
quickly flipping. It will be quite flat, but delectable.

French Apple Cake or Slices   *makes 15 cuts*

1 recipe Basic Cheese
Dough (p. 182) .... roll about ½″ thick to fit an oblong sheet
4 tart apples, peeled,
quartered .... place in thin slices in neat rows on
the dough
½ c. sugar
1 teas. cinnamon .... sprinkle onto apples

Bake, covered with foil, in 450° oven for 20 minutes; remove

cover, bake at 400° until dough is pale brown and apples are
tender.

currant jelly, heated .... brush top of cake hot from oven
with warmed jelly; glaze will be
formed; cut into oblong slices

Lemon Pie Heavenly Cloud *serves 6*

PASTRY FOR 8″ PIE SHELL

1 c. flour
½ teas. salt
½ teas. baking powder.. sift together in mixing bowl
¼ lb. butter .... add; cut into pieces the size of peas
¼ c. ice water .... add in small amounts, stir with
knife until mixture forms a dough;
chill; roll thin; place in glass pie
plate; prick with fork to keep it
flat

Bake at 450° for 15 minutes or until golden brown. Cool
before filling.

FILLING

8 egg yolks, beaten very
well
¾ c. sugar
grated rind and juice of
2 lemons .... cook in double boiler, stirring constantly until thick; cool

MERINGUE

8 egg whites
1 teas. baking powder .. beat together until peaks hold their
shape
¼ c. sugar

Add a few spoonfuls of the meringue to the cooled lemon
filling to extend it. Gently fill the crust with this filling. Pile

the rest of the meringue onto the filling in the pie shell. Meringue must completely cover the lemon filling. Sprinkle top of meringue with ¼ cup of granulated sugar to form a delicate crust. Bake at 350° until brown. Watch carefully.

Fresh Fruit Pies

Basic Cheese Dough (p. 182) is the best of all for the tops of pies; for the bottoms, use pie-shell recipe on page 273. Fruit pies may be double-crust (regulation); bottom crust only (open tarts); or top crust only (calorie-conscious).

Fruit Cobblers

The juicy fruits—apples, peaches, blueberries, strawberries, blue plums—are all fine for these deep-dish pies made either with the regulation shortcake top, or my way, with Basic Cheese Dough (p. 182).

To Make: Put fruit into greased casserole; add sugar and cinnamon; top with sheet of Basic Cheese Dough rolled out thin.

Short Cut: From chilled ball of dough, *cut* thin slices; place over sugared fruit. Almost the same as rolled dough and much quicker.

Jam Tarts *makes 24*

1 recipe Basic Cheese
Dough ....roll out very thin; cut squares 3″ x 3″

strawberry preserves ....put 1 teas. preserves in center of each square

cold water ....brush edges of squares with pastry brush dipped in cold water; fold over to make a triangle; press to seal; bake in hot oven, 450° about 10 minutes; watch carefully, as they burn readily

Apple Dumplings   *makes 12*

1 recipe Basic Cheese
    Dough .... roll out thin and cut into 12 large squares, depending on size of apples

12 small sour apples (or
    use 6 large, cut in
    halves) .... put 1 apple in center of each square

cinnamon
sugar
lemon juice .... sprinkle on each apple; fully enclose each apple in a square of dough; brush edges with cold water and bring together to 4 points; press to seal; bake in hot oven, at 450°, until apples are tender; serve warm with brandied hard sauce or brandied whipped cream

Jennie's Winthrop Pudding   *serves 12*

2 envelopes plain gelatin
¼ c. milk .... mix together until smooth; let soak 5 minutes

3¾ c. milk
rind of 1 lemon (not
    grated) .... heat together

5 egg yolks, beaten
½ teas. salt
½ c. sugar (scant) .... mix all together and combine with other ingredients; cook in double boiler; stir constantly until mixture coats the spoon; cool

5 egg whites, beaten stiff. .fold in

1 tbsp. rum . . . . add
1 pt. heavy cream,
    whipped (optional) . . fold in

Keep in refrigerator.

Chocolate Mousse   *serves 12–20*

8 oz. chocolate bits,
    semi-sweet
3 tbsp. brandy or Grand
    Marnier or strong
    coffee (liquid) . . . . . melt together in double boiler over
                         low heat; smooth; cool

6 egg yolks, beaten . . . . . add; smooth again

grated rind of 1 orange . . add

6 egg whites, beaten
    stiff . . . . fold in carefully; place in serving
                         bowl in refrigerator to set—at least
                         4 hours

The mousse is very rich and should be served in small portions. Sometimes it is served in small "pots" not much bigger than a demitasse cup. When I was testing different mousse recipes to find the best to my taste, a friend laughingly told me this story. It seems that her cousin was famous for her chocolate mousse, but could never be persuaded to give the recipe. On her deathbed, she gasped: "Now I must tell you my chocolate mousse secret: always use X chocolate."

Plum Pudding   *makes 3½ quarts*

2 lb. stale bread, cut up
1 qt. milk . . . . pour milk over bread
1 lb. citron, cut up

1 lb. currants
1 lb. raisins
½ lb. almonds, cut up
¼ lb. orange peel, cut up
¼ lb. lemon peel, cut up
rind and juice of 1 lemon
2 oranges, rind and juice
¾ lb. light brown sugar
1 lb. butter, softened . . . combine all with milk mixture

½ c. flour
½ teas. baking powder
1½ teas. salt
1½ teas. cinnamon
½ teas. cloves
½ teas. allspice
½ teas. nutmeg
½ teas. mace . . . . sift together; mix thoroughly with
bread and fruits

Put mixture into large double boiler; stir frequently; steam
2½ hours.

1 c. brandy
¼ c. rum . . . . add; stir well; cook ½ hour longer

Mold in large or small containers while mixture is still
warm; dump out of molds onto flat trays to cool; to store for
a long time, wrap cheesecloth around the puddings and oc-
casionally pour some brandy over them. Store in tightly
covered tins or in covered crocks.

California Flaming Oranges   *serves 12*

12 California oranges . . . cut slice off ends of each; scoop
out pulp
18 pitted dates, diced
18 small figs, diced
12 marshmallows, cut up
4 tbsp. shredded coconut

4 tbsp. chopped almonds
¼ c. brown sugar ......combine; add to orange pulp; stuff orange shells with this mixture; place in shallow pan; bake at 250° for 30 minutes; arrange on serving platters

¼ c. cointreau
¾ c. warm cognac .....combine; pour equal amounts over each orange; light with match and serve flaming

Fruit Cobblestones

On a large platter, place with rounded sides up, Bartlett pear halves, scoops of banana (use teaspoon), sections of grapefruit (several put together to form a semisphere). All of these may be marinated in creme de menthe or in minted cherries, bordered by a beading of minted cherry halves.

Muenster Cheese Apples

Use one shiny apple for four guests. Core. Leave the skin on, slit carefully into eighths, almost to core. Insert thin slices of cheese in each slit. Put on platter whole; serve portions of apple and cheese together.

Fruits Tri-Color   serves 30

½ gal. fresh orange
    sections, drained
½ gal. fresh pineapple
    cubes, drained
½ gal. honeydew melon
    balls, drained
1 qt. whole strawberries..wash; hull
1 bunch mint ....wash

Put half the orange sections into a large glass serving bowl. Using a flat salad plate, push the orange sections to one side of the bowl and hold them in place with the plate with one hand. Next, with the other hand pour half the pineapple cubes into the other side of the bowl. Don't remove the plate. Take a second plate and push the pineapple cubes to one side of the bowl, and thus make space for the melon balls. With some practice, you will be able to make a bowl of fruit divided into three equal sections. Now carefully remove the plates. Round out each section with more fruit, if necessary; save balance of fruit to refill. Make a center group of strawberries and fresh mint. If you are a beginner, I'd advise you to start practicing with the plates. I use this idea for other small fruits or vegetables and for relishes, too, as an easy and dramatic way to present many types of food.

Fruit-platter Basket Arrangement *for a large party*

This fruit-basket arrangement, intended as a dramatic accent for a very large platter of fruits, is made from melon halves. They form natural containers for small fruit or cottage cheese.

To make the basket, cut two melons in half and scoop out the seeds. Select one of the four halves to be the base of the basket structure and put it flat side down on the platter. The other three halves, hollow side up, are attached to the bottom one with florist's sticks.

The fruits for both platter and basket will depend on your imagination and the season. The platter fruits can either be the same as those in the basket, or entirely different.

Once for a Halloween party I used blackberries, orange sections, and pitted, uncooked prunes in the basket. On the platter were large frozen peach halves, cobble side up. Another time, for a July 4th buffet, I put raspberries, blueberries, and grapefruit sections in the containers. On the platter were alternate stripes of fresh pineapple chunks and strawberries.

Penelope's Pears   *serves 6*

2 cups dry red wine
2 c. sugar .... combine; boil 5 minutes

6 whole fresh pears,
      peeled, with stem
      left on .... simmer slowly in the sugar-wine
                         syrup until tender, about 15 min-
                         utes
peel of 1 lemon cut into
      thin slivers
½ cup port wine
1 stick cinnamon or
½ teas. cinnamon ...... add; boil 3 minutes, or more if you
                         want syrup to be thicker

May be served warm or chilled, with or without cream.

Biscuit Tortoni   *serves 6–12*

6 egg yolks .... beat

1 c. superfine sugar ..... add

1 pt. cream, whipped ... fold in

½ teas. vanilla .... add

8 macaroons, ground ... fold in most of them; put mix into
                         paper cups; sprinkle remaining
                         macaroons on top; put into freezer

Strawberry Mousse   *serves 6*

1 qt. strawberries
¼ c. confectioners suger . combine; let stand one hour; mash
                         and strain

2 c. heavy cream,
   whipped
1 teas. vanilla
¼ teas. salt . . . . combine; fold into berry mix; put
                                 into freezer

Orange Water Ice *serves 6–8*

2 c. orange juice
¼ c. lemon juice . . . . combine
2 c. sugar
4 c. water . . . . boil together; cool; add; put into
                                 freezer

Avocado Lime Ice

2 ripe avocados, peeled
   and diced
¼ teas. salt
grated rind of 1 lime
¼ c. lime juice
⅓ c. honey . . . . combine all; beat in blender or
                                 electric mixer until smooth; freeze
                                 in refrigerator tray until mushy;
                                 beat in mixer again; freeze until
                                 firm, at least 4 hours

Sauce of the Angels

4 egg yolks, beaten
1½ c. superfine sugar
½ c. pineapple juice
½ c. lemon juice . . . . . . mix; cook in double boiler until a
                                 thick custard; cool thoroughly

4 egg whites, beaten
   stiff . . . . fold in
½ pt. heavy cream,
   beaten . . . . fold in

This sauce is wonderful over fresh fruits, plain cakes, or gelatin pudding. Custard may be made a day or two ahead of your party, the egg whites and cream folded in last minute.

Hungarian Chocolate Icing

4 oz. bitter chocolate ... melt over low flame, stirring constantly

½ c. milk .... add; stir smooth

1½ c. sugar .... add; stir; cook until smooth, stirring constantly; cool well

2 egg yolks, beaten ..... add; beat; cook one minute, stirring constantly; cool

This amount will cover a sheet of cake 12″ x 18″, or will fill and ice a 9″ layer cake. Very good on the nut tortes, or on the Basic Butter Cake (p. 181).

Mocha Butter-cream Icing   *fills and frosts 10″ layer cake*

1 lb. sweet butter ...... cream

2 c. confectioners sugar.. sift; add; beat

6 egg yolks, beaten ..... add; beat

4 oz. bitter chocolate ... melt in double boiler; cool; add; beat

2 tbsp. mocha essence .. add; beat

This makes a very rich concoction, but not too sweet. You may vary it by using more chocolate to make a chocolate icing (leave some coffee flavor in, because the combination gives that certain something). Cakes filled or iced with this icing should be kept in refrigerator until ready to serve.

Boiled Icing

1 c. sugar
½ c. water . . . . boil together until syrup spins a
                    thread
2 egg whites, beaten
    stiff . . . . .pour syrup very, very slowly over
                    whites, beating all the time
1 teas. brandy or other
    flavoring . . . . .add

Party Liquids

WINES

In the not-too-distant past, wine meant just two things to the average American: champagne for gala occasions and sherry for cooking or as a late-afternoon or before-dinner drink—instead of cocktails. Serving a variety of wines with dinner was considered strictly for the French or for a society banquet.

Timidity was largely the reason many people avoided serving wines with meals. They felt they must be experts to do so—knowing the correct vintage, as well as the correct type to serve with various foods. And in those days it was unheard of to serve anything but imported wine.

In recent years all of this has changed. American wines have come into their own. And Americans have learned that it is a fairly simple matter to be knowledgeable about wines. Many American wines are delightful and even surpass the quality of some imports. American vintners have done an excellent educational job. Many of them bottle their products in splits, so that young people who are new at the art of wine appreciation can experiment with various brands and types.

Salesmen in liquor stores are now trained to be helpful in advising what types of wines to serve with various foods. But rules are not as rigid as they used to be about what simply *must* be served with what. The general guide to follow is, briefly, dry white wines with fish, seafood, chicken, dry red wines with hearty red meats, duck, goose. White wines are always served chilled—red wines at room temperature. Sweet wines are often referred to as dessert wines and are served with dessert.

Until you have picked the brands you really like in the various types, try serving *vin rosé* with everything. It is a delightful dry wine with a lovely pink color. It may be served chilled (with fish and chicken) or at room temperature (with red meats).

When not in use, all wines should be stored in a cool place where the temperature is even. All wines that have corks (some wines now have plastic tops) should be stored lying on their sides. Otherwise, the cork might dry out, letting air in and causing fermentation.

It has long been the custom for the host to be served first. His glass is partially filled so that he can taste the wine to be sure it is perfectly all right; if the host approves, he nods a "go ahead" to the server. The guest of honor, at the right of the host, is served next, and so on around the table. Some hosts insist that the ladies be served first. It is also a custom, and very practical, to wrap the bottle with a napkin. It should be done in such a way that *it* will catch the drippings—not the tablecloth.

COCKTAILS

Martini
4 or 5 parts gin or vodka
1 part dry vermouth
cracked ice . . . . combine; stir; strain into stemmed
glass
lemon twist or olive . . . . add
Use less vermouth for very dry martini.

Gibson
Make exactly like martini, but use a pearl onion instead of a lemon twist or olive.

Manhattan

3 parts bourbon or rye
1 part sweet vermouth
dash Angostura bitters
cracked ice . . . . combine; stir; strain into long
                       stemmed glass
maraschino cherry . . . . . add

For dry Manhattans, use dry vermouth and lemon peel.

Rob Roy

Make the same as Manhattan, using scotch instead of bourbon or rye.

Old-Fashioned

½ lump sugar
dash Angostura bitters
1 teaspoon water . . . . . . crush in Old-Fashioned glass

2 ice cubes . . . . add

1½ oz. bourbon, rye, or
    scotch . . . . add
pineapple stick, orange
    slice, maraschino
    cherry (optional)

Whisky Sour

2 parts bourbon, rye or
    scotch
1 part lemon juice
chopped ice
sugar to taste . . . . combine; shake well; strain into
                       Whisky Sour glasses
orange slice, cherry
    (optional)

Bloody Mary

2 parts tomato juice
1 part vodka

juice of half a lemon
dash Worcestershire
    sauce
salt & pepper to taste
chopped ice ....combine; shake well; strain into
                    small straight glasses

Daiquiri
1 part lime juice
3 parts light rum
sugar to taste
crushed ice ....combine; shake well; strain into
                    stemmed glasses

Frozen Daiquiri
Use same ingredients, but use electric blender instead of
shaker, use more finely chopped ice, and serve unstrained.

Gimlet
3 parts gin, vodka, or
    rum
1 part lime juice
crushed ice
sugar (optional) ....combine; shake well; strain into
                    stemmed glasses

On the Rocks
2 or 3 ice cubes ....put in large Old-Fashioned glass

2 oz. scotch, rye, or
    bourbon ....add

Almost any cocktail may be served "on the rocks."

TALL DRINKS

Highball
2 or 3 ice cubes ....put in highball glass
2 oz. scotch, rye, bour-
    bon, or brandy .....add
water or club soda ......add amount desired; stir

Collins

cracked ice .... place in highball glass
½ lemon .... squeeze over ice
1 teas. sugar .... add
1½ oz. gin, vodka, or
    vermouth .... add and stir
club soda .... add to fill glass; stir

Rickey

½ lime .... squeeze juice and put rind in high-
               ball glass
2 or 3 ice cubes .... add
1½ oz. gin or vodka .... add
club soda .... add and stir

Tonic Drinks

2 or 3 ice cubes .... place in highball glass
¼ lime .... squeeze juice and put rind in glass
1½ oz. gin or vodka .... add
tonic water .... add and fill glass; stir

Screwdriver

2 or 3 ice cubes .... place in highball glass
1½ oz. vodka .... pour over ice
orange juice .... add to fill glass; stir

Planter's Punch

juice ½ lemon
juice ½ orange
4 dashes curacao
2 oz. Jamaica rum ..... shake well; pour into highball glass
               filled with crushed ice; stir ice and
               drink together; serve with straws

Mint Julep

½ teaspoon sugar
4 or 5 sprigs young mint
    leaves .... place in chilled glass; mash with
               muddler

1 teaspoon bourbon . . . . add, to moisten mash; muddle until it is a paste
finely shaved ice . . . . pack in glass on top of mint mixture
2 oz. bourbon . . . . add slowly; when it has filtered
through ice, stir rapidly with long
spoon until glass is frosted (meanwhile hold glass only by rim—not
to disturb frosting)
sprig of mint . . . . stick in top of glass

Juleps can be served immediately or can be stored in refrigerator for half to three quarters of an hour. This is a convenience, as they must be made individually—and it takes
time to make enough for a sizable party. When ready to
serve, place straws next to the mint sprig and etch each
guest's initial on outside frosting.

PUNCHES

All punches are made *to taste*. Citrus fruits vary in
sweetness. Some people like charged water in their drinks;
others do not. Some like tart drinks; others prefer theirs
sweet. So I would call these recipes guides as to what to use.
Your taste is the best guide for amounts.

Quantities: figure 10 servings from a quart.
If the day is warm, better figure on several rounds; if it is
a scorcher, 4 drinks a person are not too much to figure.

GARNISHES

orange juices
lemon slices
strawberries
maraschino cherries
bunches of grapes

bunches of cherries, wired together; cucumber rind . . . pare a
narrow strip of peel round and
round the cucumber in one piece;
it looks intriguing, curling down
from the side of the bowl

Fourth of July Lemonade *makes 4 quarts*
1 doz. lemons .... squeeze juice; strain; reserve some
of the rinds
2 c. sugar
2 c. cold water .... boil together 5 minutes; cool; add
3 qts. cold water ...... add; put some of the rinds in the
serving bowl or pitcher with the
lemonade; refrigerate

Rum Punch
Rum is added to the lemonade, in varying amounts, depending on the potency you wish.

Iced Tea Punch *makes 7 quarts*
¼ lb. tea leaves
1 qt. boiling water ..... steep 5 minutes
4 c. sugar
4 c. water .... boil together 5 minutes; cool; add
1 qt. orange juice
1 qt. lemon juice
1 #5 can pineapple juice
2 qts. club soda .... add
Punch may be further diluted with more soda or with ginger ale.

Fresh Fruit Punch *makes 4 quarts*
2 qts. orange juice
½ pt. lemon juice
1 pt. pineapple juice
1 pt. grapefruit juice
½ pt. simple syrup
(sugar and water,
1 cup each, boiled)
1 pt. *white* grape juice... combine all
Garnish with mint leaves, and hang small bunches of seedless green grapes on the edge of the bowl.

Raspberry Shrub
2 pts. raspberries
cider vinegar to cover ... let stand 24 hours; put through
cheesecloth strainer; measure liquid

sugar .... take same amount of sugar as
                         liquid; boil together 10 minutes;
                         then bottle in sterile jars

To serve, use 1 cup shrub to 4 cups (1 qt.) water. Very
refreshing on a hot day.

Sauterne Punch   *allow 1 qt. for 8 people*

1 qt. orange juice
½ pt. lemon juice
1 pt. pineapple juice
1 qt. domestic Sauterne
1 qt. club soda (optional)

Pour punch over block of ice in punch bowl. If you use the
club soda, add it just before serving.

Brandied Egg Nog   *serves 25*

6 egg yolks, beaten light
½ cup sugar
1 qt. cream
1 pt. Jamaica dark rum
1 pt. brandy .... mix thoroughly; store in refriger-
                        ator two or three days
When ready to serve, pour into punch bowl.
6 egg whites, beaten
     stiff .... add to top of bowl
dash of nutmeg .... add

The egg whites float on top, and a bit is ladled out with
each cup served. This drink is so rich it could be called "Cup
of Croesus."

Fish House Punch   *serves 25 or more*

3 qts. water
1 lb. brown sugar ..... boil 5 minutes
rind and strained juice of
     18 lemons .... add to hot syrup
2 qts. Jamaica rum
1 qt. brandy
½ c. peach brandy ..... add

From an old Virginia recipe. It is very potent.

How to Chart a Party

Here are eight charts which have been found of great help in party planning. They can be left in this book for reference. Or, they can be cut out with a razor blade and inserted in a loose-leaf binder—the size that holds 5½" x 8½" paper. Be sure to get dividers when you buy the extra paper and write the names of the following eight charts on each.

MASTER GUEST CHART

PARTY PLANNING CHART

PRE-PARTY CHART

MASTER INVENTORY LIST

FOOD CHART—QUANTITIES

CHART OF WINES AND SPIRITS

CHART FOR SERVICE NEEDED

POST-PARTY EXPENSE CHART

Master Guest Chart

Some people have found it more convenient to keep a card index file of their guest lists. The same information on the chart can easily be put on 3" x 5" cards. Do it this way: Buy the cards in white and two colors. Use the white cards for pairs or married couples. Use blue ones for single males, and pink ones for single women. There are tabs in various colors which clip onto the cards (available at any commercial stationery store). Use a particular color for each party you give and clip one of the tabs onto the cards of the people who attended. This will be a quick index to whom you asked when.

Master Guest Chart

Pairs	Address	Phone	Comments	Date Entertained	
				(By Them)	(By You)
Bachelors					
Girls					

Jones, Bill & Mary   *Entertained them*
22 E. 72nd Street   9/20—cocktails
Templeton 8-1824   12/1—dinner

Comments:
                              Entertained by them
She can't eat fish.
They can't stand the Smiths!   11/6—dinner

Pre-Party Chart

The Pre-Party Chart is virtually a "work chart"—it
puts all the party details into a nutshell. It is a reminder for
you to jot down the exact date you phoned or sent invitations. If the invitations were mailed, it will make you remember to jot down the wording (or save one of the invitations)
which will be helpful and simplify your next written invitations. When you refer to it months later, you will know
at a glance what you served, to whom, and what you wore
(perish the thought that a hostess would wear the same thing
twice in a row!). Of course, this chart could also be done on
index cards—just as the Pre-Party Chart. Here's how you
do it—but first get monthly index dividers, and put a color
tab on each party chart to correspond with the ones on the
guest cards.

Cocktail Party   Date...........

When Invitation phoned

              sent................*I wore*
              (attached)

What was served:

People who came—(see other side)

Pre-Party Chart

A.................................party   Given on: ....

Invitations were sent on:......................Invitations were telephoned on: ....

Wording of invitation:

What was served: ....   What I wore: ....

Pairs	Address or Phone	Men	Address or Phone	Women	Address or Phone

Party Planning Chart

Date of Party: _____ Menu _____ Number of guests: _____

Ingredients for Each Dish	Shopping List	Quantities	Equipment	On Hand	Needed
Beverages					
Decorations					
Miscellaneous					

Party Planning Chart

People who make shopping lists for parties on tiny pieces of paper will not be interested in this chart. But they should be. When planning is done in a slap-happy way (and who hasn't been guilty of this at one time or another?), some vital ingredient or prop is almost always overlooked. There is a last-minute scrounging around to obtain it or to find a reasonable substitute. Now, my advice to you is to use the chart on p. 295 (or a reasonable substitute) and also cross-check it with a Master Inventory List—the chart following this.

Master Inventory List

Below is a condensation of the inventory list I use for each and every party. The actual list is 8½" x 17". It consists of four sheets with carbons in between. After I have filled it out, I keep the original; one copy goes to my party manager; and two copies go to my commissary (one of them later goes to the party with all of the food and equipment—to be checked off for accuracy). Obviously there are many items on my original list which are not necessary for the home party giver. I have, for instance, deleted such things as electrical equipment. After reading about my parties in business establishments, you will realize that it is not unusual for me to produce a hot meal when there is not a stove or hot plate in the place. For such circumstances, I have this category on my master list: Electric: grill, oven, jug, cord, stoves (single, double), fuses—all of which are irrelevant to a party at home.

SILVER
Bucket
Pair Candelabra
Candlesticks
Chafing Dish
Cocktail Shaker
Coffee Pot

Coffee Urn
Compotiers
Shells
Creamer and Sugar
Hot Water Dish
Pitchers

FLAT SILVER

Spoons
  Service
  Bouillon
  Tea
  Dessert
  Demi

  Iced Tea
Forks
  Service
  Oyster
  Dinner
  Dessert

Platters
  Large Round
  Small Round
  Oval
  Large Oval
Vegetable Dishes
Punch Bowl Ladle
Punch Bowl

Tea Service
Trays
Knives
  Lunch
  Dinner
  Butter
  Cake Knife & Fork

GLASS

Ash Trays
Champagne
Cocktail
Goblets
Highballs
Liqueur

Old-Fashioned
Punch Cups
Salt & Peppers
Sherry
Whiskey
Wine

LINEN

Napkins
Tablecloths
Dish Towels

Coffee Bags
Name Napkins
Name Matches

Stirrers
Thumb Tacks
Pins
Candles

Doilies
Scissors
Toothpicks
Coat Checks

CHINA

Casseroles
Tea Cups & Saucers
Demi Cups & Saucers
Bread & Butter Plates

Medium Plates
Dinner Plates
Soup Plates
Soup Cups & Saucers

FURNITURE

Tables
  Oblong
  Round

Bar
Chairs
Coat Racks

MISCELLANEOUS

Boards	Ice
Tubs	Ice Cubes
Brown Trays	Soap
Pails	Brillo
Pots	

Food Chart

This chart gives estimated amounts of food that will be consumed at different types of parties. However, there are many variable factors, so all amounts must be taken with a grain of salt. Exercise your intuition concerning the appetites of your guests. Appetites are funny things—they are completely unstable. This is particularly true of a cocktail party; some people may eat little because they are going on to dinner and others may gobble as much as possible, as they won't have enough time for supper before the theater.

Food Chart

APPROXIMATE QUANTITIES OF FOOD PER PERSON

	First Course	Main Dish	Side Dish
SOUP	½ cup (4 oz.)	1 cup (plus)	
SEAFOOD			
Shrimp	4-6 pieces*	¼ lb.	
Lobster	½ —small	½ —large 1—small or med.	
Lobster (meat)	⅓ cup	½ cup	
Crab meat	⅓ cup	½ cup	
Fish, filet		⅓ -½ lb.	
Fish, whole		½ lb.	
Scallops		⅓ -½ lb.	
MEAT & POULTRY			
With bones		1 lb.	
Without bones		½ lb.	

VEGETABLES
Asparagus   8-12 stalks*   4-5 stalks*
Canned veg.   ½ cup
DESSERTS
Ice Cream   ⅓ pt.
Pie, 9″   1/6 pie
Cookies   2 (when served
                                                  with ice
                                                  cream, etc.)

For Teas—allow 4 small sandwiches and 2 cookies per person.

For cocktail parties—allow 5–10 sandwiches and cocktail bites (exclusive of celery, carrots, olives, nuts, etc.).

Food Chart

No. of People	Seated Meal	Buffet Supper	Cocktail Party
12	3 qts. soup 12-15 lb. turkey or 6 lb. solid meat (without bones) 3 lb. string beans 2 qts. ice cream	3 qts. creamed chicken or 6 lbs. solid meats (may be assorted) 24 small portions, pick-up cake	60-150 sandwiches and cocktail bites —exclusive of celery, carrots, olives, nuts, etc.
50	2½ gal. soup 2 25-30 lb. turkeys 12 lbs. string beans 2 gal. ice cream	3gal. any stew- type dish, e.g., Beef Stroganoff 3 gal. fruit salad 100 small cookies	300-500 pieces

Chart of Wines and Spirits

People's thirsts are even more variable than their appetites. As mentioned in the Cocktail Party section, earlier, it is wise to study the guest list and try to gauge who usually

* Depending on size.

drinks what. Even then, you might be foxed. People who have been inveterate scotch drinkers may make a sudden switch to vodka. Or they may have gone on the wagon and want nothing but soft drinks. The time of the year, the occasion, the mood of the person, or the fact that yours is just one of a round of parties on the same day—all are hidden factors. So use the chart on the next page merely as a guide. Then consider the inconsistencies of your guests. When in doubt, always have more of each liquor, soft drink, beer, and mix than you think you will need. This way you will be prepared for any emergency, such as unexpected guests. And if a great deal is left over, you can always return unopened bottles to your dealer.

Chart of Wines and Spirits

APPROXIMATE NUMBER OF DRINKS PER PERSON

Luncheon	Cocktail Party	Dinner Party	Buffet Supper
2 cocktails	4 drinks per hour	2 cocktails	4 cocktails
		2 glasses of wine	2 drinks per hour after
		1 liqueur	after supper
		2 drinks per hour during evening	

STANDARD BOTTLE MEASUREMENTS

Liquors		Wines	
Pint	16 oz.	Split	6 oz. (6.4 oz., 6.5 oz.)
Fifth	25 oz. (25.6 oz.)	Half-bottle	12 oz. (12.8 oz.)
Quart	32 oz.	Bottle	24 oz. (25.6 oz.)
		Champagne	26 oz.

STANDARD GLASS SIZES

Jigger	1½ oz.	Liqueur	1 oz.	High-ball	10-12 oz.
Sherry, Port	3 oz.	Wine	5 oz.	Coolers	14 oz.
Brandy	4 oz.	Whisky Sour	5 oz.	Julep	12 oz.
Cocktail	4 oz.	Old-Fashioned	6 oz.	Champagne	6 oz.

WHAT WINES TO SERVE WITH WHAT

With	What Type	Temperature
Appetizers	Pale Dry Sherry	Room temp.
	Dry or Sweet Vermouth	Chilled or Room temp.
Soup	Dry Sherry, Madeira	Room temp.
Fish, shellfish,	Dry champagne Rhine wine, Chablis	
light meat, fowl	Sauterne, Moselle	Chilled
Red meat, duck, goose, all game	Burgundy, Claret, Bordeaux	Chilled or room temp.
Cheese, nuts	Port, Burgundy, Muscatel	Chilled or room temp.
Dessert	Champagne, Sauterne, White Port	Chilled
After Dinner	Brandy, Benedictine, Cointreau, Grand Marnier, Creme de Menthe, etc.	Room temp.

Party Service Chart

The number of servants needed for a given party depends on various factors. The chart below is a general guide. If the hostess has become extremely proficient after giving many parties, she can easily handle a small to medium-sized buffet supper without servants. The same is true of a cocktail party, if the host is an expert bartender, or if the guests are willing helpers. Servants will be needed, however, if the host and hostess are fairly helpless or are highly fastidious. Help is also needed, obviously, if the food and drink are to be served on different floors of a duplex or triplex apartment or outdoors.

Number of Guests	Seated Meal	Buffet Supper	Cocktail Party
6–8	1 person to serve (cooking done in advance)	1 to serve	1 to serve
24	3 to serve, 1 in kitchen	2 to serve, 1 in kitchen	1 to serve, 1 at bar
50	6 to serve, 2 in kitchen	4 to serve, 1 in kitchen	2 to serve, 1 at bar
100	12 to serve, 3 in kitchen	8 to serve, 2 in kitchen	4 to serve, 1-2 at bar, 1-2 in kitchen

The All-Important Guest

This book has covered many do's and don't's for hostesses. But little has been said about guests. Yet without them there is no party. They are the ultimate ingredient which makes a party successful.

I have seen a well-planned party die on the vine because the guests were blasé and indifferent. But I have also seen a modest little party, given by an inexperienced hostess, suddenly become alive with the enthusiasm and spontaneity of the people who had been invited.

Experienced hostesses have often told me that it is easier to entertain people who have lived through party giving themselves. An unthoughtful guest is usually an unknowledgeable hostess. And vice versa.

Tips to Guests

She is not difficult to please;
She can be silent as the trees;
She shuns all ostentatious show;
She knows exactly when to go.
    The Ideal Guest—Grenville Kleiser

Aside from Mr. Kleiser's good advice, I add, "Do unto your hostess exactly what you would want and expect her to do at your own party." Should you be a neophyte at being a guest, some of the tips here given may be helpful. And always remember that an ideal guest is in great demand and will be asked over and over again.

Post-Party Expense Chart

Date of party: ....   Asked: ....people   ....people came

People asked for business reasons: *Their firm names:*

Cost of party (bills attached):

Food .... (total) $........	Beverages (alcoholic) ...... (total) $........	
Meat (quantity ......) Kind .... $........	Gin (......bottles) $........	
Fish (quantity ......) Kind .... $........	Scotch (...... ") $........	
Poultry (quantity ......) Kind .... $........	Rye (...... ") $........	
Vegetables & fruit (quantity ....) $........	Bourbon (...... ") $........	
Groceries $........	Vodka (...... ") $........	
Beverages (nonalcoholic) $........	Vermouth (...... ") $........	
Club soda (.....bottles) $........	Beer (...... ") $........	
Ginger ale (..... ") $........	Wine (...... ") $........	
Soft drinks (..... ") $........	Ice (.....cubes) $........	
Decorations (flowers, etc.) $........	Service (bartender, maid, etc.) $........	
Misc. (invitations, place cards, rental	Caterer $........	
of chairs, tables, coat rack,	Over-all expenses $........	
glasses, china, etc.) .... $........		

Do's

Not only know "exactly when to go," but arrive in good time also.

Should you arrive with a present, make it one that can be stored for future use.

If you do not like some of the food set before you, make a pretense of eating it, so that no one notices.

If the hostess has little or no help, tell her that you would be glad to help in any way. If she gives you no assignment, tell her to call on you whenever needed. Be sincere in your offer; don't give it in an offhand "Well, I've done my duty" sort of way.

Be as "silent as trees" when a dangerous controversial subject comes up. But help the conversation along when there's a lapse. Circulate and talk to as many guests as possible.

Whether male or female, make it a point to be charming to the spinster or old-grandpa types.

Don't's

Be careful about where you put ashes and cigarette butts. (If the hostess has not provided enough ash trays, she really deserves whatever happens.) Don't scatter ashes on the rug (they are not *really* good for it) or put out a cigarette (ugly thought) in melted ice cream or a coffee cup. Find something else or ask for an ash tray! Don't arrive at the party with flowers—which means that the hostess has to find a vase and arrange them in the midst of her other greetings and preparations. Either have them sent ahead of time or bring them arranged in a container.

Never bring food (unless prearranged). The hostess has planned the menu, and any extra, no matter how delectable, might confuse her plans.

Shun all ostentatious show—no female should try to outdress her hostess or to outdo her in any way. (Understatment is a useful policy.)

Don't be critical—an ideal guest is "not difficult to please." Should the steak be well-done, when you particularly asked that it be rare, eat it with seeming relish. You can always have steak just the way you want it the next night in your own home! Finally, remember that it is someone else's house. Keep control and smile. Don't for a minute act as though it is yours. Keep those eager fingers from turning the hi-fi up or down or a light on or off. Just make up your mind to be the type of charming guest *you* would like to invite again and again to your own home.

Last Word to the Hostess

Pleasantest of all ties is the tie of guest and host.
—Aeschylus

Or, as a great host I used to know would say, "Welcome the coming and speed the parting guest." Actually, the dedicated hostess never wants the curtain to go down, so long as her guests are having fun. And guests are like royalty, for it is they who must suggest "parting."

If you are a hostess of today, I consider you a lucky girl. If you are sighing for grandma's day, with her staff of servants, think again. What would grandma have given to have your electric cleaner, your deep-freeze, your abundant world of canned and dried foods, instant mixes and icing that can be squeezed from a tube? And for her starched housedresses, wouldn't she have envied your washer and ironer? She might even have been glad, if she could, to trade a servant or two for your air-conditioner. And how she would have exclaimed at your gadgets and gimmicks, your stack chairs and snack stools. What would she have said to an electric starter for a charcoal grill! Imagine, if you can, preparing one of grandma's seven-course meals for a formal dinner party, with only willing hands to help. You know that the more foot soldiers there are in an army, the harder the general has to work. No, indeed, grandma wasn't as lucky as you are with all her servants. She had to be formal, too, whereas you live in the blessed freedom of an informal age.

But you do have something in common with grandma; you too know how to fling open your doors wide and welcome your guests with your own precious gift of warm hospitality. That genuine pleasure you have in your guests, that cordial atmosphere you create, that feeling of being wanted that you impart to the guest, all of this, as I said in the beginning, is *warmth from the heart,* and that is the best ingredient for any party.

INDEX

SAVE MONEY . . . TAKE ADVANTAGE OF OUR SPECIAL PRICE OFFER!

Award books retail at prices from 60¢ to 95¢ per title wherever paperbound books are sold. You may order any of these books directly from us at special reduced prices. Use the special order coupon on the last page.

Order 1 book —Pay only 60¢, plus 10¢ for postage and handling.

Order 2 books—Pay only $1.00—We pay postage.

Order 4 books—Pay only $2.00—We pay postage.

Order 6 books—Pay only $3.00—We pay postage.

Discounts up to 47%—If purchased on newsstands, books on this list will cost from 60¢ to 95¢ each. Now—regardless of cost —all at one low, low price!

Learn the Secrets of America's Greatest Chefs

DINING OUT AT HOME

James Stroman brings you, for the first time, hundreds of the most treasured recipes from America's finest restaurants—The Four Seasons, Luchow's, Antoine's, Sun Valley Inn and others.

There is something for everyone—hearty meals that can be whipped up in a jiffy, exotic Continental and Oriental meals, authentic American favorites and sumptuous repasts suitable for the most formal occasions. A387